O'ODHAM CREATION
&
RELATED EVENTS

THE SOUTHWEST CENTER SERIES

IGNAZ PFEFFERKORN, *Sonora: A Description of the Province*

CARL LUMHOLTZ, *New Trails in Mexico*

BUFORD PICKENS, *The Missions of Northern Sonora: A 1935 Field Documentation*

GARY PAUL NABHAN, EDITOR, *Counting Sheep: Twenty Ways of Seeing Desert Bighorn*

EILEEN OKTAVEC, *Answered Prayers: Miracles and Milagros along the Border*

CURTIS M. HINSLEY AND DAVID R. WILCOX, EDITORS, *Frank Hamilton Cushing and the Hemenway Southwestern Archaeological Expedition, 1886–1889,* volume 1: *The Southwest in the American Imagination: The Writings of Sylvester Baxter, 1881–1899*

LAWRENCE J. TAYLOR AND MAEVE HICKEY, *The Road to Mexico*

DONNA J. GUY AND THOMAS E. SHERIDAN, EDITORS, *Contested Ground: Comparative Frontiers on the Northern and Southern Edges of the Spanish Empire*

JULIAN D. HAYDEN, *The Sierra Pinacate*

PAUL S. MARTIN, DAVID YETMAN, MARK FISHBEIN, PHIL JENKINS, THOMAS R. VAN DEVENDER, AND REBECCA K. WILSON, EDITORS, *Gentry's Rio Mayo Plants: The Tropical Deciduous Forest and Environs of Northwest Mexico*

W J MCGEE, *Trails to Tiburón: The 1894 and 1895 Field Diaries of W J McGee,* transcribed by Hazel McFeely Fontana, annotated and with an introduction by Bernard L. Fontana

RICHARD STEPHEN FELGER, *Flora of the Gran Desierto and Río Colorado of Northwestern Mexico*

DONALD BAHR, EDITOR, *O'odham Creation and Related Events: As Told to Ruth Benedict in 1927 in Prose, Oratory, and Song by the Pimas William Blackwater, Thomas Vanyiko, Clara Ahiel, William Stevens, Oliver Wellington, and Kisto*

O'ODHAM CREATION & RELATED EVENTS

As told to Ruth Benedict in 1927

In Prose, Oratory, and Song

by the Pimas

William Blackwater,

Thomas Vanyiko,

Clara Ahiel,

William Stevens,

Oliver Wellington,

& Kisto

Edited by Donald Bahr

With a Foreword by Barbara A. Babcock

The University of Arizona Press / Tucson

The University of Arizona Press
www.uapress.arizona.edu

 Published 2001
First paperback edition 2016

Printed in the United States of America
21 20 19 18 17 16 7 6 5 4 3 2

ISBN-13: 978-0-8165-2080-0 (cloth)
ISBN-13: 978-0-8165-3415-9 (paper)

Cover design by Miriam Warren

Library of Congress Cataloguing-in-Publication Data
O'odham creation and related events / as told to Ruth Benedict in 1927 in prose, oratory, and song by the Pimas William Blackwater . . . [et al.] ; edited by Donald Bahr
p. cm — (The Southwest Center Series)
Includes bibliographical references and index.
ISBN 0-8165-2080-1 (cloth : alk. paper)
1. Pima mythology. I. Benedict, Ruth 1887–1948. II. Blackwater, William. III. Bahr, Donald M. IV. Title. V. Series.
E99.P6 057 2001
398.2'089'9745—dc21
00-013101

British Library Cataloguing-in-Publication Data
A catalogue record of this book is available from the British Library.

♾ This paper meets the requirements of ANSI/NISO Z39.48-1992 (Permanence of Paper).

CONTENTS

FOREWORD

This collection of Pima narrative, oratory, and song, which Ruth Benedict made in the summer of 1927, was her last compilation of Southwest Native American oral literature and was the product of her last solitary fieldwork in the Southwest. It is remarkable in several respects. First, Benedict actually put into practice critical ideas about the study of oral narrative that she had advocated in her Introduction to *Zuni Mythology* (1935). After several summers of collecting at Zuni and Cochiti Pueblos, Benedict argued against comparative and distributional practices in folklore studies and for the value of the "intensive study of one body of folklore" (Benedict 1935: xi). She also argued against folkorists' myth of "communal authorship," pointing instead to individual creativity "within traditional limits" and suggesting "the possibility of the study of the native narrator, that is, the literary materials which he has at his disposal and his handling of them" (Ibid.: xii). By emphasizing the literary and aesthetic qualities of stories and storytelling and the importance of studying "local literary conventions" and "regional stylistic forms," Benedict differed notably from her mentors Franz Boas and Elsie Clews Parsons, who saw myth primarily as a reflection of culture and a rich source of cultural data (Benedict 1931b: 291).

Second, this collection is remarkable because Benedict never published any of the Pima material in her lifetime, even in part, as, for example, a preliminary report or a note in the *Journal of American Folklore*, which she edited from 1925 to 1939. A third and related matter of note is that no biographers or historians of anthropology seem aware of or make any reference to this manuscript. Yet these same scholars make much of her August 17, 1927, letter from Sacaton to Boas about cultural differences: "These people [the Pimas] have more in common with the Serrano [whom she had visited in her first anthropological experience, in 1922] than with the Pueblos [especially the Zunis, whom she had visited in 1924 and 1925]. The contrast with the latter is *unbelievable*" (Mead, 1959: 206). All agree that it was this contrast between the Pueblo and their Southwest neighbors that led to the Apollonian/Dionysian distinction central to *Patterns of Culture* (1934), in which the Pima briefly appear as Dionysian because "Intoxication in their practice and in their poetry is the synonym of religion" (Benedict, 1934:85). They do not, however, quote the remainder of that letter about the Pima as Don Bahr does, and they note that she also wrote to Boas that the Pima material is "especially interesting from the point of view of literary form" (Caffrey 1989). And, in her preliminary report on her 1927 fieldwork, Benedict elaborates that "the complexity of literary form in these, their vivid use of imagery, is expecially notable and sets them off from Pueblo literature" (this volume, xxviii).

Fourth, as Pima scholar and editor Don Bahr remarks, this collection is an "unusually full and complete tribal oral literature," as well as being the most readable and felicitous translation of the three published "Pima tellings of ancientness." And from the perspective of forty years studying Pima language and culture, Bahr suggests that Benedict's text is "about as good as mythology documentation gets" (personal communication). While Benedict's earlier Pueblo volumes, *Tales of the Cochiti Indians* (1931a) and *Zuni Mythology* (1935) are reasonably full collections and do include important critical discussions or introductions by Benedict that are missing here, they are nonetheless arranged in terms of Euroamerican folk narrative categories. In contrast, in the Pima collection the narrators are identified by name, and their different versions are presented both sequentially and in a duet format. Here, we do indeed have "a native comment on native life" (Benedict, 1931a: 221), characterizations of tribal life "recorded wholly as they themselves figure them to themselves" (Benedict, 1924).

Benedict's work in Southwest Indian mythology began with a $1,000 grant from Elsie Clews Parsons and the Southwest Society in 1923. After finishing her Ph.D., Benedict had no gainful employment, so Boas arranged with Parsons for Benedict to work on her proposed concordance to Southwest mythology (Briscoe, 1979:464; Zumwalt, 1988:92; Zumwalt, 1992:216; Deacon, 1997:275–278). For the next four years, this project supported her folk narrative researches both in the Southwest and in the library.

While Benedict was obviously enthralled by Southwest Indian mythologies, by ethnopoetics, by cultural patterns, and by the Native American Southwest, she was bored with and frustrated by the endless, tedious detail and encyclopedic approach that such "useful compendia" demanded. Two Columbia students, Gene Weltfish and Erna Gunther, were enlisted to work on the project, and finally, in 1927, Benedict turned it over to Gunther. The concordance was never finished, and its whereabouts is unknown. I for one would like to see how her Pueblo and Pima material was incorporated and constructed—beyond the Zuni mythology concordance that accompanied that volume—but that's another project. There is no question, however, that it was the concordance work that engendered the research and writing that finally produced this remarkable Pima text, led Benedict to realize her own distinctive approach to folk narrative, and provided *the* difference that inspired *Patterns of Culture*.

I do not know exactly how or when John Bierhorst discovered this manuscript or if there are any other Pima materials in Benedict's papers at Vassar. She wrote many of the footnotes included here—some of which incorporate the criticisms of George Herzog, the ethnomusicologist who also worked at Sacaton—but she did not provide a title, table of contents, or chapter titles and divisions, as Don Bahr notes. Nor were Bahr and Bierhorst able to find additional correspondence regarding her Pima work or any 1927 field notes.

The latter fact does not surprise me. I had one brief day with Benedict's papers at Vassar in 1986, and because of her connection to the family I have worked with at Cochiti (especially Santiago Quintana, *the* storyteller, whom his granddaughter Helen Cordero re-presented in clay), I looked only at the Cochiti materials, in the hopes of finding both field notes and manuscript versions of *Tales of the Cochiti Indians* (1931a). I found nothing related to her Cochiti research. Finally the archivist appeared with a reporter's notebook that she had found in a "miscellaneous" box. It was dated and labeled "Cochiti," but scribbled across the front in a note to one of the people who was helping her organize the Benedict materials, Margaret Mead had written "save as a sample. mm." It was a chilling moment, especially when I realized that the archivist was not surprised and was all too aware how "weeded" and "pruned" this collection was. Someday, I hope to look for more Pima, Cochiti, and Zuni materials, but my expectations are not great. We will probably never have the inside record of Benedict's fieldwork and folk narrative scholarship beyond the letter and diary entries that Mead published in *An Anthropologist at Work* (1959).

The wonder is that this Pima manuscript was there, that it was found, and that a scholar who has spent his anthropological lifetime with the Pima was enlisted to edit it. To Bahr's and Bierhorst's credit, they agreed to produce "a book as close as possible to what Benedict would have done," and Bahr has restricted his comments to the introductions and to footnotes, which are distinguished from those that Benedict herself wrote.

In 1946, Benedict described herself as an "anthropological folklorist" (Briscoe, 1979:446). Today, she would probably be considered a "symbolic," "interpretive," or "humanistic" anthropologist, and the pioneering work exemplified in this volume would be praised as anthropological poetics. In her 1947 AAA presidential address, "Anthropology and Humanism," Benedict remarked that "long before I knew anything at all about anthropology, I had learned from Shakespearian criticism, habits of mind that at length made me an anthropologist" (Mead, 1974:173). She was referring to the literary critic's trained sensitivity to tropes and figures expressed in her own concern with paradigms, configurations, and patterns. The best known of these and the most notorious was the Apollonian/Dionysian contrast (borrowed from Nietzsche) which organizes *Patterns of Culture*. Since 1934, much ink has been spilled in enumerating the specific ways in which the Pueblo are not Appollonian, and the Pima not Dionysian. Too frequently, her "realist" critics miss the point that what matters is the contrast in overall pattern, the abstract difference. In the larger picture, the Pima *are* very different from the Pueblo.

Yeats once said that he read philosophy to give him "metaphors for poetry." Benedict obviously did the same thing, not only for her poetry but also for understanding culture. What mattered was the trope or the pattern in terms of which cultural details were meaningful. Long before the advent of interpretive or semiotic anthropology, and later of cultural studies, Benedict taught her students to read texts as cultural documents, and cultures as texts. Sidney Mintz recalled his first encounter with Benedict in a Columbia classroom as follows: "I was astonished by her, and by her lecture. It simply had never occurred to me before that a total culture might be looked upon as if it were a work of art, something coolly contemplated, something utterly unique and distinctive, yet available to be studied, analyzed, understood" (in Modell, 1983:90).

—Barbara A. Babcock

Additional References:

Benedict, Ruth Fulton.

1924 Research Proposal 2. Ruth Benedict Papers, Vassar College, Poughkeepsie, NY.

1931a (1981) *Tales of the Cochiti Indians*. Introduction by Alfonaso Ortiz. Albuquerque: University of New Mexico Press.

1931b Folklore. *Encyclopedia of the Social Sciences*, vol.6, ed. Edwin R.A. Seligman, pp. 288–93. New York: Macmillan.

Deacon, Desley.

1997 *Elsie Clews Parsons: Inventing Modern Life*. Chicago: The University of Chicago Press.

Mead, Margaret.

1974 *Ruth Benedict*. New York: Columbia University Press.

ACKNOWLEDGMENTS

Special thanks to John Bierhorst for proposing this project and for doing about half of the typing and editing; to Elinor Pascual for guiding me through the tight darkness (as she said about something else) of the tribal committees; and to Joseph Wilder for coming to the project's aid when it was penniless and unborn.

Thanks, too, for diverse kinds of aid from N. Allen, A. Bahr, C. Baptisto, G. Brotherston, M. Caffrey, C. Cassa, S. DeHaven, M. Eschief, A. Hatto, A. Hice, D. Hymes, L. Kyyitan, A. Nau, L. Paul, J. Ravesloot, M. Schweitzer, A. Sloane, M. Thomas, and P. Zolbrod; and to the American Philosophical Society Library (Philadelphia); the Archives of Traditional Music (Bloomington, Indiana); the Institute for Intercultural Studies (New York City); the National Archives and Records Center Branch at Laguna Niguel, CA; the Southwest Center (Tucson, Arizona); and the Vassar College Library Special Collections Department (Poughkeepsie, New York).

INTRODUCTION

Benedict's Choice

In the summer of 1927 the anthropologist Ruth Benedict made her first and only visit to the Pimas of southern Arizona. There she collected the texts that are published in this book. While collecting them she received an inspiration: to write portraits of cultures as arresting (as she would later elaborate the idea) as the characters in a novel by Virginia Woolf. Unlike Woolf's characters, the Benedict portraits would be true to observable reality, not invented. Also, they would be of the reality of small nations such as the Pima, not large ones such as England or the United States. Small nations have a more human scale, or, as she put it, a "cultural tradition simple enough to be contained within the knowledge of individual adults, and [in which] the manners and morals . . . are moulded to one well-defined general pattern" (1934:18). Finally, unlike a novelist, Benedict would not tell a story with her portraits. Rather, she would arrange them in a tableau where they would shed light on each other and also on contemporary America, her home culture. It would be a light show. The Pimas would be presented as "Dionysians."

The inspiration bore fruit in 1934, seven years after the Pima visit, in the book *Patterns of Culture.* The Pimas were largely dropped from the book, and so was the Dionysian way of life that Benedict felt or saw among them. The tribe is mentioned in passing in a chapter on the contrasting "Apollonian" way of life of the Zunis, and although Dionysianism is mentioned in that chapter and others, the other two full cultural portraits in the book, those of the Dobu of Papua New Guinea and the Kwakiutl of British Columbia, are not at all or not mainly Dionysian. The Dobuans are summed up as "antagonistic" (1934:139), and the Kwakiutls as "megalo-maniac paranoid" (1934:205).

Something must have happened between 1927 and 1934 to discourage a Pima Dionysian portrait. I will consider what that might have been later, but let me first note what a good book *Patterns of Culture* turned out to be. It is gracefully written, it is a triumph of the anthropological imagination (needed to construct such a tableau), and it was good medicine for America. Each sketch accentuated something Benedict felt was present in the American culture of 1934 and, one feels, is with us still: the burden of self-control among the Zunis, the meanness of the Dobuans, the self-promotion of the Kwakiutls. It was soothing and arousing to hear an anthropologist say, in effect, "These qualities exist. There are people who, thanks to their culture, push them farther than we do." None of those ways was inevitable, she said, and each of them was livable as a single band in the arc of human possibility. (This was her cultural relativism.) It was not that America should opt for one of them or should try harder to harmonize all of them. Benedict's only advice to America was negative: don't think you have to be as you are. (This was her conviction of human plasticity.)

She died in 1948. At that time the tide in anthropology was turning against studies as impressionistic (which is not to say unobservant) as hers, which select an action from here and a poem from there to make an argument about how life feels; and the tide was turning, too, against cultural personality studies of any sort, in favor of a down-to-earth materialism that hoped to show compelling reasons why peoples are as they are, at least in the practical realm. This anthropological history story is well told in the last chapter of Margaret Caffrey's book on Benedict's life and work, *Stranger in This Land* (1989:327–50).[1]

Of course what happened in anthropology didn't necessarily happen in America at large, and *Patterns of Culture* has stayed in print from its second edition in 1946 until today. Also, one could go beyond Caffrey's history, which ends in the 1950s, and note that the postmodern anthropology since the 1980s has vindicated Benedict's impressionism, on the ground that we are all impressionists; and the same anthropology has brought matters of character and morality, the feeling of life, and cultural diversity back to the fore. These were Benedict's issues.

Much as I would like to, I won't fully vindicate Benedict as an anthropologist for today. To do so would require a study of all that she did publish, not what she didn't, and in this book I concentrate on the latter: she wrote no Dionysian portrait of anyone (this lack the present book won't remedy), and she did not publish the Pima texts that triggered her interest in such a portrait (this it will). And I will vindicate her in two points of principle. I will say it was a good idea for her to turn to a literature, in this case an oral literature, in order to know the people who made it. I will also point out that all she really learned

1. Besides the works cited in the text, I read Briscoe 1979, Zumwalt 1988, and Babcock 1993 regarding Benedict's life and work. On Elsie Clews Parsons, I read Hare 1985, Zumwalt 1992, Hieb 1993, and Deacon 1997; and on George Herzog, Katz 1980. There is more to read on Benedict and Parsons. Like the works just mentioned, they probably won't say much about the subjects' Pima studies. This is appropriate, because none of the three (Benedict, Parsons, or Herzog) published much about the Pimas. (Herzog published more about them than the others, but one can find little to read about him.)

of the Pimas was their literature, and she felt, correctly, that literature alone was an insufficient base for a cultural portrait. To make a proper portrait one needs conversations and real life. One must ask people things and watch them live and share experiences with them. This Benedict didn't do with the Pimas, and this lack was a good reason to drop the idea of a Pima Dionysian portrait.

We are left with the Pima literature, then. Here we are fortunate. The texts that Benedict collected are, I believe, an unusually full and complete tribal oral literature. I will be at pains to show how this is true—that is, how the texts comprise a whole telling of ancient times that draws on the full spectrum of Pima oral means: prose, oratory, and song. As a study of a literature, this book will show how the Pimas "moulded" (Benedict's word) a world of words into a "well-defined, general pattern."

Thus this book contributes to Benedict's legacy. Unfortunately, the general Pima literary pattern we will discern is not Dionysian. I suppose this was a reason why she didn't publish the texts—they don't support the literary reading that she wished they would. I think she liked some Dionysian sparks that arose from them, but she herself must have sensed that the whole thing was not of that nature. The whole thing, I will say, is "Edenic" in quality, and this Edenism covers and controls far more than the Dionysian bits that she particularly liked.

In sum, the present book supports Benedict's idea that a people's literature belongs in an ethnography, and it concurs with her that a people's literature is not the same thing as an ethnography or an ethnographic portrait. The book gives a very good oral literature that Benedict took down, but I read that literature differently from the way she might have hoped. Also, in making this reading I have a goal more modest than hers. Where she constructed portraits of peoples who had literatures (though not of the Pimas), I study the literatures they had—that is, the portraits that the peoples themselves made, in this case the Pimas' portrait of ancientness. I seek the pattern of their portrait, just that.

DIONYSIANISM

To document the points just made, I begin with a letter Benedict wrote to her mentor, Franz Boas, in August 1927, when she was among the Pimas. The nub of it is quoted in a book about Benedict by Margaret Mead: "These people [the Pimas] have more in common with the Serrano [whom Benedict had visited in her first anthropological experience, in 1922] than with the Pueblos [especially the Zunis, whom she visited in 1924 and 1925]. The contrast with the latter is *unbelievable*" (Mead 1959:206; the italics are Mead's). Margaret Caffrey fleshed out the letter considerably in a letter she wrote to me in February 1999:

> I went back through my notes on the Boas papers, and the letter you are interested in is Ruth Benedict to Franz Boas, August 17, 1927, from Sacaton, Arizona. I did not xerox it, but I'll quote what I wrote [down] from it that has to do with the Pima:
>
> *There's a greater bulk of Pima material yet to be had than I had supposed and it's especially interesting from the point of view of literary form. Recitatives, full of figurative expressions, are incorporated into the tales as well as endless numbers of songs. The recitatives were also the stock-in-trade of the shaman in curing and war ritual.—These people had more in common with the Serrano than with the Pueblos. The contrast with the latter is unbelievable.*
>
> *I've had good luck with informants. I had a notion of going up to a Yaqui village for a bit, but I'm leaving that to Leslie and Erna [Spier]. There is enough here to keep me busy and I needed all my time.*
>
> Then [Caffrey continues] my notes say she hired an interpreter with a car and sometimes the old men came into Sacaton to stay while she worked with them.
>
> *Here I live in the Indian school guest room and am very comfortable. I shall stay till the end of the month.*

Scott DeHaven of the American Philosophical Society supplied me with the full text of the letter, which contains only one passage on the Pima visit not present in Caffrey's notes. This concerns the interpreter: "I've hired an interpreter *with a car* for 8-hours-a-day interpreting, and sometimes the old men have come to Sacaton to stay while I was working with them."

The letter to Boas lacks the word "Dionysian," but Benedict used it, along with "Apollonian," in a paper called "Psychological Types in the Cultures of the Southwest," which she presented in 1928 to the International Congress of Americanists, a gathering of European and American experts on New World peoples. First, however, I must take up the matter of Virginia Woolf. The only document I have on that is a letter from Benedict to Mead dated January 1932, four years after the Pima visit and two years before the publication of *Patterns of Culture*. The letter is about a Woolf book published in 1932 (which is why I can't actually claim that Benedict was under this novelist's influence at the time of the Pima trip or, as I put it earlier, her inspiration). The letter states:

> Did you read *The Waves*? And did you keep thinking how you'd set down everybody you knew in a similar fashion? I did. I suppose I'm disappointed that she didn't include any violent temperaments, and I want my group of persons more varied. I want them to include, not just persons who have a shrug of the shoulders like mine, but persons who haven't like you and Stanley. . . . It made me realize how Mrs. Woolf's types are circumscribed; she never does anything that isn't essentially mild. This way of setting people down seemed very exciting to me, and I wish a whole crop of authors would try it; then there'd be lots of different sorts of people included. But the talk about *The Waves* has been mostly about what it means, and it's bored me to death. Well, what is its theme? People have suggested the strangest assortments. To me of course it's just about life's being a wrapping and wrapping oneself in one's own cocoon. What you can spin is all you have to work with, and the result is altogether dependent on that. Don't you think, given the limited types she allows herself, she's done it beautifully? (Mead 1959:318)

This letter is also quoted in Judith Modell's biography of Benedict (1983:192). Modell was the first to call attention to Woolf's effect on *Patterns of Culture* and to Benedict's Dobu portrait as the hot center in a triptych framed by the cool Zuni and the calculating Kwakiutl. I believe, however, that the Dobuans are stand-ins for Benedict's original concept of the Pima Dionysians. Both would have broken out from Woolf's mild characters, but I suspect Benedict would have preferred a Dionysian breakout had one been feasible.

About Dionysians in general Benedict said the following in her 1928 paper at the Congress of Americanists: "The Dionysian pursues them [the values of existence] through 'the annihilation of the ordinary bounds and limits of existence' [this is quoted from Friedrich Nietzsche]. . . . The closest analogy to the emotion he seeks is drunkenness. With [William] Blake he believes 'the path of excess leads to the palace of wisdom'" (reprinted in Mead 1959:248). And about the Pimas as Dionysians she said:

> . . . intoxication is the visible mirroring of religion, it is the symbol of its [Dionysian religion's] exaltation, the pattern of its mingling of clouded vision and insight. [Pima] Theory and practice are explicitly Dionysian.

> *"And I was made drunk and given the sacred songs";*
> *"He breathed the red liquor into me,"*
>
> are in their songs common forms of reference to the shamanistic [Dionysian] experience. Their great ceremony is the drinking of "tizwin," the fermented juice of the giant cactus. The ceremony begins with all religious formality . . . , but its virtue lies in the intoxication itself; the desired state is that of roused excitement, and they accept even extreme violence [in drinking and religion] more readily than a state of lethargy. Their ideal is to stave off the final insensibility [after drinking] indefinitely while achieving the full excitation of the intoxicant. This is . . . in complete accord with the Dionysian slant of their culture. (Mead 1959:250)

I am not sure whether Benedict thought the Pimas or anyone else was fully Dionysian. To revert to a word in the last line of the preceding passage, she probably believed this was a "slant" in all native North American cultures except for the Pueblos, who, she stated, were an "island" of measure and sobriety in a sea of vision seekers (Benedict 1934:119). The hallmark of Dionysianism was the seeking of visions, that is, of temporarily raised consciousness. Drinking, as she said, was merely a "symbol" of the vision-seeking way of life. That the visions are temporary implies that there are no full-time Dionysians. Whether some people, the Pimas or whoever, dedicated everything to those heightened moments Benedict didn't say—and because she didn't make a complete Dionysian portrait ethnography, we cannot know where she stood on the fullness issue.

I am sure that the few months she spent with the tribe in 1927 did not enable her to get the kind of information she would have required for a Pima portrait. All she got in that time were the texts—the oral literature. But to judge from the sketches in *Patterns of Culture,* oral literature was not enough for her. She was an anthropologist, and her anthropology made it a point of method and pride to include observations of and conversations with live people. Indeed, in the one full literary study that she made, of the Zunis, she held that oral literature (perhaps written, too) is not a realistic presentation of life but is instead a compensation for life's frustrations. (I agree that the Zuni and Pima literatures are not realistic pictures of the tellers' lives, but I don't think they necessarily arose from frustration.)

I say that Benedict had little live information from the Pimas. Surely the thoughts about drinking expressed in the foregoing quotation seem like live information, but she didn't have much else to say about the tribe's doings at the time, and I am skeptical about this passage. I doubt that she ever saw Pimas struggling to maintain excitement until the moment they passed into a stupor, and I wonder whether anyone told her of a norm or personal reminiscence exactly like that. It sounds to me more like Americans talking about sex than Pimas talking about drinking. (I know something about the latter as well as the former.) I think she wrote those words for the Pimas—she didn't quote them (but see notes 38 and 42 in chapter 3, this volume, on the drinking songs she quoted in her paper).

I said earlier that the reason Benedict didn't publish the texts may have been that they were not Dionysian enough, but I also said she would have expected any literature to compensate for life's frustrations: so if life was Dionysian, the texts might be otherwise. Alas, I can only speculate on this, because she did not explain herself in any document I have found. If I may make two more guesses, they are that she thought the old Pima culture was dying, and so the connection between current Pima life, Dionysian or not, and their old literature was broken; and she felt that this literature, whatever its nature, was less important to give to the world than some other things she had in mind: let the literature be archived.

Very good, she left it for us, for the Pimas of today and the rest of us. As I implied earlier, I believe the texts make up one single, organized thing, one work of the imagination, and the imagination at work was the Pimas', in this case two Pimas named William Blackwater and Thomas Vanyiko. My job when faced with this joint work is to write criticism of the authors Blackwater and Vanyiko in just the same way that Benedict's contemporaries I. A. Richards, Van Wyck Brooks, Edmund Wilson, and Dorothy Parker wrote criticism of American literature, or as you or I can write criticism of her *Patterns of Culture:* what does the author say, and how, and what do we make of it?

The present book actually has little criticism, not because there is little to give but because when John Bierhorst and I started the project, we agreed to keep the book as close as possible to the one Benedict would have made. We would not hold forth on our own in the book. Bierhorst was unable to stay with the project, but I have tried to adhere to our bargain. I do hold forth a bit in this introduction, in the introductions to the chapters, and in some footnotes. Benedict typed the texts and did some editing on them, but her editing did not reach the stage of defining chapters and assigning texts to them. The chapter assignments and names, as well as the introductions, are my work. It is in and through them that I express my ideas on this Pima work of literature.

Those ideas are mainly two: that the entire collection *has* an order, so it comprises one work of literature—roughly speaking, a Pima "oral book of ancientness"; and that the narrated time of ancientness corresponds to the Bible's Eden in that normal human reproduction and marriage are not yet established. Benedict did not state, and might not have been aware of, these ideas, and she might not have agreed with them. Of course I wish she had agreed with them, so she would find my literary criticism congenial. I'm sure the Pimas were aware of the first idea. I doubt that they saw their ancientness as equivalent to Eden, but I think they would then have found and will now find the idea interesting.

SACATON

Sacaton, Arizona, is as hot as Egypt, and therefore not a place a New Yorker like Benedict would go for fun in the summer. It was the largest Pima settlement and the seat of the U.S. Pima Agency. Fifteen miles to the north was the town of Chandler, whose luxurious San Marcos Hotel was probably open for winter guests in 1927. (Elsie Clews Parsons, who preceded Benedict to Sacaton by a few months, spent part of the winter of 1932 there [Deacon 1997:330, 474 n. 45].) Phoenix, thirty miles northwest, had several resort hotels by 1927 (Luckingham 1989:85–91). In the hot months the guests went back home.

The Pimas slept outside in the summer and spent the hot afternoons under shade trees or their architectural equivalents, pole-supported roofs without walls—Native American stationary umbrellas. Benedict slept in a hot room in the government school and took down the texts across the street in the Presbyterian church. That is about all we know of her activities among the Pimas. We don't know when she first arrived and finally left,[2] only that she made side trips of a few days to visit the Mojaves to the west (hot) and Cochitis to the northeast (cooler). The working-place information comes from a letter that she sent to George Herzog, who followed her to Pima country and took down from Thomas Vanyiko basically the same texts that Benedict did. He took them down in both Pima and English, however, and she only in English. (His texts remain unpublished.) The side-trip information comes from a preliminary

2. We know that she was still in New Hampshire on July 8, the day she sent a letter to Boas about her travel plans. (My thanks to the American Philosophical Society for the letter, from the Boas correspondence.) We don't know when she left Sacaton—probably in September in order to be back in New York for the fall school semester.

report that Benedict sent to either Boas or Parsons when her visit was finished. Both of these documents are reproduced in the next section.

Thus, from Parsons to Herzog there was a flurry of anthropological visits to the Pimas. All the visitors were associated with Columbia University, as was their master, Boas. Parsons published her information, which was on kinship, chiefship, and traditional religion, in a brief paper in 1928. She included a genealogy naming some of the same people who gave Benedict texts. Also included in the genealogy was Johnson Azul, Benedict's interpreter, as her letter to Herzog states. He was a remote nephew of the tribal chief at the time, also named Azul. Undoubtedly Parsons paved the way for Benedict.

Herzog closed out the Columbia visits with his work with Vanyiko. (Parsons, it seems, didn't return to Sacaton during her 1932 visit to Chandler.) He came in the summers of 1927, 1929, 1933, and 1936 (Herzog n.d.*a*). He didn't publish the Vanyiko texts, but he did publish his Ph.D. dissertation, a study of Pima and Pueblo music (Herzog 1936). (He also reviewed Benedict's typescripts for her and sent her sixteen pages of comments [Herzog n.d.*b*, n.d.*c*], some of which are put into this book's footnotes.) The Pima side of his dissertation has many song texts (see the second section following on the place of song in Pima oral literature). His publisher was the *Journal of American Folklore,* of which Benedict was editor and to which Parsons contributed many articles and some financial support.

After those visits, anthropology left the Pimas alone until the 1960s, but Ruth Underhill, also from Columbia, started working with the Papagos (Tohono O'odham), basically the same people, in 1931. Underhill continued her studies until 1935.[3] From her came a wealth of books—on a woman's actual life (1936), songs (1938), social organization (1939), a fictional man's life (1940), and religion (1946). Also, in 1929 Leslie Spier studied the Maricopas, a distinct people who shared the Gila River (Sacaton) and Salt River (east of Phoenix) reservations with the Pimas.[4] These polities, now separately self-governing, are today called the Gila River Pima—Maricopa Indian and the Salt River Pima—Maricopa Indian Communities. Spier wrote a book (1933) on the same span of Maricopa topics that the others covered for the Pimas and Papagos: material life, economy, family, kinship, government, ceremonies, songs, and mythology.

3. June–October 1931; September–October 1932; February–October 1933; November 1934–January 1935; October–November 1935 (Underhill 1939:v).

4. The Pimas and Papagos speak the same language, Pima-Papago, but the Maricopa language belongs to a different family. Mythologically—that is, in telling the ancient past–the Pimas and Papagos are about the same, and the Maricopas are different. And note that in her "Dionysian" letter to Boas, Benedict said she expected Spier and his wife in the summer of 1927. My date of 1929, actually the winter of 1929–30, comes from Spier's book on the Maricopas (1933).

Why did anthropology go to the Pimas in the first place, and why did it stop so abruptly? Actually, the beginning wasn't in 1926 but in 1901–2, when Frank Russell spent a solid seven months, November to June, documenting the same full spectrum of Pima life as was treated by the others. (Russell's study was published in 1908 by the Smithsonian Institution.) His visit came early in the history of anthropological studies, that is, of studies intended to add to the record of and reckoning about the world's cultures. Benedict had an inspiration on the reckoning *about* these cultures in 1927. But the idea of building an objective record of the world's tribal cultures had taken hold about sixty years earlier, in the writings of Edward Tylor in England and Lewis Henry Morgan in the United States. One can say that the work on that record for the native cultures of the United States didn't really start strongly until the 1890s, with Franz Boas, Frank Cushing, Alice Fletcher, James Mooney, and others, including Frank Russell, who contributed studies of arctic and subarctic peoples in 1891. (He died young from tuberculosis shortly after his Pima work, according to Bernard Fontana in his introduction to the 1975 re-publication of Russell's monograph [pp. xiv–xv]).

If anthropology went early to the Pimas, why did it abandon them in the 1930s? Let us see what the Pimas' visitors did afterward. Benedict turned to writing against racism in America in the 1930s (Caffrey 1989:286–301); then during World War II she turned to large nations with which the United States had unsettled political dealings: Thailand, Romania, Germany, Finland, Denmark, Norway, Poland, and Italy. After the war she made a splendid long study of the culture of Japan. Parsons turned to Mexico and Ecuador, again to large and politically strategic societies. Herzog continued to study tribal peoples' musics and languages, but he didn't publish a great deal. Underhill went to work for the Bureau of Indian Affairs in education and teacher training—that is, in practical matters as distinct from the recording of old-timers or the description of the full span of contemporary life. Spier turned to historical, document-based studies of native peoples. These appear to be pretty representative reasons, for in general anthropologists stopped studying Indian life in the 1930s. Like Benedict and Parsons, they turned to places and peoples of greater political importance, or they went into Indian "applied anthropology" like Underhill, or into "ethnohistory" like Spier.

What anthropology stopped, then, was the study of full Indian cultures as people lived them. It stopped writing Native American ethnographies or culture portraits based on live observation. Having said that, I will now say, first, that I am sorry it happened (insofar as it did), because those lives were still part of the human story, not to mention the American one; and second, that since the 1960s a new factor has been added. The tribes don't like anthropological snooping. Probably they never did, or at least some people didn't like some snooping, but they had no way to stop it.[5]

The publication of Benedict's texts has been long delayed, but has anyone suffered because of that? I doubt that the Pimas suffered, because in general they haven't read what anthropology has written about them. I wish, however, that the texts had been published in the lifetimes of the people who gave them, so they could have seen them in print whether they wanted to read them or not. Nor, finally, can I say that the world's scholars of oral literatures have suffered. They had the version of Pima literature that Russell published, and in 1994 they received a second version (Bahr et al. 1994). I hope that this third version will rouse them and the Pimas—the scholars who never paid much attention to Pima literature and the tribe who seem largely to have forgotten it. Both will see something good.

I must explain one more thing about Benedict's times which I don't know if I have exactly right, but which is important because it involves politics and white-and-Indian relations. This is the institution or office of "chief." Benedict and the others came at the end of the no doubt always changing old style of Pima chiefship, the time of what Lloyd Paul of the Salt River Reservation (then administered from Sacaton) called "self-appointed chiefs." What Paul meant was that those chiefs were not elected by the vote of all the people. The election of such officials began in 1936 when the people accepted a constitution modeled after that of the United States. These new-style officials are called governors. With them came an elected tribal council, also new.

One difference between the old and the new form of government is that the old did not require a council's approval of anthropological visitors, whereas the new style requires it, at least in principle. Thus, the council as well as the governor was notified of the present work on the Benedict texts.[6] I have no documents on the earlier anthropologists' procedures, but it is safe to assume

5. In the last section I implied a criticism of Benedict for writing for the Pimas rather than quoting them. In fact, they probably didn't want to be quoted, by her, at that point.

6. They did not know of Benedict's visit or the texts' existence, which is not surprising because her visit took place seventy years earlier and was low key, although, I am sure, not secret or hidden. I should add that I hope the tribe will honor the people with whom Benedict worked, her interpreter, and the six givers of texts. I learned bits about them while editing this book, but not enough to write proper sketches of them. I hope the book pleases their descendants and will cause the tribe to take full notice of who they were.

that Benedict, Parsons, and Herzog all wrote to and appeared before the white Pima Agency superintendent, who consented to their study and directed them to the chief, to the white head of the Presbyterian mission (for a place to work), and to the white head of the school (for housing). Whether the chief could have refused them permission to interview Pimas I don't know—perhaps only the superintendent could do that. (Under the new government, at least nowadays, this is the prerogative of the council.) The chief could have refused to help the anthropologists himself, and in fact he gave no texts. But he approved of and perhaps suggested his nephew as Benedict's interpreter, and he probably also recommended the people who did give the texts.

Two final comments on self-appointment. First, although the people didn't elect the old chiefs, they acknowledged them and expected the chiefship to pass from father to son. Second, so far as I know, these chiefs had no specifically *Pima* signs, symbols, or privileges of office, but they did have such from the Spanish, Mexican, and American governments: a staff or cane of office, the title *kowinal* (from the Spanish *gobernador* or perhaps *gobierno* and now the title of the elected governor), and, in U.S. times, postal letters and no doubt other things sent from Washington—apparently no salary, however. Thus, the old chiefs, if not appointed by Washington, were at least recognized more concretely by the United States than by the Pimas. The latter acknowledged the chiefs and no doubt used them, but the whites gave them their titles and symbols. That was colonial. The next step for the Pimas, and probably all colonized peoples who survived, was not to throw off the foreign symbols and ideas but to assimilate themselves to and take as their own a constitutional form of government.

This probably affected the forgetting of the texts, for they do seem largely to have been forgotten. No one is pleased with this now, and everyone seeks someone or something to blame for it. The missionaries? They surely railed against the texts and assured people that they were no longer necessary. By the 1930s there were Pimas preaching Christianity to Pimas in Pima, a dramatic redirection of talent. The penetration of the American popular media—movies, television, and music? People did take these up, and they drew talent away from the old forms. Nor should we overlook the rise of constitutional government, whose here-and-now practicality and liking for pomp leave little use for the old-timers' way of telling of their kind of Eden. I hope the goodness of those texts in this book will lighten the hearts of the council.

A LETTER AND REPORT

Two documents that I mentioned earlier fairly well exhaust what I have found on paper about Benedict's field trip to the Pimas. First, a letter to George Herzog:[7]

Sacaton, Arizona
Aug. 5, 1927

My dear George Herzog,

I've been here for two weeks, and they gave me your letter only yesterday, nearly a month old. There's something rotten in Denmark.

I am so hoping you will get here while I'm here. I have heard countless songs and have longed to record them. They have the song-story cycles [about which Herzog may have asked] that I suppose are related to the Navaho and Diegeno pattern.

About the Serrano [the California tribe Benedict first went to], Mr. Strong would have fuller and more recent information. My advice would be to go to the Morongo family who live a few minutes walk from the Agency compound (about four miles from Banning). Old Rose may have died, but her daughter Annie would give you help. She was my main interpreter. I think she said the Morongo "singer" was Joe Morongo—he was off the reservation when I was there and I didn't see him.

There were a couple of families of Chemehuevi on the Banning Reservation when I was there. I doubt if they would have been much good—they'd knocked around a good bit. In California they'll know better where there'd be a good example [not sure that's the word she wrote].

I am hoping to try a Yaqui settlement up by Tempe, and I may be up there by the time you get down this way. I hope not, for I should hate to miss you. There's a train—S.P.—that leaves Phoenix 8:45 A.M. and a bus at 4:30 P.M. [from Phoenix] for Sacaton. (From the train stop called Sacate [not sure that's the word] you have to get the train hand's wife to drive you over four miles.) I shall tell the Presbyterian missionary (!!), Dirk Lay, about you if I'm not here, and

7. Thanks to the Archive of Traditional Music (George Herzog Correspondence), Indiana University, for this letter.

> he will take you to Johnson Azul, my interpreter, who will get the old men. Vañiki [her spelling] is nearer by and certainly sang better in his story telling, but Wm Blackwater has many more songs and might let his voice out better to the phonograph than he has to the interpreter. Ask him for a "Corn Song"—they have a special pattern of their own—they'll all begin with the creation songs. Both old men will come to the church basement, and if the school guest rooms are vacant you can be housed there (gratis [not sure that's the word]. Ask for Mr. Smith) and eat at "the Club" [dining room for Agency employees].
>
> I do hope I'll still be here when you come.
>
> Best wishes—
> Ruth Benedict

Second, Benedict's "Preliminary Report on Anthropological Fieldwork Summer of 1927":[8]

> The principal field of my investigations during the past summer was the Pima tribe. They are a very numerous people living contiguous to and under the same geographical conditions as the Pueblo peoples which have been the subjects of my field investigations in 1924 and 1925. They are nevertheless a strikingly contrasted group, having cultural relationship with the tribes of northern Mexico rather than with the Pueblos. This impression had already been suggested by Russell's notes [book] on the Pima some twenty years ago, and further work has overwhelmingly confirmed this inference.
>
> I was able to obtain long ritualistic myths, orations, and song sequences which are now known only to a handful of the old men and which will be completely lost at their death [not true]. The complexity of literary form in these, their vivid use of imagery, is especially notable and sets them off from Pueblo literature. The collection I obtained establishes also the cultural affiliations of the Pima with the people of Southern California, notably the Yumas and Mojave, and is

8. Thanks to Vassar College Library, Special Collections Department (Ruth Benedict Papers), for this report. I am aware of no final report anywhere, nor of any correspondence official or personal on the Pima study between Benedict and any Pimas, the Bureau of Indian Affairs, or any colleagues other than Boas, Herzog, and Mead.

essential to the understanding of the influences that have shaped Navajo and Apache culture in the same region.

In continuance of my field work of 1925, I returned also this summer to Cochiti, the Rio Grande pueblo, to obtain the more esoteric tales from an informant who had promised them to me. These tales are carefully guarded from the whites in the Rio Grande Pueblos, and yet are indispensable for a comparative study of myth. I obtained accounts of the emergence and the katchinas that had been withheld from me on my first visit.

I made a trip also to the Mojave to investigate the special problems of their relationship [kinship] system. This had been insufficiently recorded some years ago, and it presented some very striking and puzzling features. It proved to be quite an unprecedented system, based on fundamental ideas which are not known in this form in any other kinship nomenclature that has been recorded.

THE VALUE OF THE BENEDICT COLLECTION

In chapter 2 I note how one text in this collection, called "The Feud," resembles a treasure of New World literature called the *Popol Vuh*. The resemblances may be judged minor, and I don't claim that "The Feud" is the equal in size, beauty, or majesty to the Quiche Mayas' *Popol Vuh*. Still less would I claim that the Benedict collection is better than the Maya text simply because the collection includes, as just one of its many stories, an equivalent to the *Popol Vuh*.

"The Feud" seems a worse text to me because the genealogy of its characters is almost impossible to follow. The *Popul Vuh* is good in comparison because its characters have a simpler and clearer genealogy. The Pima text, although far shorter than the other, is a sort of genealogical and geographical tongue twister, but it echoes the *Popol Vuh* in having something like a ball game, in featuring decapitation, and in telling of a conflict that continues for three generations (two in the *Popol Vuh*) between people living in different places—a feud.

I bring this up now because the publication of the present collection gives us three independent, comprehensive tellings of the ancient past from Pimas or Papagos (Tohono O'odham), and the present one is the fullest yet. The other two are also from Pimas. From the Papagos there are anthologies from several narrators, but there is no telling of everything by a single person, which is the way the histories or mythologies actually existed—in the memories of experts who thought about them constantly, who rarely told them completely (except silently to themselves), and who accepted no greater living authority over them than themselves.

It so happens that "The Feud" exists only in the present collection. I have no explanation for that, and I don't think we should seek one at this point. We should simply see where "The Feud" fits in the overall Benedict collection and be content to have the two Feud-less tellings to compare the present collection to. We are fortunate because from the Mayas we have only the one text, the *Popul Vuh* itself, written at an unknown time, probably around 1550, in Maya with Latin letters, and brought into Spanish keeping about 1701 (Tedlock 1987:469).

I am sure there are *Popol Vuh*-like texts featuring ball games, decapitations, and transgenerational feuds from peoples between the Mayas and the Pimas; and there may be more such texts from the Quiche, the source of the Popul Vuh. They are the ones to compare with the *Popol Vuh*. We may eventually find a chain, or at least a series of dots, of them from the Quiches northward through Mexico to the Pimas and beyond. Anticipating that, and not just because of "The Feud," I now discuss the fullness of the Benedict corpus, and how we are fortunate that it makes the third full book of ancientness that we have from the Pima-Papagos. With the three, plus the not insignificant odds and ends that exist in addition, we have enough to begin to understand the integrity of this one small nation's whole literature—not just its single stories, but the whole picture of ancientness the old-timers made with their texts. The old-timers, I hold, were acting as authors with those texts. They had a tradition of the oral book of ancientness, and with those books, which all more or less resembled one another, they were constantly tinkering.

The other two full tellings are from Thin Leather, who was actually recorded twice, first by Frank Russell in 1901–2 and then by J. W. Lloyd in 1908 (published in 1908 and 1911, respectively),[9] and from Juan Smith, whose translated words were taken down by Julian Hayden in 1933 and published by Bahr, Smith, Allison, and Hayden in 1994. We don't know whether the principals of the present book, William Blackwater and Thomas Vanyiko (they cooperated in telling the longest texts), knew Thin Leather and Smith. They may well have; for example, a William Blackwater was listed as a minor consultant

9. A few of Thin Leather's stories bearing on Casa Grande Ruins National Monument were also taken down by J. W. Fewkes in 1906–7 and 1907–8 and published in 1912. Fewkes may have taken down more of Thin Leather's stories than he published.

by Russell (1908:18). He could be the same person as, or possibly the father of, the William Blackwater of this volume.[10] No matter, and despite the duet appearance of some texts given here, telling is basically a solo matter. If two tellers are present, then when one talks, the other listens—and sometimes adds things or says differently, as will be seen here.

To tell fully means to use more than prose speech. In fact, such speech is the softest, weakest, most tenuous part of a full telling of ancientness. Harder, more durable stretches of language are distributed throughout the prose. These stretches are considered to be quotations from the ancients verbatim. There are two forms of this, one more stringently memorized than the other. The stricter form is song, which is memorized down to the individual, metered sound. Such songs exist, it is held, because important ancient characters burst into song at operatic high moments: the songs were heard then, it is believed, and have been retained perfectly ever since. The less strict form, remembered down to the word or perhaps only the phrase, is what Benedict called "recitative," a term she took from operas, where the reference is to declaimed speeches that come between songs. In this book those Pima speeches are called orations. They are longer and less stringently memorized than songs, but they are more firmly retained and more strongly voiced than plain prose. Like songs, they are quotations from ancients. The prose of a story is, in effect, the explanation of such quotations. Prose is like the writing historian's voice, being what someone now understands of the events from which certain precious preserved documents originated.[11]

Thus, one aspect of the fullness of the present telling is the abundance of its songs and orations. Thin Leather and Smith supplied many, but the present telling has more. Another aspect is that the present telling simply has more stories than the others, especially more in certain of the categories that correspond to this book's chapters. Moreover, the categories have an order to them, which is the order of the Pima literary knowledge of the whole of ancientness.

Just about every story in this collection's main category, which I call "The Rafter Hauled," was also told by Thin Leather and Smith and by at least some Papagos. The collection has several stories in its other chapters that either Thin Leather or Smith lack, but the interesting thing is that except for Coyote stories, which all the prior collections grievously lack, there is only one long story

10. Russell says he was "elderly," and that was twenty-five years before Benedict's visit.

11. I say "like" a modern writing historian's voice because wholly prose stories *were* memorized and handed down. My point is that they were handed down with less precision than Western written documents have been, and with less precision than were Pima orations and songs.

that is absolutely unique to this book, namely, "The Feud." Again and again, as my notes will attest, a somewhat obscure story in the present collection corresponds to another one from either the Pimas or the Papagos.

There is another aspect to the fullness. This is the quality of the written English relative to the original spoken Pima. This collection has almost no Pima in it—just isolated words such as the names of important characters and places. That is true of the two other full versions, too. Until Herzog's manuscript of Vanyiko's telling is published, there will be no native language version of a single narrator's full telling of ancientness. (A bilingual anthology of Papago narratives equal to a full telling was published by Saxton and Saxton in 1973, and two longish bilingual Papago stories appear in Evers 1980:110–22 and 128–49.)

That is a serious lack. The *Popol Vuh,* as I mentioned, was written in Maya. (It has been translated and retranslated into several languages.) Knowing some Pima-Papago and having done some translating from it, I can say that the four translations of full tellings (Benedict's collection, the two versions of Thin Leather, and the one of Smith) are about equal in conveying the flavor, idioms, and cadence of Pima.[12] None of them is really close, but the translations in Benedict are the nicest to read in English. This is partly because of her skill in English, but her interpreters and the tellers did their share, too. There must have been good feeling between everyone.

Finally, some comments on the importance of full tellings such as these and what scholarship can learn from or about them. The Pima-Papago were a small people or nation. (Now they are four independent tribal governments on four distinct reservations, called Salt River, Gila River, Ak Chin, and Tohono O'odham.)[13] In the past it was their mythology, if I may use that term, that made them a nation. They had no governing authority beyond the village council of elders (the Pima chiefs, for example, had little power), and they had no official telling of ancient times. Yet their practices in government and their mythologies were largely the same everywhere. Although they told their mythologies only at home among family members, the families told the same

12. All of the translators for the early ethnologists were Pimas, and none of the whites who wrote down the interpreters' translations understood Pima. Herzog, who took down Vanyiko's telling in Pima, had a grammarian's understanding of the language, and Dean Saxton (Saxton and Saxton 1973) had that and could converse in Pima as well.

13. In my opinion, the division of them into four was a cultural setback. It occurred because land between the reservations was taken from the Pima-Papagos by the United States. Of course at the time the land was taken, from 1850 to 1900, there was no single overarching Pima-Papago government, and moreover most of the taken land had no villages in it.

things, some families no doubt at greater length and with more love of the telling than others.

I suppose most tribal peoples had uniform but decentralized political and mythological cultures. I wish we knew, though, how commonly their mythologies were ordered like that—or those—of the Pima-Papagos, with a master chronicle spanning nearly the whole of ancientness and with documentary, or quasi-documentary, songs and oratory to bolster the prose. Other tribes' narrators must have found or put some order to their stories, but scholarship hasn't looked hard for it yet. The tendency in scholarship, in anthropology and literature, has been to compare versions of single stories (generally prose) across different narrators and tribes, not to study single narrators' arrangements of everything as we study the great authors of the Western tradition.

Benedict did what I ask in her way, not in her unfinished work on the Pimas but in her book *Zuni Mythology.* I don't know that Benedict's approach to that study has been summarized before. I will do so now quickly by constructing her answers and mine to the three questions on criticism that I asked in the earlier section "Dionysianism":

What did the native authors say (or tell)?

Benedict: What they said was either the accurate "reflection" of (1935, 1:xxvii) or an "idealization" of (xv) or a "compensatory daydream" about (xvi) "the conditions of everyday life" (xv), that is, "custom" (xv) or "behavior" (xxviii).
Bahr: What they said was histories of Edenic ancientness ("Edenic" meaning "before the time of normal sex and marriage").

How did they say it?

Benedict: They said it in many separate stories (of the size and autonomy of the short story of Western tradition). The stories have traditional "incidents" (e.g., "brides appear old in the morning" [1935, 1:xxv]) and "themes" (e.g., a "man's fear of submitting to a woman" [xxv]).[14] The tellers skillfully and individualistically adapted incidents to themes (xxxiv) and plots (xxxii).

14. Benedict gives a twelve-page index of incidents (1935, 2:334–45), of which there are about three hundred. I counted thirteen themes in volume 1's introduction, which is her critical essay: polygyny; abandonment of children; triumph of abandoned child; overworked children; death sought by summoning Apache; violent action based on secret enmity; triumph of the despised and weak; marriage taught by supernaturals; abduction (of women); erotic invitation (of men, by women); man's fear of submitting to a woman; reunion of families; and mildness—overall a pretty grim list.

Bahr: They composed long works using stories that past authors had used. (Note that in answer to the next question I count authors of neighboring tribes as formative influences: authors tend to stay true to their own peoples' stories, and they like to differ with stories from neighboring tribes.)

What do we make of it?

Benedict: We see and say how the culturally standardized frustrations of everyday life are compensated for, and find relief in, story-daydreams.
Bahr: We get familiar with the long works. (In other papers not to be discussed here I have read neighboring mythologies as parodies of each other. I hold that the current tellings of neighbors are as influential on mythologies as are the real pasts and personalities of the tellers. See Bahr 1998, n.d.*a,* and n.d.*b;* and note well: if mythologies are basically parodies of neighbors' mythologies, they can hardly be ethnographies of the tellers.)

In sum, Benedict's program was to connect the characters in texts to personality or character traits in real life, with emphasis on the frustrations entailed in everyday living. I see the characters in texts as having their own world, and I want to know what that whole world is. I find her literary criticism too atomistic. She might find mine trivial, first because it is merely about literature and second because I suppose that the two principles, those of overall mythic organization and Edenic content, apply to all mythologies. (She would prefer tensions between opposites.) I accept the first objection, and to the second I say that sex and marriage (the subjects of my Edenism) are not trivial, nor are they presented uniformly. Indeed, it seems that neighboring peoples made a principle of presenting them differently.

EDITING

Benedict had a fine "mental" ear for English poetry, which is why her texts are so pleasant to read, but her "regular" hearing was poor (Caffrey 1989:7, 102–3). This shows in the way she spelled Pima words. There was no Pima dictionary in her time, but Russell had written the language better than she, and Herzog, a musician, did better than Russell soon after her. An excellently heard and spelled Pima-Papago dictionary (but mainly Papago, or Tohono O'odham) came out in 1969. This was the work of the missionary linguists Dean and Lucille Saxton, and it was augmented by Susie Enos in a 1983 edition. Saxton, Saxton, and Enos are the state of the art for spelling Pima-Papago, a language which, from the scientific point of view, has several dialects on the "Papago" side and perhaps more than one among the "Pimas."[15]

When Benedict's spelling is not far from that given in Saxton, Saxton, and Enos, or even when she is far but she got the right sounds by an idiosyncratic means, I have left her versions alone. When I think she was misleadingly far from the Pima, I have put the Saxton, Saxton, and Enos version or another one in brackets after her version. To avoid undue bracketing, three frequent and important words are respelled for Benedict as if she had written them that way herself. These are Ho'ok (she wrote Haak), the name of a character; Nasia (she wrote Naasa), another character's name; and *va'aki* (she, *vaaka*), the name of a type of ancient house.

The letter-to-sound system—in other words, the orthography—used here is explained in Bahr et al. 1974:1. It is better to consult that source for the orthography than Saxton, Saxton, and Enos 1983 because some of my claimed improvements on the latter work are no more than the use of different letters for what all would agree are the same sounds. (I must add that this book uses the letter *v* for a sound written as *w* both by Bahr et al. and Saxton et al. This sound distinguishes Pima from Papago.) The spellings can be read aloud as Spanish is read. The main two symbols that can't be so read are the letter *e*, which is pronounced like the *o* in the English word *cool* but with the lips straight instead of rounded, and the apostrophe, which stands for a glottal stop, as in the English *oh-oh* (I would write that word as *o'o*). The letters *ḍ* and *ṣ* indicate that the tongue is curled back in pronouncing the sound. Finally, to pronounce Pima-Papago, put the stress (emphasis) on the first syllable of every long word.

To Benedict's wordings, English spellings, punctuation, and line divisions (in orations and songs) I have made changes only where I thought clarity or present-day writing conventions were better served by a change, and where the meaning would be the same. There is, however, the following change in punctuation. Benedict used quotation marks in the prose portions of the texts, but

15. Nowadays the Pimas call themselves and like to be called the "Akimel O'odham," River People, in complement to the Papagos' "Tohono O'odham," Desert People. Old-timers also refer to each other by village, district, or direction—for example, "Santa Rosa People," "Gila Bend People" (a district), and "Downhill People." What binds them together is the native word for "people" (the same word also means "male human" and "Native American")—"O'odham."

she did not place them around the songs and orations that are incorporated in many prose tellings. I have done this in the understanding that Pimas consider those songs and orations to be the very (quoted) words of the characters of a story.

When I prefer an English word translation significantly different from the one Benedict used (when either she gave or I think I know the Pima "original"), I keep her word and put my preference in brackets. When I have added new subheadings to a text, these are in brackets, too. Sometimes I have changed the title of a text but to avoid clutter don't give hers. Finally, as I mentioned earlier, Benedict didn't order the texts in an overall sequence and didn't form them into chapters. I did that, as well as inventing the chapter titles and the book title.

Benedict took down four long and important texts conjointly from Vanyiko and Blackwater. I don't know how she did this—whether in separate or joint sessions—because I don't have and haven't seen her field notebooks. In her edited typescripts, however, and in the penciled revisions she made upon them, one finds a fascinating and rare product, namely, a kind of duet or duovocal text. In certain passages the two men are presented in unison (I have marked these in boldface as "TV&WB"). But throughout most of these texts either Vanyiko or Blackwater speaks alone, as if, however, the other was listening. Usually these individualized portions are just a sentence or two. The two narrators rarely contradict each other (such that the truth of one statement would rule out the truth of the other). Rather, they supplement each other, so where one has something to say the other remains silent. This seems to be typical of oral literatures—they resolve into differences that don't contradict. But this quality, if typical, is rarely shown in publications. Here we see the telling as Benedict heard it from the two men. This was a more important feat of hearing than that which she was poor at, the hearing of picayune sound differences in Pima-language words.

When Vanyiko speaks alone, I put a "TV" in boldface, and correspondingly a "WB" for Blackwater (Benedict identified the narrators as "a" and "b," but her notes make clear who was who). And I have imposed on the duet texts the following additional convention of punctuation: I mark with a dash the end of each passage followed by a "solo" (single-speaker) passage, as well as the end of each solo passage itself. The dashes therefore indicate that one of the narrators is going to say, or has just said, something "on his own." Benedict did not do this.

Besides the four duets, which are rather long, Benedict took down some additional full but shorter texts from both Vanyiko and Blackwater, and sometimes from a third person as well. These she typed separately, not in duet format, and I publish them that way. In general these shorter, freestanding variants are more different from each other than are the long Vanyiko and Blackwater duets, mainly because the latter share so many passages in unison.[16]

Benedict wrote many footnotes to her typescripts. I have retained nearly all of these and leave them unmarked, as the book's "main" footnotes. When I have added something to them, the addition is bracketed. All the bracketing in this book is mine, whereas all the parenthetical materials in a text or a Benedict footnote, including the parentheses themselves, are Benedict's. My additional footnotes (in some chapters there are almost as many of them as there are of Benedict's) are marked at the end by "—*Ed.*," except in this introduction and the chapter introductions, where they are all my own.

16. I can't believe the two men said exactly the same words. I believe they said essentially the same thing, probably on separate occasions, and in making the typescript from her field notebooks, Benedict perceptively and creatively rendered them as if spoken in unison.

O'ODHAM CREATION
&
RELATED EVENTS

1

THE RAFTER HAULED

The Long Telling of Ancient Times

Introduction

Donald Bahr

One way Pimas and Papagos say "to tell of ancient times" is "to haul the rafter" (*vavandag i mo:t*). The word *vavan,* a verb, means "to stretch straight," "to span," "to be in a line." The suffix *-dag* makes the verb a noun, roughly "the straightness," "the spanner"—and this is the word used for ridgepoles, rafters, and crop rows.[1] *Mo:t,* or *mo:to,* means "to haul on the head (or back or shoulder)," "to lug."

To speak of the past as a rafter is to speak linearly—no question about that. The past, or ancientness, is conceived as a line of events in the long ago. To speak of telling the past as lugging or hauling implies work: the speaker lugs it from memory and speaks it out; the listener takes it on. This is correct. The text that Benedict called "The Creation" and I retitle "The Rafter" is long and in one piece. It stretches from the creation of the physical universe (earth, sun, moon, stars) to a point not quite in recent memory when the Pimas and their native neighbors settled in their present locations.[2]

If the rafter is the main line of the past, the rest of the chapters of this book are not exactly joists and studs, but the metaphor holds in a general way because the other chapters depend on—lean on, take their position from—the text of this chapter.[3] To understand the relation between the rafter and the rest

1. This last is actually *vavañim,* a related word.

2. But not the whites. It is said that they originated locally, but they left. The telling of ancientness ends just before their return.

3. Note that such a metaphor is used near the end of the Rain Ceremony oration in chapter 5, under the heading "Spreading the Heavens."

of the stories, we should recognize, first, that *all* of the stories in this collection belong to a period called "ancientness" (of which more later), but the stories of the rafter belong to the *Edenic* (analogous to Eden) portion of ancientness. By "Eden" (it is my analogy, not the Pimas') I mean the time of creations, which was also the time before normal human procreation and marriage. ("The Feud," the *Popol Vuh*–like story mentioned earlier, is exceptional for its fully human genealogy.) The two elements, creation and absence of marriage, are coordinated. Instead of marrying and procreating normally, the characters in Eden (whether in Pima texts or in the Bible) create miraculously. The Bible actually has little of this. Its narrative of Eden is short, and the main thing is the Original Sin. The Pimas in their rafter have much creation and, as it happens, nothing quite like the Original Sin. The key to understanding all this creation, or at least a great help, is the realization that it takes place in a time before there was human marriage.

Reading the text is a bit like solving a "what's wrong here" puzzle, where much of a picture looks normal but a close look reveals oddities. In this text the revelation comes in two stages. First, although stories with families and children are common enough, there are few accounts of the *formation* of these families—they are just "there." And when the formation is told, there is usually an inhuman parent. Second, the various acts of creation in the text are understandable as abnormal *pro*creations. Combining the two observations, one realizes that a hidden rule governs the text: tell no story in which a human man or boy meets a human woman or girl, the two like each other, they make love, and nine months later the woman has a baby whom the parents raise and who falls in love and marries in turn—tell everything but that, tell story after story differing from that. In these stories, gods make people from mud; a man gives birth through his penis; a woman is impregnated by a ball; a man sprouts feathers after drinking a girl's offered gruel; a man-eagle kidnaps a woman and fathers a child with her. This is a long Eden with no genealogical continuity; it either comes before or takes place outside of normal family life—the former, I think.

I next sketch the whole and note how this text and those of Thin Leather and Smith resemble the Bible's Eden. All the texts start with a character named Earth Doctor (actually Smith starts with God, called "Jeoss," from the Spanish *dios;* after creating, Jeoss stays in heaven, outside of the story). In both Pima texts, Earth Doctor is first narrated as existing in a space with no light or solidity, just as God does. Unlike God, however, Earth Doctor takes something solid from himself and causes it to grow into the earth, on which he (like God) dwells for a time (= Eden). Also unlike God, he makes the sun, moon, and stars from water or his spit. Then he causes a few beings almost as powerful as he to exist: a man named Elder Brother, a Coyote man, a Buzzard man, and, in this text, a woman named Nasia (the Blackwater-Vanyiko text is unique in introducing her at this time). Like God, Earth Doctor next makes a pair of humans—from mud in the Pima story—and like God during Eden, Earth Doctor stays for a time near to the first humans.

The people multiply. The women's fecund promiscuity alarms Earth Doctor. He makes an additional man (never named, to my knowledge) to ruin the creation. The man goes from woman to woman, impregnating them into ever shorter intervals until childbirth. Finally he gives birth through his penis, which causes a flood (from the baby's tears, some texts say). After the flood, humanity is created again, this time from mud molded by Elder Brother, not by Earth Doctor. Earth Doctor sinks into the earth, but Eden continues, now with a different principal man-god. The ball pregnancy and man-eagle stories come in this period. There is trouble again, but this time it is aggression from the people. They kill Elder Brother. He is resurrected (like Jesus, God's miraculous son) and eventually gets the people all killed, or at least conquered. These people are the Hohokam (Pima *Huhugkam,* "The-finished-ones"). They are conquered by the Pima-Papagos.

The Rafter

Thomas Vanyiko and William Blackwater

[Earth and Sky]

TV&WB In the beginning there was darkness. Darkness spun round upon itself and from it was born Earth Doctor. He went west, south, east, north, up, and down, looking everywhere, but there was nothing.

He created first the greasewood plant, and after that big black ants to form the gum of the greasewood. But Earth Doctor was not satisfied. He considered. He created termites to live also on the greasewood. They formed dust,[4] and he took it in his hand and shaped it into a ball. He went to a great height and placed it, but it would not

4. They make a light dust on decaying wood. The same Pima word is used for body lice [*hiopc,* "body louse" (Saxton, Saxton, and Enos 1983:91), "termite" (Russell 1908:207)].

remain steady. The dust blew around the earth, and the ball would not hold together—

WB It fell and Earth Doctor caught it again—

TV&WB He laid hold of darkness in the west and stretched it toward the east. He laid hold of darkness in the east and stretched it toward the west. He laid hold of darkness in the south and stretched it toward the north. He laid hold of darkness in the north and stretched it toward the south. Upon the place where the lines joined, he set the earth he had made and it rested there.

The earth was not large enough and he was not satisfied. He stood upon the top of the ball where he had placed it, holding his torch,[5] and he sang:

"The earth is spreading, spreading.
Earth Doctor made the earth,
Standing upon it he spread it in all directions.
The earth is spreading, spreading.
Earth Doctor made the earth,
The earth spread flat in all directions."

Still the earth was not large enough. He stood a second time upon it and sang: (repeat [the previous song]).

He stood a third time upon it and sang: (repeat).

The earth became large and he was satisfied. He rested.

Water covered the earth. Earth Doctor took his cane. He spread the water and pushed it in all directions, leaving bare the surface of the earth. For this reason water does not cover all the land.

The earth was not solid. He made the sky, but this did not steady the earth. He made a second sky lower than the first, but this did not steady the earth. He held his torch behind him and cast his shadow before him. He reached out and laid hold upon his shadow. He seized it in his hand, and of this he created Buzzard.

He caused the heavens to come down and strike the earth, and from the union of sky and earth was born Elder Brother. Again he caused the heavens to come down, and of the joining—

WB out of the water—

TV&WB came the first woman, Nasia. They were brother and sister and they live forever.

5. Vanyiko interpolated that the torch was the first creation of Earth Doctor.

There was no light but the torch of Earth Doctor. He put water in his mouth and spewed it out upon the sky and formed the little stars. It was not enough. He took his crystal and threw it into the sky. It broke and formed the large stars. It was not enough. He put his power on the point of his cane and drew it in a great circle across the sky and formed the Milky Way. It was not enough. He took a bowl of water—

TV: and set it overnight to form ice. He formed a man and gave him the mask of ice and a feather headdress. He threw him to the north. He fell back to the earth. Earth Doctor threw him to the west. He fell back to the earth. Earth Doctor threw him to the south. He fell back to the earth. Earth Doctor threw him to the east—

WB He threw [the bowl of water] into the heavens. [It became the moon.]—

TV&WB [The water, or the man, became the moon.] The moon stayed in the heavens and began to cross the sky. It was not enough. He took another bowl of water—

WB and set it overnight to form ice. He formed another man and gave him the second mask of ice and a larger headdress—

TV&WB and threw him [or the water] to the east. He sang:

> *"I have made the sun!*
> *It rises in the east and gives light to all people."*

The sun remained in the sky.

The sun traveled over the heavens, but it was high and traveled slowly. It was four days before it came to the sunset. Earth Doctor took the sun from the sky and threw it up again, but it was so low it scorched the land. He took the sun again and threw it to the sky, and it traveled a middle course, and it gave light to the earth.

During the day the sun gave light to the earth. And during the night, the moon. They were of equal power and there was no darkness. Therefore, Earth Doctor placed—

WB darkness—

TV his power—

TV&WB upon the face of the moon so that during the night there should be rest. He sang:

> *"I am going, I am going,*
> *To form darkness to cover the earth."*

He hung the moon so that it went down in the west as the sun rose in the east. There was no break between the light and the darkness. He sang:

"I am making the early light (dawn),
I am making the early light.
Toward the east the early light is shining."

The moon preceded the sun across the sky and the sun pursued her. The rays of the sun reached to the moon. The sun impregnated her[6] and she bore Coyote. At noon the moon dropped her baby on the mountain Aatkawitka and laid it on top of the bush *korhops.*[7] For this reason the bush is called Coyote's *korhops*—

TV Coyote rose and came down the mountain. He came to Earth Doctor and Elder Brother—

TV&WB There were five beings now in the world: Earth Doctor, Elder Brother, Nasia, Buzzard, and Coyote. But the earth was not steady. Earth Doctor made great rocks to steady the earth and placed them around its edges. He made all plants to steady the earth, but the earth was not firm. Therefore Earth Doctor and Elder Brother went together toward the east. Earth Doctor said, "Use your power to make the earth steady." Elder Brother put his hands upon the earth and sang:

"In the east the earth is shaking.
I put my hands upon it steadying it.
I watch till the earth is made firm."

At the east the earth ceased shaking and became steady. They returned to the middle point of the earth. In the west it was still unsteady. They went to the west and Earth Doctor said, "Use your power to make the earth steady." Elder Brother put his foot upon the earth and sang:

"Toward the west the earth is shaking.
I put my foot upon it steadying it.
I watch till the earth is made firm."

6. Because Pima pronouns have no gender, the English translator must choose feminine, masculine, or neuter according to context. Here, the moon's gender seems to be female, so "her" is appropriate, but it is impossible to square this passage with Vanyiko's previous statement that the moon was made as a man.—*Ed.*

7. Evidently misheard as "korhops," the word is *tohaws,* "brittlebush." The mountain name is unrecognized.—*Ed.*

The earth at the west was still. They returned to the middle point of the earth. In the far west the earth still shook. Earth Doctor became Mockingbird.[8] He lit on every tree and on the tops of the mountains, speaking all the languages of the world, and it quieted the earth. He became Spider and spun his thread from the sky to the earth and around the edges of the world. And Earth Doctor sang:

"Spider with his ropes makes the earth steady.
Spider with his ropes makes the mountain steady."

He made a canopy for the clouds to rest on. For this reason we see the clouds still resting upon the canopy of the spider, and after the rain we see in the sky the white thread with which the spider bound the earth to the heavens—

TV The earth remained firm and steady. The earth was level, without a crease. There were no rivers, no mountains. Earth Doctor called Buzzard and sent him to give features to the earth. Buzzard sang:[9]

"Buzzard is the bird who gives shape to the earth."
(4 times)

Buzzard dropped from the sky, and with the edges of his wings he cut the river beds and the canyons. Still the ridges of the mountains stretched without a break. Buzzard sang:

"Buzzard is the bird who gives shape to the mountains."
(4 times)

With the edges of his wings he cut the peaks and folds of the mountain ranges.

Earth Doctor considered the rain. He cut four pieces of bamboo and painted them black. He threw them into the sky and they formed the black clouds, and from them fell black rain. He was dissatisfied and wiped them out. He made four pieces of bamboo and painted them white and threw them into the sky and they formed the white clouds, and from them fell rain white like lime. He was dissatisfied and erased them from the heavens. He made red clouds, and from them fell rain like blood, but he was dissatisfied and wiped them

8. The Rain Ceremony oration [chapter 5] touches on these events.

9. "We call this Buzzard's song, but they were all sung by Earth Doctor and he created all things." Both narrators explained at length that though Earth Doctor worked through Mockingbird, Spider, and Buzzard, he alone had created the world. "Like the Trinity," the interpreter said.

out. He took all the colors of the rainbow and made white clouds, and from them fell clear water. He was pleased, and therefore we have white clouds and clear rain in this world—

WB But the colors he had rejected were smudged across the heavens—and the clouds are still colored in the sky.

The clouds were too high and he made them settle lower toward the earth. He called the winds from all directions, but there were no winds so strong as South Wind. He called South Wind[10] to bring clouds full of seeds from the Green Snake (ocean) that lies around the earth—

TV He caused low clouds to come up out of the ocean, filled with seeds—

TV&WB [The clouds] were low and hung below the tops of the mountains; and when they covered the bottomland with seeds, the seeds did not fall on the tops of the mountains. For this reason there are no trees on the tops of the mountains. Earth Doctor caused another cloud to rise from the ocean, filled with seeds of the large brush of the desert. This stood higher in the heavens and the seeds fell higher upon the mountains. Again he caused a cloud to rise from the ocean, but it still lay below the tops of the mountains. He caused a fourth cloud to rise full of the seeds of the small desert plants. This stood even with the tops of the mountains and for this reason the smallest plants grew to the tops of mountains.

[Humans]

After this they made the crawling creatures of the earth and the birds of the air. Earth Doctor took red clay and made images. He breathed into them and they became men. He told them what was right and what was wrong and gave them the power to carry out their plans—

TV For this reason anyone who makes up his mind to undertake anything, goes through with it—

TV&WB People multiplied till they covered the whole earth. There was not enough to eat—

TV the roots of the trees made the ground hard as a board so that people could not plant in the earth—

10. This phrase and the preceding two sentences are unassigned in Benedict's manuscript. Following the sense of the passage, I have assigned them to WB.—*Ed.*

TV&WB and they fell upon each other and ate each other. Earth Doctor was angry with his people—
WB and he sent out his power[11]—
TV and he took his cane and pulled down the heavens upon them—
TV&WB and destroyed them. Again Earth Doctor took red clay and made male and female, and they multiplied. Their lives were too short, and he was not satisfied—
TV He took his cane and pulled down the heavens—
WB he sent out his power—
TV&WB and destroyed his second creation—
WB Again he took red clay and made man and woman. They multiplied and had children. But the children began to smoke before they were grown and Earth Doctor was angry with his people. He sent out his power and destroyed his third creation. A fourth time he took out his power and made two images, male and female. They multiplied but the women lived loose lives and Earth Doctor was angry. He did not want to destroy his people again—

[Flood]

TV&WB He talked to them saying: "Live good lives or I will destroy you." But again they sinned, and he said, "I will send a flood upon you." But they would not listen. He said to them again, "When you see the waters spring up from the roots and stumps of trees, then you will believe what I tell you now." Still they would not listen. Therefore Earth Doctor made a plan to destroy them.

Earth Doctor and Elder Brother and Buzzard and Nasia consulted together. They said, "We will destroy the people of this earth, but we will save the creatures of the earth and the birds of the air." Earth Doctor directed the animals—
TV to climb on drift logs to save themselves from the flood—
WB to live in the foam on the top of the waters—
TV&WB He called the birds and he sent Hummingbird, Woodpecker, Kiosop, and Kootovitc[12] to the sky to remain there while the earth was flooded—

11. "A power like poison gas."

12. *Gi:supi,* "black phoebe," and *kul-wicigam,* "curve-billed thrasher" (Saxton, Saxton, and Enos 1983:16, 36).—*Ed.*

WB Nasia went into the heavens, and Earth Doctor and Elder Brother remained on earth—
TV&WB Earth Doctor took his cane and waved it in the air. He made an ark in which to save himself. Elder Brother made an olla in which to save himself. He tested it, and it was watertight and it would float upon the water—
TV Coyote said to Earth Doctor, "What shall I do?" Earth Doctor said, "You knew what was about to happen. You should have been getting ready." Coyote had a flute with him. Earth Doctor said, "Give it to me." He enlarged it and shoved Coyote inside. He stopped both ends so that they were watertight and threw it upon the ground—
TV&WB In the west, Wind Covered Medicine Man (Hüwamaiac Maaka)[13] called his people together. He stood and cried, "Listen. This earth will be destroyed. It will take fire and burn us all." He sang:

> *"Earth is burning and the mountains are melting down to the plain."*

The people went to their homes, and Wind Covered Medicine Man received knowledge and called them again saying: "I know now surely that the earth will not burn, but it will be overwhelmed with flood. Choose now the highest mountain, so that when the waters come we may escape." He sang:

> *"Flood, flood, I know now,*
> *The world will be destroyed with flood."*

Now Earth Doctor made a plan and he created a handsome young man to come from the east. The handsome young man went into every house where a young girl lived. Next morning the girl with whom he had slept gave birth to a child. Wind Covered Medicine Man had a daughter, and she heard what was happening in the world. She cried. Her father said, "Why is it that you weep?" "Because a stranger has come and he sleeps with the daughters in every house, and in the morning they give birth to children." Her father said to her, "When he comes to this house, do as I tell you—
TV "Take his bow and arrows from him and hang them up"—
WB "Make broth out of corn and give it to him"—
TV&WB "Then we shall know if we shall overcome him"—

13. Hewel Ma'iṣp Ma:kai, "Wind Covered-up-by Medicine-man."—*Ed.*

WB Her father made for her a woman's apron of sharp thorns, and she tied it around her waist—
TV&WB She did as her father had commanded her. The stranger came and spent the night—
WB The thorns pricked him so that they did not lie together—
TV&WB Next morning her parents heard the cry of the baby, and her parents went to see the child. The baby had been born of the man and not of the woman. The young man picked up the child and started for his home in the east, singing:

"I have discovered something.
I have discovered that water is oozing up through the earth."

He returned to Earth Doctor.

The whole earth became damp. Water ran from the wood they brought for their campfires. The people gathered and went to Broad Mountain (Momatc) and to Breezy Mountain (Moadek) and to Crooked Mountain (Gakotc).[14]

Wind Covered Medicine Man led his people and went to Crooked Mountain. He sang:

"With sadness we are traveling under the sun.
With all my people we are traveling"—

WB Some of the people who believed went to Earth Doctor; and he bored a hole in the earth, and he sank them so that they were safe during the flood. These were the only people who were saved from the flood[15]—
TV The stranger returned to Elder Brother with the baby. He laid the child down at a little distance. The child cried, and his tears ran over the earth. Elder Brother said, "What did you do with the baby?" He went back to get the child and already the baby's tears had formed a lake. The water rose and drowned the young man and spread over the surface of the earth—
TV&WB The waters rose until they came almost to the tops of the mountains—

14. The three mountain names should probably be Komaḍk, "Broad," Muhadag, "Greasy" (misheard by Benedict as "breezy"?), and Gakoḍk, "Crooked" (correctly identified by Benedict as Superstition Mountain).—*Ed.*

15. Many accounts (e.g., Russell 1908:210, 226) say that these were ancestors to the Pimas.—*Ed.*

TV The ark floated on the surface of the waters; and the olla, with Elder Brother; and the flute, with Coyote—

TV&WB Wind Covered Medicine Man drew a white line along the ridge of Crooked Mountain. He used his power and said to the waters, "When you have reached this line, cease rising." The waters came to that place and covered it, and still they rose. He sang:

"The water is rising over the land.
The water is rising over the land.
It increases.
Here I stand above the waters."

Four times he used his power upon the waters and he said, "I have used all my powers over the waters. I will use my power over the mountains." He stood on the top of the mountain and he sang:

"The mountain is shaking with the rising of the water.
The mountain is shaking with the rising of the water.
It is growing.
Here I stand on the top of the mountain."

Four times he used his power over the mountain. And he said, "I have used all my power over the waters and over the mountains. I must use my power upon you yourselves."

The people went down to the mark he had drawn on the mountain to see if the water was still rising, and they came back saying, "The water is rising fast." A little dog came with them, and the dog spoke and said, "The water is rising fast."

Wind Covered Medicine Man said, "Now I know that something will really happen. When did a dog talk before? Stand close, for it is upon you I must use my power." He stood holding his medicine man's flint stones, and he sang:

"I the medicine man,
With my medicine man's stones,
I turn into stone." (4 times)

He clapped the stones together suddenly and everyone turned into stone. That is why we still see Wind Covered Medicine Man and all his people standing at the top of Crooked Mountain, and the white lines that he drew upon the mountain.

The waters rose and covered the whole earth—

TV The ark, the olla, and the bamboo whirled four times around the edges of the world. Earth Doctor was floating about in the ark, and he sang:

> *"White* va'aki *in the east!*[16]
> *I am floating about in the water!"*

Elder Brother floated about in his olla, and he sang:

> *"Black* va'aki *in the west!*[17]
> *I am floating about in the water!"*

The ark and the olla and the flute floated four times around the world, and Earth Doctor sang again:

> *"The waters have covered the driftwood that is piled on the edge of the world."*

All the animals that had taken refuge were destroyed. The four birds that Earth Doctor had sent to the sky hung by their beaks from the heavens. The water rose and rose. It reached the tails of Woodpecker and Kootovitc [thrasher]. That is why there is a dark mark on the tail of these birds. But when the water reached this point it stopped rising and it did not touch the tail of Hummingbird and Kiosop [black phoebe]. Kootovitc was frightened and cried. The others plucked their downy feathers and made a nest for him. To this day he lives far to the west in his nest of downy feathers, and we call him Downy-feather-nest Medicine Man (Vikoshkam Maaka).[18]

Hummingbird began to cry, and he sang:

> *"It is almost morning:*
> *God* [Dioṣ],[19] *my Father,*
> *Come and help me."*

When he heard the song, Earth Doctor came to Hummingbird. The rain was pouring down and he said, "Come, Hummingbird, make this water go down, and I will stop the rain." He gave Hummingbird power to make the flood go down. Hummingbird sang:

> *"Hummingbird is making the waters go down." (4 times)*

16. The ark. [Normally *va'aki* means "great-house," that is, a large building of sun-dried mud, made by the prehistoric Hohokam. For a discussion see Bahr et al. 1994, index entry "Great-house."]

17. His olla.

18. Vi:g Koṣkam Ma:kai, "Down Nest-having Medicine-man," is looked upon as one of the personifications of the Creator, Earth Doctor (Herzog n.d.*c*).—*Ed.*

19. *Diosh,* the narrator insists, is an ancient Pima word.

He kept on singing. The rain stopped and the waters began to go down. He asked Kiosop to help him. Kiosop said, "I cannot do anything but sing your song." He sang:

"Hummingbird is trying to make the waters go down." (4 times)

Earth Doctor sang:

"Hummingbird, hanging above me,
Has power to make the waters go down.
He is causing the waters to fall."

The waters were falling fast, and the ark and the olla and the flute were whirled in a whirlpool of the receding water—

TV&WB Earth Doctor's ark grounded first, in the east, and Elder Brother's olla next, near the ocean in the west. You can still see the big flat mountain in the west country. Coyote's flute grounded last, toward the west.

Earth Doctor came out of his ark and stepped into the water. It was breast-high, and the foam settled in a line upon his breast. Elder Brother came out of his olla and stepped into the water. The water came almost to his waist, and a line of foam settled across his thighs. Coyote came out last and stepped into the water, and the foam only washed his heels—

WB Earth Doctor, Elder Brother, Nasia, Buzzard, and Coyote wandered over the face of the earth until they came together—

TV Earth Doctor and Elder Brother set out to look for each other. Earth Doctor went to the west, and Elder Brother went to the East; and they passed each other without meeting. When Earth Doctor had come to the west and Elder Brother had come to the east, they turned and Earth Doctor went to the east and Elder Brother went to the west. Four times they passed each other before they met, going from east to west and west to east. They were both singing:

"On this whole earth I see the tracks of the medicine man."

At last they met, and Elder Brother said, "Here you are, my younger brother!" And Earth Doctor answered, "Why do you call me younger brother? It was I who came out first after the flood. See the mark of the foam breast-high on my body, and yours is across your thighs. Nevertheless, if you wish it, I will be your younger brother, and I will call you Tksir'xa [S-e'ehe] 'Elder Brother'"—

WB Earth Doctor gave Elder Brother power to rule in this earth and gave him the Elder Brother—

TV They started out to find Coyote. In the distance they heard him howling. He came, saying, "How do you do, my younger brothers?"

"Why call us your younger brothers? See the marks of the foam on our bodies, and yours is at your heel!"—

[New Creation]

TV&WB They said to each other, "We must find the center of the earth." They sent Woodpecker east and Hummingbird west to see if they were at the center of the earth. Hummingbird came back first, so they moved toward the—

TV east—

WB west—

TV&WB and sent him out again. Again Hummingbird returned first, and again they moved toward the—

TV east—

WB west—

TV&WB Four times they moved farther toward the—

TV east—

WB west—

TV&WB and at last both birds came back at the same moment, and they settled there.

Earth Doctor sang:

"I came from the east;
I came and discovered the navel of the earth." (repeat)

Elder Brother sang:

"I came from the west;
I came and discovered the navel mountain of the earth." (repeat)

Earth Doctor gathered all the waters and made them sink into the ground, that springs might well up. The earth was still wet and he created ants to dry the ground. They dug down into the dry earth and brought it to the surface, and out of the dust the ants brought up they built a *va'aki* of many rooms at the navel of the earth. Earth Doctor sang:

> *"Wonderful* va'aki *that is made of adobe.*
> *In it we begin life again."*[20]

He sang again:

> *"Strong* va'aki *that is made of adobe.*
> *In it we begin life again."*

They sent the ants down to bring up red earth, and they made [three] balls of clay—

TV Earth Doctor took one and sat down facing the east. And Elder Brother took one and sat down facing the south. Coyote took the [third] and sat down facing the west—

WB Elder Brother and Coyote [both] faced west with their backs to [Earth Doctor]—

TV&WB They began to make clay figures. When they were finished—

WB Earth Doctor sent Coyote to look at the images they had made. He came back and reported that they were all good—

TV&WB Elder Brother went to Coyote, and when he looked at his figures he saw that some were made with one leg and some with long ears that hung down to their heels and some with webbed hands—

TV? He said to Coyote, "What's the good of these? How can this one walk with one leg?" "He can hop." "What's the good of these with webbed fingers?" "They can use their hand for a dipper to drink." "What's the good of ears down to their heels?" "They can use one for a bed and the other for a covering."

There were some that had no vents, and Elder Brother said, "What good are these that have no holes? How can they eat?" Coyote said, "They don't need to eat. They can smell their food and it will be just the same."

Elder Brother was angry, and he threw all Coyote's figures to the west into the ocean. And that is why we see ducks and beavers and mermaids[21] and fish with long ears in the ocean—

TV&WB Elder Brother went to Earth Doctor and looked at the figures that he had made, and most of them were wild beasts and he did not like them, and half of them he threw away. Earth Doctor was angry—

TV He lifted his cane and was about to pull down the skies to destroy the earth—

20. Or, [we are] made over again. (The location of the *va'aki* is not known.)

21. So translated. Pimas are said to have seen mermaids in the Gulf of California. From the descriptions they are probably seals.

TV&WB "If we cannot agree, let us return to darkness and no existence"—
WB Elder Brother with his power put aside the darkness—
TV Elder Brother put his hand upon the sky and held it in place—
TV&WB and said to Earth Doctor, "Let us have peace." But Earth Doctor sank into the earth. Elder Brother snatched at him, but he had already sunk beneath the surface[22]—
WB and he caught only a thick sticky substance—
TV&WB When he opened his hands, sickness spread over the whole earth—
TV "I did not think my people would live with sickness and suffering. But what has happened has happened"—
TV&WB Elder Brother took up the clay figures that he had made. He carried them into the *va'aki* that they had built and went off a distance. In four days he sent Coyote. Coyote heard talking in the *va'aki*. In one corner a group had come to life. In four days he sent Coyote again. In another corner a [second] group had come to life. He sent him a third time and a third group had come to life. He sent him a fourth time and a fourth group had come to life. They were all talking. So all languages came to be—
TV Still there were no Pimas. They waited a long time and built a fire and warmed the clay figures. When the images were hot, they began to talk, and they were Pimas—
WB They were always talking so that nobody could sleep with the racket. Coyote said to Elder Brother, "Do something so that they may rest." Elder Brother caused them to sleep with a deep sleep. He divided their hearts, one side the half of sleep, the other of wakefulness. The one half they used in the daytime and the other half at night.

Again Coyote said to Elder Brother, "Do something to make them see things when they are asleep, so they will have something to talk about."

Earth Doctor sang:

"In the darkness my people sleep.
In their sleep their spirits (duak)[23] go journeying over the earth.
In darkness they receive their wisdom (dreams)."

22. Most versions of the story have Earth Doctor stay in the underworld after his sinking. But TV and WB treat the sinking as a demonstration of Earth Doctor's power, not his actual departure.—*Ed.*
23. Probably *duakag*, "life."—*Ed.*

He sang again:

"In the daytime when my people dream it shall not be powerful.
The night dream is powerful.
(In the day) their being may wander but without receiving knowledge."

After he had sung, that night all the people dreamed, and when they woke they told their dreams—

TV Coyote said, "Do something so that even in their sleep the people will travel and see things (receive knowledge)." Elder Brother agreed and he sang (as above). After he had sung that night all the people dreamed. Next evening they stayed up late telling each other their dreams. All night they kept Earth Doctor and Elder Brother and Coyote awake. Earth Doctor said to Elder Brother, "We must do something to keep them still at night." And Elder Brother caused them to sleep with a deep sleep. He divided their hearts; one half they were to use in the daytime, and the other half at night. After that, when they began to tell their dreams at night, the half that was filled with drowsiness overcame them and they fell asleep—

TV&WB Coyote said to Elder Brother, "The people are naked. We should do something to cover their nakedness." Elder Brother took clay to make aprons for the women. He sang:

"This clay is the best I can do" (repeat)—

WB Next he gave them the inner bark of the willow for clothing. Second, the skin of animals. Third, fabrics of native cotton. Fourth, silk—

TV&WB Earth Doctor said, "These people multiply too fast." It would be better to make some plan. Let us give them death—

TV for as a tree dries up at certain times and nothing remains but the stalk, and when the rain comes again it leafs out, so let it be with these people. And as a bird when it is plucked looks ragged, but in time its feathers grow again as before,[24] so it shall be with my people"—

TV&WB They thought, therefore, how they should give their people death—

24. The narrator explained that this referred to a family that has lost an only child and is as a stalk or plucked bird, but when another child is born it is as the tree that is leafed out again, or as the bird whose feathers have grown.

TV They made a plan. They caused a quarrel between an Apache child and a Pima child, and the Apache child cried and came to its mother. She was angry and whipped the Pima child. Then the Pima mother fought the Apache mother, and the Pima father came to help her, and the Apache father came and fought also. So there was a fight between the Apaches and the Pimas, and Earth Doctor taught the Apaches to live on the north side of the Gila Valley. Earth Doctor sang:

"On the tops of the mountains you shall live.
You shall live on the roots and plants on the mountains."

He gave the Apaches bamboo arrows, and the Pimas arrows of arrow weed. He told them to test the power of their arrows, and the Apache arrow went through wood and stone, and the Pima arrow went only through wood and did not penetrate the stone. Earth Doctor said, "This will not do. One has too much power."

(Recitative [Oration]: Ritual of the Apache Arrow)[25]

"Do you feel the power of the enemy's arrow?
Did you feel it when it hit you?
Did you groan and roll about?

***In the east is a shining crystal* va'aki.**
In it lives Kootovitc Medicine Man.
He went out onto the roof of his house;
He sat there and sent out his power, searching to see if all was still (peaceful).
He felt the power of the bamboo arrow and went down into his house.
He took the bamboo of darkness and out of it he drew darkness.
With it he painted a black horizontal band across his face.[26]
He went out and followed the trail of the bamboo arrow, and by the far ocean he overtook the arrow.

25. The following is the first of the recitatives [orations] that are incorporated in the myths and that are used in curing, rain, and war ceremonies. They are always distinct in literary form from the more informal narrative. This one is used to heal anyone wounded by an Apache arrow.

26. The *kootovitc* [thrasher] has this black horizontal line across its face.

He picked it up and he bit the eyes (of the bamboo, the joints of the reed) and he weakened its power.
He retraced his steps to his own home, bringing with him the (captured) power of the bamboo."

And he sang the song of Elder Brother:

"Bamboo has no power,
It is hollow inside,
It has no strength,
It cannot wound.
Strengthen yourself and overcome the danger."

Elder Brother asked the Apaches and the Pimas to shoot again, and both of their arrows went through wood and stopped short at the stone, and Elder Brother said, "It is very good."

He put power between the Apaches and the Pimas, so that when the Apaches were victorious they acquired the power; and when the Pimas won, in their turn they acquired power. Elder Brother said, "I did not think this enmity would come between these tribes but since it has happened, it has happened. Let it be so"—

[The First Death][27]

WB The people lived at the navel of the earth and there was no death. Earth Doctor returned to his people as a poor man, and no one knew that it was he. He built a village council house and gathered the people together. He spoke to them as a great orator, and people came from all directions to hear him. He made a snake for his pet and the snake had rattles but no poison. The people played with this snake. They would throw it into the air and listen to its rattle. One day when they were alone, Earth Doctor said to his snake, "Does it hurt you to have them throw you about?"

"Yes, but I do nothing about it."

27. This story and the next one, down to the "Navitcu" section, are practically the same as stories told by the Maricopas (Spier 1933:347–52). Although they were widely known among Pimas and Papagos, WB and TV were the only narrators of record who considered the story to belong to the Pima-Papago as distinct from the Maricopa past, that is, as pertaining to the Pima-Papago god Earth Doctor. I think it likely that many Maricopas and Pimas would have criticized them for stealing, or, as an academic would say, "plagiarizing," this story from the Maricopas.—*Ed.*

"I will do something to help you." Before sunrise he went out and built a fire. When the sun came up he took one of his [the sun's] rays and made a fang. He took another and made another fang. And he put the heat of the sun in the teeth of his pet snake. He took more rays and decorated the snake's back, and he said to the snake, "When anyone troubles you, bite him. If you kill him you will also be the one to help him back to life again."

Next day the people came again to the council house and played with the snake. He bit at them and the people left him alone. Rabbit came, however, and he was not careful. The snake bit him. He lay without moving and the people said, "What is the matter?" Rabbit answered, "Snake bit me and the pain is growing worse." They took him to his house and at exactly the time of day when the snake had bitten him, he died. This was the first death. They wondered what they could do. The people went to Yellow Buzzard and asked, "What can we do to avenge our friend?"

Yellow Buzzard answered, "There is nothing you can do. Only Earth Doctor could have given him [the snake] his power. There is nothing I can do. But I can avenge you." Yellow Buzzard sent Green Frog. Frog waited till Earth Doctor went out to defecate. She sat on the ground and sucked out his heart (through the rectum) and Earth Doctor became ill. This was the first sickness. Earth Doctor gave himself to show the people how to prepare for sickness—

TV Earth Doctor came among his people as a sick man—

WB? All the people and crawling people and birds came to care for him. He asked for this and that, and when it was brought he refused it.[28] He said, "I want the finest sand. Perhaps I will lie on it and feel better." They gathered the finest sand of the arroyo, but he refused it. Again they went to a more distant arroyo and brought the finest sand, but he refused it.

Coyote said, "He means the fine sand of the ocean," and his people went away to the west and brought the fine sand of the ocean. When they had brought it he said, "Yes. That is what I want." He had them make the bed, and he lay on it[29]—

28. "Like a sick person. Medicine men are always hard to understand, too; they speak in riddles."

29. [Vanyiko] said that some people had fine sand beds, and those who had them might lie on them when they were sick or in childbirth, but they are not especially connected with curing.

[Farming and the Calendar]

TV He taught the people to dig holes and plant seeds, that they might live. He took the tail of Kiosop and spread it out and told them to count the feathers in his tail. There were twelve. And he said, "There shall be twelve months in every year"—

WB His people who had gathered together to care for him said, "Earth Doctor is recovering." So some of them [went] to their homes. He said, "Where are the people?" "They thought you were cured and they have gone to their homes." "I think my time is come, and I have something to say to them." "Some are here."

He called those who had remained and told them how to plant the earth and gather the crops. Those who heard him are the ones who know how to do these things, and those who went away are the shiftless ones—

TV&WB So Earth Doctor died. The people gathered together to decide what to do with his body. Some said, "Let us dig a hole and bury him"—

WB Others said, "No. There is this man Coyote, and he is likely to scratch up the ground and desecrate the grave." "Let us put him in a high place." "No. Coyote can climb up." "Let us put him in deep water." "No. Coyote can dive." "Let us burn the body." Nobody made any objection—

TV&WB They burned Earth Doctor's body—

WB They stood around the pyre in circles. When everything was burned but the heart, Coyote jumped through the row of people and seized the heart. He ran with it and the ashes of it scattered as sickness.[30]

This is how we know there are other ways of disposing of the dead, and they are wrong. All these ways are used by other people, and in this way sickness has been scattered—

TV Earth Doctor's ashes were scattered in the winds. From that time all the people who had lived together were scattered like his ashes, the Yumas, the Maricopas, the Papagos, the Pimas. The birds also, who had lived together, were scattered over the face of the earth. The people lived happily. Everything grew without cultivation and they were

30. It should be remembered that the Pimas never cremated the dead, except on the battlefield under forced circumstances so that the Apaches should not desecrate the bodies. [Cremation, however, is the standard Maricopa funeral practice. See Spier 1933:414–15.]

at peace. They built the *va'aki*s [great houses], and Elder Brother appointed the chiefs to live in those *va'aki*s and to be medicine men and to have more power than the rest of the people—

WB Next year the people began to plant seeds, but there was no rain. They had no crops and nothing to eat. The second year, also, their crops failed. And the third and the fourth. There was famine so that the people scattered all over the earth looking for food.

Nasia started for the west.[31] She came to a fertile land and remained. There plants grew without labor and springs ran over with water. Every month she swam in one of the springs and became young again. When at the end of each month she was old, she swam again in the spring.

One day, on going to the spring to bathe, she saw something on the opposite bank. Nasia said to the gopher, "You can do nothing to me." She went into the water to bathe and forgot all about Gopher. Gopher entered the water and impregnated her. She was frightened and came out of the spring. She started home. On her way, there were four mountains to cross. As she came to the last she gave birth to twin boys.

From the sun there came down a bowl in which to wash the children, and cradles in which to put them. The sun named them Parahaki and Parahang. She brought them up until they were old enough to use the bow and arrow. She taught them; and they killed the wood rat, the rabbit, the jackrabbit, [and birds,] each time a larger bird, until they had killed a deer.

One day they were hunting and shot a deer but it did not fall down. Their mother chased everywhere over the mountains following the deer. They suffered hunger and thirst and weariness. They came home sorrowful. So their mother taught them that whoever hunts deer suffers hunger and thirst and weariness. It is not an easy thing to kill the deer.

[Navitcu]

And this was the last of the works of the five helpers:[32] she taught them how they should multiply.

31. This story is given separately and at greater length under the title "Nasia's Twins" in chapter 2.—*Ed.*

32. That is, childbirth, the gift of Nasia [who—with Earth Doctor, Elder Brother, Buzzard, and Coyote—is one of the five helpers, also called five beings earlier in the text].

Elder Brother made Turtle out of frog spittle, and out of driftwood he made Navitcu.[33] He gave him a smooth face and round eyes, no nose.[34] And he gave him the power of beautiful blossoms and of flowering vines. He sent Turtle and Navitcu toward the west, and Turtle sank into the earth and tunneled through to the ocean; therefore Turtle is in the ocean. Navitcu went also, but he came up from the earth before he reached the ocean and returned and lived here among his people.

After Navitcu had been here for a time, he felt the earth shaking. He searched all over the earth looking for the cause. In the east he came to a whole country of people like himself. They were dancing and causing the thunder and rain, and that is why the earth was shaking. It rained all the time. He learned their rain ceremonies. He stole from them some of the corn pollen they used to make clouds and ran back to this country. The dancers chased him all over the earth to recover the pollen, and he dropped some in different places as he ran. For this reason it rains more in some places than in others.

Elder Brother took a bag of deerskin and made Mountain Goat. He made him live on the tops of mountains. He dropped one of his hairs on the top of each mountain, and the hairs he dropped became mountain goats; therefore we have goats on every mountain, and whenever anyone kills a mountain goat it is sure to rain.[35]

Elder Brother ruled this earth and taught the people to dance and sing and hold ceremonies. He appointed the chiefs and built the *va'aki*s. They lived in peace and there were plenty of rains. The chiefs were given the powers of medicine men, more than those of any other human. Elder Brother showed them how to clear the land and bring water in ditches. And the people dug irrigation ditches and they sang:

"Big rippling waters through the land rippling." (repeat)

There was one place where the land was hard to dig. They went to Elder Brother and he said, "Go to Nasia." They went to Nasia and asked for help. She caused a strong wind to blow through that land and sang:

33. See the Navitcu oration and "Notes on the Navitcu" in chapter 5.—*Ed.*
34. That is, the Navitcu mask.
35. See the Mountain Goat orations in chapter 5.—*Ed.*

"The river shakes and causes water to run down into the ditch."

They completed the ditches.

People were dissatisfied that Elder Brother had sent them to Nasia for help. They began to make complaints against Elder Brother. They complained because he had created Ho'ok [see next story] and Man Eagle [see subsequent story],[36] and because women came to the singing ceremonies—

[Ho'ok]

TV They fought among themselves, and Elder Brother considered what he should do against his people. He made a plan. He made an orphan boy and sent him to Blue Turquoise Medicine Man (Tsealtenk Sivanyi),[37] the chief of Casa Grande.[38] The chief said, "I shall sink you into the earth." The boy sang:

"My name is Turquoise [probably just "Green"] Child.
You have given me the soft downy feathers of the eagle,
And from me will come (stone) blue as the rainbow."

He sank into the ground beside the house. In four years the people dug, and they found that the body of the child had turned to turquoise. The rumor went all over the earth that Blue Turquoise Medicine Man had turquoise, and far in the east Sun Power Medicine Man heard of it.

Sun Power Medicine Man (Tacanamkan Sivanyi) had a parrot,[39] and he sent it to the medicine man at Casa Grande, saying to the parrot, "Take none of the food that he offers you until he gives you turquoise. Eat it and return."

The parrot went that night, and the two daughters of Blue Medicine Man saw him outside the house. They told their father, and he said, "It is a parrot. Put a stick in his bill and bring him in."

36. This is Blackwater speaking. For his versions of these stories, see chapter 2.—*Ed.*

37. Si'al Cehedag Sivañ, "Morning Green (or Blue) Chief," is an important character in the traditional history of the Hohokam period. See Bahr et al. 1994, index entry "Morning Green Chief," for references on him. Pimas call the mineral turquoise "green/blue rock" (*cehedagi hoḍai*). "Rock" or "Turquoise-rock" is not actually part of this character's name.—*Ed.*

38. Present-day Casa Grande Ruins National Monument, at Coolidge, Arizona.—*Ed.*

39. Interpreters always translate this "peacock" [probably *a:ḍho,* "peacock," "macaw," "parrot." Sun Power Medicine Man is Taṣ Namkam Siwañ, "Sun Meeter Chief"].

They brought in the parrot and they offered him corn and pumpkin seeds and everything they had, but he would not eat. The medicine man said, "Perhaps he will eat charcoal." But he would not eat it. He said, "What is the matter that he will not eat?"

The parrot walked about, and whenever he saw a tiny bit of turquoise he ate it. They said, "Perhaps he will eat turquoise. Bring some and see." He ate all the turquoise they brought, and at last they brought out their rings and necklaces and fed him the turquoise from them.

At night the parrot went home to his master, Sun Power Medicine Man. His master placed a dish and the parrot vomited all the turquoise that he had eaten. Blue Medicine Man caused a cold wind and rain. The parrot was frozen dead. The people built a fire to warm [Sun Power Medicine Man], and when the cold ceased they built a pyre and burned his parrot. With the ashes Sun Power Medicine Man made a kick-ball, and he drew down the rays of the sun and decorated the ball with them. When it was finished, he gave it to a young man and told him to run with it past the house of Blue Turquoise Medicine Man.

The boy started, kicking his kick-ball. Blue Medicine Man's daughter was sitting outside, making a mat of reeds. As the ball rolled past her she picked it up and put it under her skirt. The boy saw what she had done, but he pretended to look everywhere for it. He said, "Where is my ball?" "I didn't see it." "I will have to give up." He started back to his home, and the girl called after him to come back, saying, "I've got your ball." But he kept on.

In a month she had a child, and they called her name Ho'ok. The child had claws and a great beak. Ho'ok used to go out with one of her uncles when he hunted. Whenever he killed any game, Ho'ok grabbed the animal and swallowed it raw. One day she set off to the south. Her uncle followed and he sang:

"Your mother, your grandfather, want you to come back." (4 times)

"How is that [she asked]? They wanted to kill me. I cannot go back with you, my uncle." And she sang:

"Why do you call my mother's and my grandfather's name?
For my people do not want me.
My uncle, you cannot prevent me."

She went far to the south and lived in a cave in the mountains. From there she came back and caught the little children and took them to her cave and ate them. The people suffered, and they went to Elder Brother and asked him to help them get rid of Ho'ok. He told them to have a big dance and invite her to come. She came and danced for four nights. She was tired, and in her sleep the people took her up and carried her to her cave and put her on her bed. They piled wood at the mouth of the cave and burned her to death. She became a hawk. And she began to kill the old men and the old women.

Again the people went to Elder Brother and asked for help. He told them to take a cooking pot and put it over the fire and heat it very hot right under a little opening in the roof of the house. The old men and old women made this fire and gathered there. They went outside once in a while so that the hawk saw them. She dived for them in the hole in the top of the house. She fell into the boiling pot and was burned to death. They took the pot and threw it outside. The little children found it and took it home and cooked greens in it. Their mother found out that the hawk had been killed in that pot, and she took it out and dumped the greens at the back of the house. Two young men had been hunting all day. They came by and saw the greens. They sat down and ate the greens. As soon as they had finished eating they both turned into bears.

So the people were punished, and they lived at peace for a time.

[Man Eagle]

But again they became bad, and the women lived loose lives. Elder Brother went to a man who had a daughter and asked her help. Her father agreed and Elder Brother told the girl to take all kinds of feathers, strip the ribs, roast and grind them, and make pinole. There was a man who liked that girl and whenever she went for water he went and talked to her. Elder Brother told her, "The next time he speaks to you and asks you to marry him, tell him he must drink your pinole first."

Next day when he spoke to her she said, "Drink my pinole and I will tell you then." She went back to her house for the drink she had made and gave it to him, and he drank. He felt chilled and he shook himself. All over his body, feathers began to come out. He said, "Can it be that my dream will come true? For when I was a boy I often dreamed I would become a bird." He became an eagle.

The girl ran home and told her father and her neighbors, "There is an eagle at the spring." They got their bows and arrows and went down. The eagle flew up and grabbed the arrows and flew back to his home in the east. There he stole their children and even those who were grown up. He stole a young girl and took her to his cave to be his wife, and she had a baby boy. In his house were big piles of the dead that he had killed.

The people went to Elder Brother for help against the Man Eagle, and Elder Brother said, "I will go to that mountain myself against the Man Eagle. If you see clouds rise over the mountain you will know that I was successful." He went to the foot of the mountain and waited all night. In the morning when the eagle started out to catch people, Elder Brother climbed up the steep precipice, putting sticks against the rock. When he got to the top he spoke to the eagle's wife and said, "What does Eagle do when he comes home?"

"He lies down to sleep." Elder Brother turned into a big blue-fly and he hid. He said, "Could he see me here?" "Yes." "Could he see me here?" "Yes."

He couldn't find a place. At last he flew as far as he could, rapidly up into the air, singing:

"Fly, oh Fly, oh Fly, oh Fly."

He said, "Am I quick enough? Will he catch me?" "I think you are quick enough. You will be quicker than he is." "When does he come home?" "About the middle of the day."

So Elder Brother hid as a big blue-fly under the bottom heart of the corpses of the people that Eagle had killed. He said to Eagle's wife, "Pile all the bodies on top of me. When he has gone to sleep, whistle and tell me." About the middle of the day Eagle came with his prey. They were still groaning, and he threw them down on the top of the pile. Eagle's baby boy began to talk. He was trying to tell his father what had happened.

"What is he trying to say? He never did that before." His wife said, "When babies are learning to talk they always babble." Eagle got up and turned the bodies all over, but he stopped before he got all the way to the bottom. He went to sleep and his wife whistled. He woke up. "Why do you do that?" "I am happy because of the food you brought home."

He slept again. Again his wife whistled, but he did not move. She whistled four times and he did not move. Elder Brother came out, and with a great knife he cut off the head of Eagle and the head of the child. When Eagle's body fell, it shook the whole mountain, and clouds gathered over the peak. The people saw the clouds and knew Elder Brother had been successful.

Eagle's wife said, "What shall I do with the dead bodies?"

"Warm some water." She put the pot on the fire, and when the water was warm Elder Brother sprinkled the bodies and they came to life. He said to each one of them when they began to move, "Where did you come from?" When they answered him, he told them to go back to their own country. Some were very old bodies and had been dead a long time. When they came to life they were very pale and couldn't talk so anyone could understand them. Elder Brother took a feather and cut it to a point like a pen, and he peeled off the skin from the palm of his hand and made marks upon it with the pen he had made. He gave the marked skin to the pale people and he said, "Go east. This is how you will talk to each other."

The people who had been brought to life made a litter out of wood and put eagle feathers on it and downy feathers on top. They put Elder Brother on it and brought him down singing:

"On my litter of feathers
I look big and wise like a medicine man."

Four winds went out from him and covered the mountains. They carried him a little way and set down the litter, and he sang:

"On my bed of downy feathers I am lying
And my heart is light as the wind.
Thunderclouds went out from me
And covered the mountains."

After this the people behaved themselves for a long time and were at peace.

[Killing Elder Brother]

At that time all things grew without labor. But Elder Brother wanted his people to work and irrigate. He held back the rain so that there was a great drought, and the people blamed Elder Brother—

TV&WB They made up their minds to destroy him.
Every night they met together and sang their songs, and the women came and sang with them. They made their plans to kill Elder Brother, and they sent young men out against him. They killed him and cut his body in pieces and mixed the pieces with dirt, but next day he was alive again. They boiled his body in a great pot and threw the flesh out with the refuse, but next day he was alive again. They took him to the top of Mount Mwaadik[40] and threw him down, but when they looked down to the foot of the precipice, they saw him stand up unhurt at the bottom—
WB They bound him and held him all day underwater. He was dead, but when they loosed him at night he swam ashore, and next day he walked about among them. They built a great fire and put him in the center. He stood there till the fire had burned itself out, and he walked home unharmed—
TV&WB They could do nothing against him. They went to Buzzard's House (the *va'aki* west of Tempe). Buzzard said, "It is very hard to kill Elder Brother. He has all power and you do not know what you are doing. I have as much power as he has, and perhaps I could kill him, but if I do, it will not end there. You and your children will suffer." They said, "Have you power to kill him?"

"Come to my house and I will show you." He drew darkness over them. He raised his hand and lifted the darkness. Below it he showed them the earth and the clouds and the rain and the sun and the moon and the lights of the sky, all the creation of Elder Brother. But they said, "Go ahead, kill Elder Brother"—
TV Buzzard put on his nose ring of turquoise and flew high up into the sky and looked down and saw that all the earth was green with growing things, and he knew he could not kill Elder Brother. He came down and put on his nose ring of pearl and flew far up into the sky, and he looked and saw that all the world was white and withered.[41] And he knew that he could kill Elder Brother—
WB Buzzard flew high up in the air, and he sang:

"The earth below shines green with the power of Elder Brother."

40. Probably the same as Moadek [Muhadag], mentioned earlier in the section on the flood.—*Ed.*

41. The nose ring of turquoise is connected with green growing things, and the nose ring of pearl, with drought. [Not pearl but a slimy stone about which nothing seems to be known (Herzog n.d.*c*).]

He flew again into the air and sang (repeat). He flew four times into the air and sang. At last he rose straight to Earth Doctor—

TV&WB He said to him, "The people wish to kill Elder Brother whom you left to rule on earth. I was appointed to do this and I have come to ask you for the power." Earth Doctor said, "Are you going to destroy his clouds and his rain?" "Yes." "It would be better to leave these. I can only tell you to borrow Sun's heart. With that you can overcome Elder Brother." He returned and said to the people, "I have been given power to kill Elder Brother." He sang—

TV *"I have a gun, my cane, with which I shall destroy the heart*
of the medicine man (i.e., Elder Brother).
I have been to receive the gun from the sun"—

WB He sang:

"I am the Buzzard who will kill." (repeat)

He sang again:

"I am Yellow Buzzard going to the sun to travel with him across the sky."

Buzzard traveled with the sun. Four times he accompanied the sun across the sky—

TV&WB Elder Brother knew that his time was come. He sang:

"What have I done? What have I done
That you should seek to kill me?"

The earth grew hotter and hotter. Elder Brother went south and tried to escape the heat. There were four pools of water that belonged to him. They were covered with ice. In all of them the water was boiling—

WB Elder Brother sang:

"Let them kill me.
The sun will die with me and the moon will die with me"—

TV He could not bear the heat of the water, and he returned and he sang:

"In this land of Ol,[42]
I shall be killed with the iron gun this afternoon"—

42. I don't know what this means.—*Ed.*

TV&WB He found shelter for himself under a tree, but he could not bear the heat and he fell down dead. Buzzard came and stood over his dead body and he sang:

> *"I have done a great wrong in killing Elder Brother" (repeat)*—

TV He sang:

> *"But I have saved your power over the wind;*
> *I have saved your power over the clouds"*—

[His Resurrection]

TV&WB He lay there four years. After four years a strong wind from the—

TV west—

WB west, south, east, and north—

TV&WB blew over him and the clouds came and rained upon his body. He moved and stood erect. He said[43]—

TV ***"You have followed me through this earth, and through this mountain, and through these trees,***
The birds of the air, and the crawling creatures of the land.[44]
You have killed me and left me for dead.
I lay there under the tree many days and nights.
I put my hands on the ground and raised myself and stood up.
Toward the west by the green snake (the river) grew the arrow weed.
I took the reeds and cut them into short pieces and made **aamina.**[45]
Toward the east I made four steps:
At the first step I set my foot upon the medicine man;
At the second step I set my foot upon the war chief;
At the third step I set my foot upon the speaker;
At the fourth I set my foot upon a brave.
I started toward the east and came to Mount Vaakamoiakut,[46]

43. It seems as if Elder Brother made this speech at the moment of his resurrection, and yet the speech will also tell what he did immediately *after* the resurrection.—*Ed.*

44. That is, these natural objects, his powers, had to be overcome before the people were able to kill him.

45. [Or *o'omina,* "broken-sticklike-things."] These are the banded and bundled sticks cut to short lengths, which correspond to the Pueblo prayer sticks, but they were used among the Pimas to keep count of the days. [Illustrated in Russell 1908: plate 14.]

46. Probably Ba'ag Muakud, "Eagle Killing-place."—*Ed.*

And the mountain spoke and asked why I came there;
And I answered, 'I want to destroy the people of this earth.'

I put my hand on the flowers of the mountain and
strengthened myself;
I put my hand on the springs of the mountain and
strengthened myself;
I started toward the sun; and toward the sun there were
four steps
Difficult to climb, full of clouds and strong winds.
I followed the trail toward the west;[47]
Along the trail were the sacred feathers and beads,
And I overturned them and destroyed them.
I came to the medicine man[48] *and I tossed him aside.*
I came to the Talking Tree and I put my hands on the tree
and strengthened myself.
I stripped the bark from the tree, and with the rays of the sun
I ornamented it and put it on my head for a headband.
From the middle branch of the tree I made a war club,
And out of the knothole a canteen to carry my water.

I threw aside the four sticks of arrow weed,
And I laid hold of the south branch and made again four
sticks of the wood of the Talking Tree,[49]
And I carried them in my hand.
I continued my journey to the west, and I came to a bowl
of water.
I knelt and drank.
I put my right hand into the water
And took out the sacred obsidian that was in that water.
And I went on toward the west and came to the end of
the trail where the sun goes down.

47. That is, from the sunrise in the east over the heavens along the trail of the sun.

48. Of his enemies (Herzog n.d.*c*).—*Ed.*

49. Because the four days were accomplished that were denoted by the sticks of arrow weed. Compare, however, Russell 1908:343, where this same account is symbolic of thrusting aside the power of the enemy.

I went down and came to my brother medicine man
(Earth Doctor).
He said to me, 'What is your desire that you come here to
me in the manner of the sun?'
Four times he asked me, and I answered, 'I want to
destroy the people of the earth.'

When I had spoken, a strong wind from the west blew me
to the east
And dropped me in the middle of the world (i.e., at the
feet of Earth Doctor).
A strong wind from the south blew me to the north
And dropped me again at the same place.
A strong wind from the east blew me to the west
And dropped me again at the same place.
A strong wind from the north blew me to the south
And left me there for dead.
And you, Earth Doctor,
Picked me up as a child.
With your sacred pipe you blew the smoke over me,
And gave me strength, and brought me back to life.
I set up my crystal (transparent) mirage
As a round windbreak[50] *around me.*
I sent out the blue roadrunner with his blue darkness,
And I caused the enemy to forget his dream,
And left him there without understanding.
I sent Gray Owl with his gray darkness,
And I caused the enemy to be in a stupor,
And left him there without understanding.
I spread out a mat for the medicine man to sit upon.

(Earth Doctor said,) 'How many people are there upon
the earth?'
(Elder Brother answered,) 'There are many.'
(And Earth Doctor said,) 'How can it be that there are
so many?'

50. *Unama* [or *onma*], old Pima windbreaks.

He sent his pet gopher down to bring him word.
He went under the earth and came up to the surface.
He made four springs and spied out the number of people on the earth.
He returned to Earth Doctor and brought him word. And he said:

'Master, you sent me, and I went under the earth.
In the west I made a water hole of black water,
***And above it I planted* kawak *(bulrushes?).*[51]**
I heaped the surface of the water with raven's feathers.
I went to the south and I made a water hole of blue water,
***And I planted* kokpotk.**
I heaped the surface of the water with the soft feathers of the bluebird.
I made the red water-hole of red water in the north
And caused bulrushes to grow out of it
And heaped the surface of the water with macaw feathers.
In the east I made the fourth water hole of white water
And covered it with the downy feathers of the eagle.
***So I prepared the way for you.*[52]**
I looked and saw the ancient pueblos,
And their tops reached to the sky.
I could hear the cries of the boys and the laughter of the girls,
And I knew there were many people in them.
It will be hard for any enemy to approach them without being seen'"—

TV&WB When Gopher had spoken, Earth Doctor said to Elder Brother,[53] "Go, war against the people of the earth. Those who are to go with you will follow"—

51. Probably *uḍawhag,* "cattail." According to Herzog (n.d.*c*), the *kokpotk* mentioned three lines later is "bulrushes"; compare *ko'okpoḍk,* "bulrush" (Rea 1997:104–5).—*Ed.*

52. The existence of water holes is an important consideration for a war expedition. (The narrator explained that the use of the feathers was a figure to indicate the creation of the different colors seen on the surface of still water.)

53. Yet Elder Brother seems to have delivered this speech right after he came back to life on the earth's surface. It is as if speaking the speech has brought him to the underworld.—*Ed.*

[Passage to Earth's Surface]

WB So Elder Brother received power to fight the people of the earth. He made a windbreak about him and practiced his powers. He called together the medicine men and gave them the powers of the wind and rain and of overcoming the enemy—

TV Elder Brother gathered together the medicine men to help him. To the chief medicine man (going-in-front-of doctor)[54] he gave the power over the thunder; to the second, power over the lightning; to the third, power to use snakes against the enemy; to the fourth, power over the fog; to the fifth, power over the wind; to the sixth, power over the cold; to the seventh, power over the rain; to the eighth, power of the rainbow; to the ninth, power of the false dawn; to the tenth, power of the mirage of water; to the eleventh, power to cast sleep upon the enemy; to the twelfth, power to tie together the long hair of the enemy; to the thirteenth, power to tie in knots the muscles of the enemy; to the fourteenth, to be as himself and see far into the distance[55]—

TV&WB He gave to each of them the power that he had decreed, and they gathered in council and practiced their power. In the day the sky was darkened, in the night there was fire upon the sky, because of the practicing of the medicine men—

WB Elder Brother said to his people, "This world (i.e., underworld) is too cold for you. There is a country called earth and we will go there and conquer it." He sent one of his messengers from the east to the people on the earth. The man had a strange face and strange body, and the people of the earth laughed at him. He disappeared. Elder Brother sang:

"From my crooked cane a man appeared to my enemies,
And they laughed at him."

[Again] a man appeared to the people of the earth, from the west, and the people laughed at him. He disappeared. Elder Brother sang:

"From my thin cane a man appeared to my enemies,
And they laughed at him"—

54. *Apa itc e minum maaka* [*ha-ba'ic himdam ma:kai,* "them-in-front-of going-one medicine-man"].

55. Elder Brother is conceived as having a special power to see the people of the earth through the earth's crust; until the emergence he is thought of as being in an underworld. The last four powers listed are common to all war magic. The medicine men sought to cripple the enemy by leg cramps and to tie together the long hair of those sleeping under one cover.

TV Elder Brother set out upon his shining road. And he sang:

"Toward the east a shining road I am following" (4 times)—

WB Earth Doctor said to Elder Brother, "Do something so that your people, when they are traveling, will not be tired. Elder Brother made the shining road[56] from the north toward the people of the earth—
TV&WB Elder Brother formed his people into companies to go against the people of the earth—
WB He formed the first company and called it Maam, and he gave it the color red.[57] He formed the second company and called it Apap, and gave it the color white. He formed the third company and called it Vaav, and gave it the color red. He formed the fourth company and called it Apk, and gave it the color white. He formed a fifth company and called it Onkl, and gave it the color red. He formed a sixth company and called it Aapapa, and gave it the color white. He formed a seventh company and called it Paapaakam, and gave it the color red. He formed twelve companies, and he gave them the red and white velvet wasps for their pets. Those that had the color red were his own people, and those that had the color white were the people of the north—
TV&WB The chief medicine man had gone part of the day's journey without his carrying basket. Earth Doctor said, "Go on. I will send it after you. But do not look behind." By his power he caused the carrying basket to go by itself till it came to the chief medicine man. All the company went on ahead and caused their loads to follow them. Coyote was with them and he looked behind: "See what's following us." All the carrying baskets dropped to the ground. They could not make them go by themselves again. "See what you've done," they said to Coyote, and they scolded him—
TV Coyote went back to where the carrying baskets had dropped to the ground; and he raised one of them and lifted it to his head, and he said, "This is the way carrying baskets shall be carried." He adjusted it on his head and walked off with it—

56. "Railroad."

57. These companies are what most people speaking English would call "clans." Technically they are what anthropologists call sibs or gentes. Inherited from the father, clan membership had only one important purpose among the Pimas: to provide people (of both sexes) with the word to use in addressing their fathers. See Russell 1908:197; Parsons 1928:445–47; and Bahr et al. 1994:310n13, 310n14, 325n5.—*Ed.*

TV&WB One of the medicine men said, "No, this is the power of the women. Henceforth women shall carry the carrying basket"—
WB As they came near this country the chief medicine man told them not to look behind them. Coyote was with them. He looked and said, "See our great army! How can our enemy stand against so many?" As soon as he had spoken the army broke in two, and that is why we have lost so many of the companies—
TV&WB Elder Brother looked over the earth (i.e., through the earth's crust) and he saw that it was parched with drought. No rain had fallen since he had been killed there. All living things were burned: the flowers, the shrubs, the trees. "How can we fight when there is nothing for our people to eat? We must rest here and cause plants to grow or we will starve on our journey." Elder Brother instituted the ceremonies for rain. He taught them the songs and it rained for many days—
WB It flooded the earth, and the rain did not stop. Elder Brother brought forth a rainbow and it stopped the rain. This was the first rainbow, and they were frightened. Elder Brother sang:

> *"Here beside me the rainbow appeared and the people were frightened." (repeat)*

He told them, "Don't be afraid. I've made this rainbow to stop the rain." He sang:

> *"I made the rainbow out of my heart.*
> *Do not be afraid."*

He gave his people everything they make use of in the rain ceremonies and taught them the songs. He told them when they needed rain to do as he had taught them—
TV They were ready to go to the surface of the earth. The first company, Maam, went up, and the second, Vaav. When all growing things had come to maturity and the earth was green, the third company, Apak, came up. When all plants were ready to bear, the fourth company came up, Apap.

As they were coming up, Coyote said, "Look at our company. What chance has the enemy? They will be overcome." The chief medicine man was singing, and he made a mistake in his song; Coyote laughed, and the fourth company was cut in two so that half remained in the world below. The people blamed Coyote, but Coyote said, "Why do you blame me? It is not my fault. It is the fault of the chief medicine man who made a mistake in his song." The half of Apap who remained behind continued to live in the world below. They gave red to Vaav and to Maam; white to Apk and to Apap and Onkl—

WB The army divided into four sections. One went to the south and spread from east to west, and Earth Doctor was its chief. The second went through this Gila Valley from east to west, and Elder Brother was its chief. The third went to the north and spread from east to west, and Coyote was its chief. The fourth went to the north and spread from east to west, and Nasia was its chief. Some went down into the earth and became gophers. Some went into the air and became eagles. Wherever the buzzard can take refuge Elder Brother sent people to populate the earth. Elder Brother said, "It is necessary to have some way to communicate with each other." And he made lines of light[58] and stretched them from north to south—

TV When they had come to the surface of the earth, they settled there at that place for a long time. Every day the people of the earth saw their dust in the sky, and every evening they saw their smoke, and they said, "There will be rain," for the light of their fires in the smoke looked like lightning. In that place they had plenty of rain, but the people were homesick and wanted to return under the earth. Elder Brother thought to himself what he could do to amuse them, and he caused the earth to bring forth paints. He told the people to paint themselves and hold ceremonies and enjoy themselves—

[Elder Brother's Campaign]

TV&WB Elder Brother started out with his people against the people of this earth—

WB He sent out scouts. One of the medicine men had the power of Coyote, and Elder Brother said to him, "Go out and see what you can see." He went far over the surface of the earth, but he could not see anyone. He stopped and dug a hole to show how far he had been. Coyote sang:

58. "Telephone wires."

"See the medicine man you have made.
He went ahead and dug a hole."

After four days Elder Brother said to one of the medicine men, who had the power of raven, "Go out and see what you can see." He put on his raven's skin and went as far as he could fly. He could not see any of the people of the earth. He piled up rocks to show how far he had been. He returned and said, "I have not seen a human being," and he sang:

"See the medicine man you have made.
He went ahead and piled rocks"—

TV&WB They journeyed, and there was no water. For four days they were without water. They stopped and called upon the medicine men. They felt the earth tip and straighten again, and they looked and beside them there was a river running. (Song:)

"Earth is coming close bringing water." (repeat)

When they had drunk, they went on to the west again. Again there was no food to eat. Elder Brother called the wood rat and said, "I am going to cut you in many pieces and you will be multiplied into many large food animals"—

WB Elder Brother cut the throat of the wood rat and he became sheep and cows. He called the mouse and he cut his throat and he became mountain goats and deer. So he gave meat to his people—

TV The wood rat agreed, and Elder Brother brought his stone knife to cut his throat. Wood Rat was frightened and escaped. Elder Brother called Deer Mouse and he consented. Elder Brother cut his throat and covered him with a cloth. Next morning he uncovered him and there lay tiny fawns that spread all over the earth. That is why deer have the color and the bristles of the deer mouse. Elder Brother kept them till they were full grown and very tame, and anyone who wanted meat took one of the deer as he needed it. (Song:)

"Over this broad land there are many deer going to the water holes.
The mountains shall be full of its young."

At last Elder Brother said, "Let the deer be scattered, so that whoever wishes to eat shall have trouble to obtain them and shall encounter danger and much labor." He rubbed power (of keen scent) on the tips of their antlers and on the tips of their tails, so that they could smell human beings at a great distance. He made a great noise and frightened them, and they scattered, and that is why deer are so difficult to trap—

WB Among the people there was a cripple, and Elder Brother told him to kill his older brother and cut him in pieces: "Out of him shall come an animal to carry you." The cripple told his brother, but he did not want to kill him. The brother said, "Do as Elder Brother told you. Kill me as he said." He did, and out of the pieces came all the different kinds of horses.

Elder Brother told the horse to run a day and a night, and he said, "A horse shall have power to run a day and a night without exhaustion." Therefore horses are our elder brothers, because it was the older brother of the cripple who was killed to create the horse.

There were two brothers, one crippled and one blind. One day the blind man said to his brother, "How shall we make our living? If you were not crippled you could support us both. If I were not blind I could support us both." Elder Brother heard them talking and he sent thunder. It cracked above them and frightened them. The one who was blind opened his eyes and the one who was lame ran away. After that the blind man could see and the lame could walk. They started on again—

TV&WB They went on against the people of the earth. Elder Brother appointed Sunkeeper (Tac'kamaaka)[59] to call the march, morning, noon, and evening, and sent out scouts to look for the enemy. They did not find them till they had come to the east,[60] and there they found the first people—

TV The four companies formed to give battle. Maam formed in the south and spread out to the west; Vaav spread to the south of them; Apk in the Gila Valley; and Apap formed in the north and spread to the west—

TV&WB They startled the people in the villages out of their sleep, and the people tried to take their weapons and fight with them, but they stumbled and fell; the power of the medicine men had knotted the muscles of their legs, and those who slept together could not fight, for they were tied together by their hair through the power of the

59. The first part is *taṣ*, "day" or "sun." The rest might be *kwintadag*, "counter" (from Spanish *contar*). There was an old man with that as his last name (from which the present-day family name Tashquinth derives). I don't know of an office called sunkeeper, but it is said that this old man kept watch on the sun and also kept a yearly calendar carved on a saguaro cactus rib.—*Ed.*

60. Said to have been in New Mexico.

medicine men. Elder Brother's people laughed. They took the power of birds and descended upon them and killed them—

WB They started again toward the west. Elder Brother sent two scouts ahead and they came to Casa Blanca. There was a girl there who knew that enemies were coming against them. She said to them, "You come from our enemies' camp. I have heard of you and I am afraid. Help me." "Yes, we were sent to help you."

She had a pet eagle, and they threw the pet eagle into the air. They said, "Follow your eagle, and wherever he alights, alight also." The eagle flew to the west, and beyond the ocean[61] he lit on a cholla cactus. He caught a snake and held it in his mouth, and from this came the emblem on the Mexican dollar.

The men returned to Elder Brother and told him what they had done. He sent out two more scouts. They came to a forest where there were many birds singing. They mistook them for human beings, and they came back and reported that there were many people. When the people came, they found only birds.

He sent out two more scouts. They came to a mountain where there were many crows. They mistook them for human beings and came back and reported that there were many people. When the people came, they found only crows—

TV&WB They came close to the country where the people of this earth lived. The medicine men, who had power to see a great distance, saw ahead of them the *va'aki* of the ocotillo cactus hedge (near Florence). The chief was Sun Power Chief [Taṣ Namkam Siwañ]. While they were still far to the east they sang against it:

> *"I see it ahead. I really see.*
> *I see it ahead. I really see*
> *The* va'aki *with the ocotillo hedge.*
> *I see it ahead. I really see.*
> *I see it ahead. I really see*
> *The* va'aki *with ocotillo growing on the top."*

They came close to the *va'aki*. They called a strong wind and it blew down their [enemies'] houses. It blew down the ocotillo hedge—

WB They came to another *va'aki* that stood close by. Strong Man Chief was their leader. Elder Brother asked to go against Strong Man

61. Said to be China.

Chief and wrestle with him. He said, "I have never killed an enemy." Therefore the chief medicine man gave him the power to overcome the chief of the enemy.[62] He fought with him and killed him—

TV&WB They came to the *va'aki* at Casa Grande. Blue Turquoise Chief was their [enemies'] leader and he tried his power against them. He sent out his first medicine man and he used his power over the thunder. But the chief medicine man of Elder Brother's company, who had power over the thunder, kept the clap of the thunder high above their heads so that it did not harm them.

The second medicine man used his power over the strong wind; the medicine man with the power over the strong wind in Elder Brother's army kept the wind blowing far above their heads so that it did not harm them.

The third medicine man used his power again over the strong wind, but Elder Brother's medicine man turned it back upon the people of Casa Grande.

The fourth medicine man used his power over the lightning, but the power of Elder Brother's medicine men caused his power to fail; it hit to one side and destroyed nothing.

The people of Elder Brother's company waited to feel again the power of the medicine men of the enemy, but there was nothing, and they knew that the enemy had come to the end of his power. Elder Brother said, "That is all his power. Let me have my turn." He made the sun and the moon stand still. He sang:

> *"With the powers of all the medicine men we have made the sun and the moon stand still."*

Again he sent thunder. When it hit the ground, it shook the stones of the *va'aki,* and Blue Turquoise Chief knew it was the power of Elder Brother. Elder Brother sang:

> *"When the moon and the sun stood still*
> *And thunder shook the walls,*
> *The Blue Medicine Man had no more power against us."*

Blue Turquoise Chief told his people, "I can do nothing more. It is best for us to flee." He sang:

62. Note that at this point in the traditional history Elder Brother is like one of the mortal Pimas. The episode is unique to Blackwater and Vanyiko but is consistent with other Pima accounts of the Hohokam conquest in having the ancestral Pimas, not Elder Brother, do most of the magic and the conquering. One can say that at this point Elder Brother is portrayed as a chief and leader, not as a god.—*Ed.*

"I do not know what more to do.
The sun stands still in heaven,
And the walls are shaken."

And he said, "I will go to my brother in Santan [a present-day Pima village] and die with him." So the [enemy] people were left without a leader. They were divided and some wished to fight—

WB The army [of Elder Brother] came against the outlying houses and destroyed them. But they left the *va'aki* of Casa Grande because those people who had remained there surrendered to them. The chief medicine man said, "There is a woman of the enemy who has a shawl of many colors." One of their women said, "I will have that shawl." The women came and fought for three days until they won the victory and took the shawl.

They lived at Casa Grande for a long time, and sickness came upon them there. Elder Brother said, "I must do something to rid us of this sickness." He took elbow-length sticks of ironwood and stuck them in the ground. There was no more sickness[63]—

TV&WB They came on (to Sacaton) and came to another *va'aki*. Burning Poles Chief (Tcuudik Sivanyi)[64] was their leader. Both sides called upon the rain and fought with the power of water. After many days Elder Brother won the victory.

They came farther to the west and they came to another *va'aki* (the one four miles below Sacaton). Tciohou'okum Sivanyi[65] was their leader. They had a great treasure of beads there, and Elder Brother won the victory and took all their beads. Blue Turquoise Chief had fled to this *va'aki* and he helped them, but it was of no avail.

They went on and came to Casa Blanca. Tcutcu'tatakamol[66] Sivanyi was their leader. The people camped outside the *va'aki*. The medicine man of the enemy sent a strong wind, but it did not reach them. Four times he sent the strong wind, but it did not harm them—

63. There is no similar ritual known at the present time. The sticks were set in no particular order, separately, and were unpainted. [A ritual called *a'ada,* "the sending," is described for the Papagos, or Tohono O'odham, by Underhill et al. (1979:81, 83), in which sickness is driven into the ground with an ironwood stake.]

64. Cu:dagi Siwañ, "Ember Chief."—*Ed.*

65. Probably Cew Ha'okam Siwañ, "Long Gourd-having Chief."—*Ed.*

66. Black Bird (TV). Black Sinew (WB). [WB is correct: Cuk Tataikam Siwañ means "Black Sinew-having Chief" (see Bahr et al. 1994:287).]

WB He made a deep canyon between them, but by their power Elder Brother's people crossed it. Elder Brother sang:

> *"Black Sinew Chief has used his pet, the wind.*
> *My power will be greater than his."*

He sang again:

> *"I am about to destroy the house of this medicine man.*
> *Poor medicine man, he has made trial of his power, and it is exhausted"—*

TV&WB Elder Brother called on the medicine man who had power over the thunder. He went to the north and flew up in the air. He came down on top of the *va'aki,* but he did not overturn the walls of the city. He returned to Elder Brother and said, "I have done. I have used my power and I can do nothing more." Elder Brother called the medicine man who had power over the lightning. He went to the south and went up in the air and came down upon the *va'aki,* but he did not overturn it. He returned to Elder Brother and said to him, "I have done. I can do no more." He called on the medicine man who had power over the snake. He went to the west and became a black snake—

TV Snake encircled the *va'aki* in his coils and all the people were caught in them—

WB Snake threw himself toward the *va'aki* and hit it, but he broke in pieces and did not overturn the walls. He returned to Elder Brother and said, "I have failed. Give me another chance and I will try again." He went to the east and became a white snake and threw himself against the walls of that city, and the walls fell in ruins.[67] Only the chief of that city saved himself by sinking down into the earth.

Elder Brother called upon the medicine man who had power over the mirage. He called it up and they saw the chief of the enemy appear in the mirage. They tried to snatch him, but he disappeared into the earth.

He called upon the medicine man who had power over the rainbow, and he caused a rainbow to form over the whole earth. The chief of the enemy appeared again upon the rainbow. They rushed

67. "The black snake was a stick of black powder. The white snake was dynamite, and it has much more power."

upon him, but before they could reach him he had sunk under the earth again.

Elder Brother called the medicine man who had power over the dawn mirage, and he spread it. The chief of the enemy came up upon the dawn mirage and they rushed against him, but he sank again into the earth.

Elder Brother called the medicine man who had power over the water mirage, and he spread it. The enemy chief came up again on the mirage and they rushed against him, but he sank again under the earth.

Elder Brother called the medicine man who had charge of the fog, and he spread it. When the chief of the enemy came out of the earth again, the fog was so thick that the company rushed upon him and killed him.

After they had conquered Casa Blanca the people looked pale and weary and Elder Brother directed them to purify themselves. He established the purification ceremony and the rain fell, and they conquered all that country[68]—

TV Snake came to Elder Brother: "I have never killed an enemy. Do something for me so that I may kill an enemy." He [Elder Brother] called Gopher and said to him, "Help him." "I will." Gopher sank into the earth and tunneled to the center of the *va'aki*. He came to the spot where the crier stood to address the people. Snake followed him under the ground. Gopher said to him, "Stay here till the crier comes to speak to the people. Bite him twice and return through the tunnel to your own people." Next morning Chief Centipede-Necklace came to make proclamation against the enemy. Snake bit him twice and escaped. Elder Brother sang:

"There is a land before me full of centipede necklaces.
When I reach there, my heart will be strong."

The people fought, and after the fight Chief Centipede-Necklace lay dead in the stone city they had conquered. Everyone rushed forward calling, "I killed him, I killed him." Elder Brother answered, "No. It was Snake who killed him. He is the first victor." Elder Brother sang:

68. That is, the ceremony was equally a rain ritual. (The text above follows the order of Blackwater's version. Vanyiko gives the conquest of Casa Blanca and the institution of the purification ceremony at the very end of the story of the settlement of this world, following the conquest of Decorated-Feather Va'aki and of Chief Centipede-Necklace.)

"Our ancestors are with us.
We see their land in every direction.
And now our enemies are with us"—

WB They went on. They fought Tcuacat Sivanyi and overcame him. They fought Two Whirlwinds Chief and overcame him. They fought Tswahaini Medicine Man and overcame him. They came to Curling Downy Feathers Medicine Man and overcame him. They came to Braided Feathers Medicine Man and overcame him.[69]

They came to Decorated Feathers Medicine Man. He was a great chief and had taught the people irrigation. He had a medicine man's bag, and when he knew that the enemy was coming he hid an orphan child and gave him his bag. He took the child into the field and dug a hole and buried him. He covered him over with his medicine man's bag: "When the battle is over, if I am killed, come out at night, go to the enemy and give yourself up to them. You are only a child. They will not harm you." They fought. They had killed all of his people, but Curling Feather [i.e., Decorated Feathers] Medicine Man they could not kill. Whenever he was hard-pressed he sank down into the ground and all his enemies could not seize him. Four times he escaped them; but the fifth time they took his life. By night the child came to them with the medicine man's bag. Elder Brother said, "Let us take the child. He has good medicine." The bag was filled with strong wind and it is now in the Papago country and still sends strong winds down the Gila Valley[70]—

TV&WB? They lived there many years, for they had used up their supply of bows and arrows, and their power was exhausted. They sent word to the people who had gone to the south under Earth Doctor and said, "We have used up our bows and arrows, and our power is exhausted." Earth Doctor's people cut down arrow weeds and gathered feathers. From these, Elder Brother's company made a new stock of bows and arrows and obtained power again. When they were ready to start again, Chief Medicine Man sang:

69. Jenaṣt Siwañ, "Lizard Chief"; Go:k Sisiwelig, "Two Whirlwinds"; "Tswahaini" (unanalyzed); Vi:g Iol Ma:kai Siwañ, "Down-feather Turned-over Chief"; A'an Hi:tpagi Siwañ, "Feather Braids Chief" (Bahr et al. 1994:260, 287–89).—*Ed.*

70. The same episode is told at the beginning of the story "Koolhaa (or, The Orphan Boy)" in chapter 3. There the enemies are said to be Apaches. The two names for the father used here, Decorated Feathers and Curling Feather, may be different translations of the same name.—*Ed.*

"Yellow-headed old deer, my enemy shall go crazy."

They did not know what the song meant, and they called a man who had his power from dreams. They asked him to tell them the meaning of this song. He sang:

"See my medicine man's bag.
My sacred stones are about to fall out (of the bag)"—

WB Then they knew that he needed a new bag made of the skin of a full-grown deer. They sent out their two best hunters to get the deer. They brought it and tanned the skin and gave it to the medicine man and [he] made the bag—

TV&WB They started on again. They came to another *va'aki,* where they had many eagles for pets. They sang:

"Mountain with many eagles in the west, I am approaching.
My heart grows white."[71]

They fought and overcame the *va'aki* and took the eagle feathers. They came to another *va'aki,* where they had many macaws (*aadok*) for pets. They sang:

"Mountain with many macaws in the west, I am approaching.
My heart grows red."[72]

They fought and overcame the *va'aki* and took the macaws. They came to the left-handed people. Chief Medicine Man told his people, "We have come to Kwiuk,[73] where the left-handed people live. They will give us a hard battle."[74] They fought many days and overcame them.

They went on toward the west and came to Big Mountain (Kadoak) [Ge'e Duag]. In this *va'aki* the people kept themselves and their houses very clean. The people said, "Shall we kill them or take them along as one of us?" Chief Medicine Man sang:

"We must fight the people of Big Mountain." (repeat)

They fought, and Elder Brother's people won the victory.

They went on again toward the Colorado. They came to a *va'a-*

71. "I am about to have many down eagle feathers."
72. "I am about to have many macaw feathers."
73. Probably Kuiva, or Kuivo, "Downstream," "Westward."—*Ed.*
74. That is, they are good shots.

ki that had large fish for pets.[75] Chief Medicine Man sent spies ahead to see if it were so. [One of] the fish saw the scouts approaching. He inhaled and drew them in with great power. However, they caught hold of the branches of trees and saved themselves. When Fish shut his mouth they went home and told what had happened. Chief Medicine Man told them to gather much brush and, when the fish inhaled, to let go of the bundles of brush. They did, and the fish choked on the brush and died. (When the source of their power was gone) the people in that *va'aki* were conquered easily.

They went on to the Colorado River, and they could not cross. They said to the medicine man, "Do something so that we may cross the river." He took his cane and laid it on the water. The river separated and they went across on dry land.

They went on to the west. Near the ocean they came to people who dug holes and hid themselves in the ground. As Elder Brother's people marched over the country where they had hidden themselves, one of them hit Chief Medicine Man with his arrow from his hiding place; for the campaign was coming to an end, and for this reason in every great undertaking there is always an accident that brings it to its close. Chief Medicine Man was wounded. The people went on toward the ocean. They pulled the arrow from his body, but the arrow point remained in the flesh. They came back and crossed the Colorado River as they had done before.

Some of the people were far in the rear, and the waters closed before they had crossed. Chief Medicine Man said to them, "Stay where you are." And that is why there are Indians on the other side of the Colorado River.

They came to Komotk (Broad Place, very near Sacaton).[76] They still had the Chief Medicine Man with them. He died there, and they buried him in a seated posture in the earth.[77]

There was one enemy still to be overcome. They had not killed Yellow Buzzard. They looked for him in the air and under the ground. The eagle people found him in the air and brought him down from above. They brought him bound to Elder Brother. He

75. These would be *ñe:ñbig* (singular *ñe:big*), "sea monsters," "whales." See Bahr et al. 1994:244, 323n.—*Ed.*

76. It is about twenty-five miles to the northwest.—Ed.

77. As medicine men are still buried. [The place is Komaḍk, not "very near" but actually thirty miles west of Sacaton.]

said to the people, "Tie him." And they tied him. Elder Brother took his knife and scalped him so that he died. Elder Brother and Buzzard were brothers, and from this we learn that brothers kill each other.

All the four companies that had gone in different directions under Earth Doctor, Nasia, and Coyote came together at Broad Place, and from there they scattered to those parts of the country where they had staked out land. As they had traveled, wherever they had seen good land, they had marked it so that they could return. That is why we are scattered all over the country.

[Departure of Elder Brother]

So Elder Brother left his people. He went east to the country of the dead. He started another kingdom there and left Coyote on this earth.

After Elder Brother left, we could not build *va'aki*s anymore. We lived on as we do now.

Coyote made a man like himself and went about showing people how to make their houses (*ki*)[78] and to make the doors face southeast. He showed them how to make mats of wild reed for sleeping. After this, Coyote also followed Elder Brother to the east.

The people lived here. A woman died and left her husband and children. He mourned for four years. Elder Brother came and told him that his wife was happy with him [in the country of the dead], but the husband would not believe him. Therefore Elder Brother sent the woman back to her husband. She went to the place where they had lived. She said, "I have come to prove that I am alive. You were told but you would not believe. There are many people where I come from. Everything is good in that country." He believed her. She said, "I am not going back. I will stay with you. But during the day I will be invisible. Only at night will you see me. For ten years we will live together and we will have no intercourse. After that I will live with you as I did before." All day he was alone but at night she was with him in the house and they talked together. At last he tried to embrace her. She said, "If you cannot wait till the ten years are up, it is better for us all to go together." The house fell down and killed them all.

78. The old-style Pima dwelling, or *ki:,* is circular with a flat roof, "resembling an overturned wash basin" (Russell 1908:153).—*Ed.*

They went with all their children to the land of the dead. That is why the dead never come back after death. If he had waited ten years our dead would return—

WB Before Elder Brother left them he had said, "When the people will not listen to their leaders they will die and there will be no more rain. There will be famine and the tree will grow out of the earth that will reach to heaven. Earth Doctor will climb down this tree and the dead will rise from their graves and mingle with the living upon the earth. Earth Doctor will make a new earth that will be better than the old. People will live again and Earth Doctor will rule them"—

TV Elder Brother led his people to the south. He brought all the Pima into this country and they settled the Gila Valley.

2

PIECES LEFT OUT

Introduction

Donald Bahr

The thirteen stories of this chapter stand apart from those of the last, but they belong to the same Edenic time period as the rafter text. Why are they apart? I believe the narrators kept them out because with three exceptions they lack the two characters who preside over the whole of the rafter, Earth Doctor and Elder Brother. In effect these are jealous gods, and the rafter, as the narrators saw it, is their property. If they are not in a story, then the story is not in the rafter; and if a story has one of them, even in a minor way, then the story is included. They give the rafter its complex continuity: Earth Doctor is on scene alone first, later Elder Brother usurps the title "elder" from him, both gods create people, and by the end of the story Elder Brother is on scene without Earth Doctor.

Actually, three texts in this chapter do feature one of the gods, but these stories are either longer versions of ones told briefly in the rafter ("Nasia's Twins," enlarged from the "Farming and the Calendar" section), or they are Blackwater's versions of stories that appear in the rafter as Vanyiko told them ("Blackwater's Ho'ok" and "Blackwater's Man Eagle"). Those three, then, don't violate the jealous god rule but are extra versions of stories that adhere to the rule. Nor do the rest violate the rule. Three of them, all by Blackwater, expand on a topic covered by the rafter, the origin of corn. This locates them temporally in the time of origins—Edenic time—that is covered by the rafter. Consistent with the rule, however, they lack the key gods. Another text, "The Feud," which also lacks the gods, is on the topic of marriage, which is linked in Pima thought with the origin of corn. The feud is over a marriage at a time when corn farming is already in existence, and as is explained later, this text might equally have been placed in next chapter, on post-Edenic warfare. (Benedict, it will be recalled, stated no opinion on where it belonged.) The rest of the texts in this chapter, six of them, I am content to call "miscellaneous" or "leftovers." They lack the key gods, they don't treat origins or creations particularly, and yet they have something Edenic about them (no marriages that stick, a large amount of miracle, and a feeling of "first times").

Of the whole ensemble, "The Feud" and three of the "miscellaneous" items ("Dove Makes Magic for a Race," "Girl Becomes Star," and "Girl Becomes Saguaro") have not been published before. I have heard the last two from a Papago (but didn't record them), so they are not unique to Blackwater, who told them in this instance.

Blackwater's Ho'ok

William Blackwater

[The Parrot and the Turquoise]

At Casa Grande the women were playing double ball.[1] One of the players sank down into the earth and they stopped the game. They began to dig. Blue Turquoise Chief said to them, "No, she is dead already. It is no use to dig for her." Several days passed. They saw that the ground had turned blue. They dug and found it was solid turquoise.

Sun Power Chief (Tacanamkan Sivanyi)[2] lived to the east, and he was an enemy of Blue Turquoise Chief. He was jealous that his enemy had turquoise, and he prayed to Elder Brother for help. Elder Brother said to him, "Cut the vein in your hand and make a parrot, and send it to Blue Turquoise Chief."

Parrot came to Casa Grande. Blue Turquoise Chief's daughters were outside the house, and Vaam[3] saw the bird. She told her father. "Bring it in." She picked up a stick and the parrot took it in his mouth and followed her. They

1. *Toka,* a women's game like field hockey, also called tied ball, is played with a pair of balls attached to each other by a thong and thrown by a stick (Culin 1907:648, 660). Another story featuring this game is "Girl Becomes Saguaro," in this chapter.—*Ed.*

2. Sun Meeter Chief. See Vanyiko's version of the Ho'ok story in chapter 1 for this and also for his opponent's name, which is Morning Green Chief.—*Ed.*

3. This is the first recording of this story to give a personal name for the daughter. We don't know what the name means. There is a Pima word *va:m,* meaning "too-much" or "overdoing-it," but it is an adverb and in general Pima personal names were not adverbs.—*Ed.*

did not know this bird, and they brought all kinds of grain to feed him. But he would not eat. They called the wise men, but they did not know his proper food. At last a man who was very wise directed them, "Let him alone for four days. If he is a common bird he will die of hunger."

They did not feed him for four days, and as he wandered about he saw bits of turquoise. They saw that he picked them up and swallowed them. They brought him all the turquoise they had and fed him. Then they brought their earrings and necklaces.

At night, Parrot returned to his master, and Sun Power Chief set a dish, and the parrot vomited all the turquoise he had gathered. So Blue Turquoise Chief lost all his turquoise. When he saw it in his enemies' city, he knew that he had been tricked. He was angry and caused a cold wind and rain and great sickness. The rain put out all their fires, and they were freezing to death.

[The Kick-ball's Child]

Sun Power Chief sent Roadrunner and Gopher to the sun to get fire. Lightnings were guarding the fire, and Gopher tunneled underground and passed them. Then Gopher called out, and all the lightnings turned their faces toward the noise. While they were looking for him, Roadrunner seized the fire. He ran home. The lightnings chased him over the mountains and the hills, and sparks dropped from the torch into all stones and all woods, and that is why there is fire in stone and wood. He reached home. Sun Power Chief lit the fires again and warmed his people, but the parrot was dead.

Sun Power Chief burned his parrot and made the ashes into a kick-ball. He decorated it with the rays of the sun and gave it to the best runner of the village. He said to him, "Run with it past the house of Blue Turquoise Chief. If you lose it, return home immediately." Vaam was sitting outside weaving a sleeping mat of reeds. As the ball rolled past her she picked it up and hid it under her skirts. "I have lost my ball. Have you seen it?" "No. I don't know anything about it." "I have lost it. I will go home." He started back. She called to him, "Come back. I have it." But he would not turn back.

The girl was with child. The people began to talk about her and said, "We thought she was a good girl, but she must have been with the young men." The child was born. She had long arms and long fingernails, and the people did not know what to do with her. Some said, "Let us kill her." But others said, "Let us see what will come of it." When the child grew to be a young girl, she was hard to get along with, and she liked to eat raw meat. When the men went hunting, she would go along and chase rabbits. When she caught one, she ate it raw. One day she killed a baby and ate it in the same way. The people said, "Now we must kill her."

Her uncle knew of this and he came to her and said, "The people are giving us much trouble on your account. Do not kill any more children." She answered, "If I am causing trouble, I will go away for good." She started away from the village. Her uncle followed her, singing:

"How can I make my niece return with me?" (4 times)

He said, "I am not scolding you, I am only asking you to come back with me." He sang:

"Your mother, your grandfather (ask you to return)."[4]

She sang:

"Why do you call my mother's and my grandfather's names?
They do not want me to return."

She sang again:

"My poor uncle, you can do nothing to make me return with you."

Her uncle returned home, and she went to the mountains looking for a place to make her home.

[The Witch's Child]

She went far to the south and came to a cave in the mountains. She lived there and hunted wild animals and ate them raw. One day a man came hunting in that direction. He found her and came often to see her. He married her. They had a child, a daughter; and when the child grew to be large the father left, and the mother and daughter lived together.

When her daughter was grown, Ho'ok saw another hunter. She called him and gave him her daughter in marriage. The man was afraid to refuse, though he had a wife and children in the village. He lived with them a long time, but at last he left. Ho'ok's daughter wanted to go with him, but he said, "No, if you stay here I will return." She insisted, and when they came to the village his wife saw him coming with another woman. They fought, and Ho'ok's daughter killed the other woman and her sisters.

They went back to Ho'ok. Ho'ok's daughter would not eat. She would not talk. She lay around like a sick person. Ho'ok said to her daughter's husband, "What is the matter with my daughter?" He told her how she had killed the

4. This and the preceding song are used in mourning for the dead.

two women. Her mother scolded her, and she went away and hid in the cliff. Her husband followed her and called, but she would not come to him. Ho'ok went with him, and they tried to pull her out, but they could not. They left and went back home. She lived in the mountain as a *tcaac' top* (a lizard that resembles a Gila monster but is smaller).[5] The man went back to his home and Ho'ok lived alone again. When Ho'ok had eaten all the small animals in the region where she lived, she returned to her own country and caught children for food.

[End of the Witch]

The people came together and took council. They decided to ask Elder Brother for help. They went to him and he promised, "In four days I will come." They waited four days and he did not come. They waited four years and at last he came. Elder Brother said, "Where is Ho'ok?" "She comes from that direction." He went toward the south and turned himself into a rattlesnake. Ho'ok came by. She heard rattles. He tipped the earth and frightened her. She ran back. Elder Brother returned to his people and said, "She will not trouble you anymore," and he made rattles for the children so that when Ho'ok heard the rattles she was frightened and ran away.

After a time Ho'ok became used to this rattle. Again she caught the children and ate them. The people went to Elder Brother again. He said, "In four days I will come." They waited four days and he did not come. They waited four years and he came. He said to them, "Gather plenty of wood and take food and water into your houses. Stay there and she will think you have moved away." At last Ho'ok thought the people had moved and did not come hunting there anymore. Then an old woman went out of her house and Ho'ok saw her and returned and caught more children.

The people went again to Elder Brother. He promised to come in four days, and in four years he came. He made himself into a baby and went to the south. Ho'ok came and took the child. "I am going to take the baby to give to my grandchildren." She put the child in her carrying basket. Elder Brother shook the feathers that were in his hair and made thunder and frightened her. She threw the child on the ground and ran away. Elder Brother returned to the people and said, "I have frightened her. She will not trouble you anymore."

For a long time Ho'ok did not come to hunt children. But again the people had to go ask Elder Brother for help, and in four years he came. He made himself into four boys. Ho'ok came and threw the boys into her carrying bas-

5. At this point the narrator said that her [the daughter's] father's name was Tcaac' top. [It might *be* "gila-monster," which is *ciadag* in Pima.]

ket. The oldest said to her, "Grandmother, give us some stones to play with." She picked up several stones and threw them up for the children to play with. As she walked under some trees the oldest boy told them, "One of you catch hold of the branch and save yourself." Then he said to Ho'ok, "Throw us more stones to play with." Next time they went under trees he said to the boys, "Another of you catch hold of the tree and save yourself." When Ho'ok discovered there were stones in her basket instead of children she started back to get them, but she could not find them.

Then Ho'ok began to catch the older people and eat them. The people came together in a council, and they went again to Elder Brother. They said, "This thing has gone on for many years. Our children are almost gone and she has begun to eat the older people." Elder Brother answered, "There is nothing to be done but to kill her. It will be hard to accomplish, but we will try. Go close to her cave and hold a ceremony. Invite her to come. If she accepts, I can overcome her."

The people went to the south and found a place for a dance. They brought wood and food, enough for a long time. Elder Brother sent a man to Ho'ok and told her, "We are going to sing *maatk* (a dance in which one line dances up to the other and back again). Come to our ceremony." Ho'ok said, "No, I don't like that dance."

They sent a second man and he said, "We are going to sing *kaxyovitutckut* ('swing leg dance,' a round dance said to be unfamiliar).[6] Come to our ceremony." She said, "No, I don't like that dance."

They sent a third man and he said, "We are going to sing *cürl nya* (there are two forms of this dance, one similar to *maatk* and the second a round dance in which the dancers clap rattles above their heads).[7] Come to our ceremony." "No, I don't like that dance."

They sent a fourth man to say, "We are going to sing *tsikoimkutc nya* ('going round with song')."[8] "That is the dance I like." He went back and told Elder Brother, "She is coming."

Elder Brother said to his people, "We shall hold the dance, and after a while I shall light my cigarette and pass it around. Only pretend to smoke it. If she smokes, you will know that I can overcome her."

People said, "Ho'ok is coming. Hear the bones rattling."[9] Elder Brother started to dance. He lit his cigarette and passed it about, but Ho'ok did not

6. *Kahio wiḍut* . . ., "leg swing. . . ."—*Ed.*
7. Probably *ṣel ñe'e,* "straight (not circular) sing."—*Ed.*
8. Probably *sikol himcudk ñe'e,* "circular make-go-and sing."—*Ed.*
9. Bones of children she had killed, her dress decorations.

smoke. Again he passed it. At last she smoked. She went to sleep. As soon as she had taken a puff of the cigarette, Elder Brother sent men to pile wood at the mouth of her cave. He put her over his shoulder and carried her there. He put her far at the back. They lit the wood and it burned. She called out, "My grandchildren, what have you done? I have been dancing with you. I have been having a good time with you." She struggled and cracked the rock roof of her cave. Elder Brother put his foot upon the crack and it knit together. The print of his foot is still there on the mountain. They saw that she was dead, and an old woman sang:

> *"You have done everything well.*
> *Hereafter the earth will shake and the night will shake."*[10]

Out of the burning blue smoke Ho'ok rose, a blue hawk.

[Time of the Hawk]

The people went home, but they did not have peace, for Blue Hawk killed even the grown people. A woman was cooking greens outdoors, and Blue Hawk dived to strike her. Blue Hawk missed and fell into the pot and died. The pot kept on boiling, and it made a hot spring. The people went to Elder Brother and said, "How shall we get rid of the hot spring?" He answered, "In the early morning, when it is cool, go to the place where Blue Hawk was killed and empty the pot of greens."

Next day two men came by, returning from a hunt. They saw the greens tipped out upon the ground, and they stopped and ate. Immediately they became bears. These bears also began to kill people. People went again to Elder Brother and he said, "These bears can be killed with a bow and arrow." They took their bows and arrows and killed the bears, but their power went up into the clouds and it became dangerous lightning.[11] People went to Elder Brother. "How can we get rid of this dangerous lightning?" Elder Brother answered, "This is as much as I can do. Lightning often does not kill. What has happened, let it be." For this reason lightning sometimes kills.

[The Parrots and Tobacco]

Elder Brother took a portion of the power and cut it in pieces for each family to keep in their houses (as rain medicine), and for this reason we have wind,

10. With the jumping and playing of children.
11. Before this time lightning was harmless.

clouds, rain, everything. They distributed these, but there was one old woman with two granddaughters who did not get any. She considered, and she split bones and took out four red clots of blood. She put these under brush and they became macaws. After this, whenever they held a dance, her granddaughters would go wearing the red macaw feathers. Everybody envied them and wished for feathers. Some of the people said, "We will kill these girls and their grandmother and get the feathers."

The grandmother knew what the people had planned, and she said to her granddaughters, "Take the birds and escape with them. I am old and I will stay." The people came but there were no birds, no girls. They killed the grandmother and they followed the girls till they came to Steep Pitted Mountain (Vaapv tsejudjuk).[12] The girls saw the people coming. They opened the cages of the macaws and the birds flew up to the holes on the face of the mountain. So they escaped. The granddaughters returned home and buried their grandmother in a sandy place. In a few days they returned, and a plant was growing from her grave. It was tobacco.

Ever since, people have said to their children, "Stop crying. Ho'ok will get you."

[A Slightly Different Version of Parrots and Tobacco][13]

Black Ant Old Woman had four grandchildren, two girls and two boys. The boys were fast runners and the girls were good tied-ball players,[14] so that whenever their village challenged other villages, they came off victorious. Therefore the people in the other villages wanted to kill Black Ant Old Woman.

All the people of the country were gathered together at the killing of Ho'ok. They feasted and sang triumph songs. The old woman went down also, but no one offered her anything to eat. They all feasted on Ho'ok, and the old grandmother got nothing. She went to the place where they had burned Ho'ok and took two pinches of the ashes. She planted the ashes she had taken and hilled the earth around them. Her grandsons asked her for Ho'ok's meat. She said to them, "In four days go to the hills that I have planted, and you will find it."

The next day they went, and they could see nothing. The second day there were beautiful red feathers growing out of the earth. The third day there were

12. *Vawp S-cecedk,* "Rocks rough."—*Ed.*

13. Blackwater told this story separately from the previous one.—*Ed.*

14. Also called double ball, Pima *toka.*—*Ed.*

baby macaws. The younger [boy] said, "Let us take them now and show them to our grandmother."

The elder said, "No, she told us to wait four days." They went the fourth day. The birds were the most beautiful things they had ever seen. They took them back to their grandmother and everybody said, "These are the most beautiful feathers we have ever had." They tied the soft white downy feathers to their hair, and the girls used the long feathers for a headdress (like a crown).

The people still tried to kill the old woman. She said to her grandsons, "The people will kill me. Take the macaws to Mount Kiwatkam[15] and hide them. Make the ground soft and put my body in the ground. In four days you will find something growing there." The boys took the macaws to Mount Kiwatkam, and when they were returning they heard the cries of the people. They ran in among them, but their grandmother was already dead upon the ground. They made the ground soft and buried their grandmother. In four days they saw something growing. They did not know what it was. They picked the leaves and dried them, and that is how we came to have tobacco.

Blackwater's Man Eagle

William Blackwater

[Braided Feather]

Braided Feather (Aanhaitpak) [A'an Hi:tpagi] lived beyond the Gray Mountains.[16] He seemed feeble-minded, and the people did not pay much attention to him. He dreamed that he saw light shining in the west. He dreamed often, and at last he saw light in the daytime, too. He decided to follow it, and he started toward the west. Toward evening he stopped and cut brush for a shelter. Buzzard flew into his shelter. "I did not make this for you." Buzzard spread his wings to fly away and the boy saw white spots on his breast. They shone like medicine men's crystals. "I did not know you. Don't go." All the birds and beasts came and they began to talk. Next morning he went on toward the west in the direction of the bright light. At evening again he cut brush for shelter. The birds and beasts came again. Four nights he listened to their council.

Next day he came to a strong wind. He could not walk against it. It talked to him and blew him over all the earth. It showed him everything in the world.

15. Unrecognized name.—*Ed.*
16. The Toothbrush Mountains.

After this the wind carried him to the shining light that he had seen. It was a great *va'aki* and empty.[17] In the middle room he found a turtle.

He returned to his home. He made bamboo flutes and all the musical instruments that had not been known before. He did everything that others could not do and became a great man.

He saw red lights in the south and set out to follow them. He came to an ocean. Lightning was playing over the ocean. He started across it, and the ocean became fog. It gathered together and formed a great pearl. He returned home with it and everybody respected him more than ever. He was a great man. He seemed to know everything and could answer all questions. The medicine men came to ask him all the things they did not understand.

[Making the Gambler]

There was a boy named Vaante[18] and he seemed feeble-minded and made a great deal of trouble. He came to Braided Feather Medicine Man and sat silent all night beside him. Braided Feather did not speak to him. In the morning he went to his own home. Three times he came and sat all night beside him, and Braided Feather did not speak to him. Next morning his wife said, "There is a young man who comes here and you do not talk to him. I am sorry for him." "I do not think he has much sense." "Talk to him anyway."

Next night Vaante came again. Braided Feather went to bed. He woke and saw the young man still sitting beside him. "When did you come?" "I have just come in." Braided Feather got up, and the young man lit a cigarette. Braided Feather said, "Are you going to smoke it alone?" Vaante lit another cigarette and gave it to him. Braided Feather said to him, "You came here last night, and for four nights. I saw you." "Yes, I wanted you to tell me something. I wanted you to teach me." He taught him.

The young man went home, and the next night he came again. Every night Braided Feather taught him. He told him, "Whatever the people say, do not talk back. Listen and let them say what they wish." After that, people made fun of him, but he said nothing.

One day Braided Feather made a bow and arrow for him and said, "When the men go out hunting, go with them. If anyone else touches your arrow, leave it and come home." It was a poor-looking bow and arrow; the bow had bark on it. The hunters laughed at it and handled it. Vaante left it with them and

17. A *va'aki,* it will be recalled, is a large building of sun-dried mud.—*Ed.*

18. "Väntre" in the version given by Thin Leather to Russell (1908:218). Perhaps not a Pima name, because the word has no known meaning in the Pima language.—*Ed.*

returned home. Three times he went out on the hunt and the men handled it and he came back to his home. The fourth time, the leader of the hunt said to the hunters, "Whenever this boy goes on the hunt with his arrows, and we handle them, he leaves them behind. Today we will not touch them and we will see what he is able to do." They went hunting and no one touched his arrows. He killed many rabbits and gave them all to the old men. The last few that he caught he took to Braided Feather, and Braided Feather knew that he had followed his instructions.

The people used to come to Vaante to ask him to play with them, but he refused. One day Braided Feather said to him, "Do the people still tease you, asking you to gamble with them?"

"Yes, they still ask me to play with them." "I have told you to refuse everything. But now, if anyone asks you four times, come and tell me."

A man came and asked him to gamble. He refused four times and went to Braided Feather. He said, "A man has asked me four times to gamble with him." "Go back and accept." Braided Feather made the sticks for him to gamble with.[19] He said, "Always use these whenever you play. If anyone refuses to use your sticks, do not play with him." He played and won every game. Everything that he won he gave to Braided Feather. The people talked together and said, "Why is it that this boy always wins? Let us go to Elder Brother to ask for help against him."

[Gambler to Eagle]

They went. Elder Brother made gambling sticks and said, "Always use these when you gamble." They came back and set a day when they should gamble together. They brought out the sticks that Elder Brother had made. The boy would not play with their sticks and at last the people had to use his. They lost to him. They went back and said to Elder Brother, "He has won against us." "He is a good player, but I will do my best for you. Go into the forest and get feathers of the big meat-eating birds and bring them to me. Set a day, and from that day he will play with you in four days."

Elder Brother took the feathers the people had brought to him and he said to one of the men, "I need the help of your daughter." The man went to his daughter and said, "Elder Brother needs you." Elder Brother said to her, "Roast these feathers and take the ribs of them and grind them. As the feathers roast,

19. Evidently for the game called *kints,* or *giins,* which also figures in the stories "Corn Woman," "The Coyote Brothers," and "Nasia's Twins," this chapter.—*Ed.*

they will pop like corn. Take ironwood and mix it with the feathers. Grind it to meal and make pinole. When you have finished, take it to the spring and give it to the boy when he comes to take a drink."

The fourth day came. They were about to play. Vaante said, "I will go and drink." Braided Feather said, "Drink the water here." But he answered, "No, it is fresher at the spring." He went down the path to the spring. The girl was there. She called to him, "I have pinole. Drink it before the game." When he had taken the first sip, he was cold. He wondered what was happening to him, but he drank. The girl went home. He looked at himself and saw that feathers were growing on his body. He saw a bill sticking out where his mouth had been. He saw he had yellow legs and claws like the yellow pith of ironwood. He said to himself, "I wonder if I shall fly?" He flew up into the air and he sang:

> *"Pinole made of feathers you gave me to drink.*
> *You caused feathers to grow upon my body."*

The gamblers were waiting for him to play, but he did not come. They said to one of the men, "Go and see where he is." He went to the spring and saw only an eagle. He came back and said, "I could not find him. I saw only an eagle." "Perhaps he has become an eagle." "Yes, that is he. He is going to cause trouble. Get your bows and arrows." They shot at him, but the eagle caught the arrows in his claws. That is why there are eagles with arrows in their claws on the Mexican dollar.[20]

The eagle flew south to Vaavstoiya.[21] He lived there and killed deer. When the game was exhausted he came farther north. Again he moved and came nearer to his people. He seized them and took them up to the mountain. He saw the woman who had given him the drink at the spring, and he took her to his home and married her. They had a child.

[The Eagle Undone]

The people were in great trouble because of Man Eagle. They went to Elder Brother and asked for help. He said to them, "I will try. I will come in four days." They waited, but he did not come. They went again. In four years he came and said, "Bring me pliant sticks (*vasiv*)."[22] They gathered all the pliant

20. In this case, actually the United States dollar. In the rafter there is an episode of a battle for a *va'a-ki* at Casa Blanca, with an account of the origin of the design for the Mexican dollar.—*Ed.*

21. Vaf S-do'i, "Rock Raw," so named because of the bloody smell of the people whom the Man Eagle ate there.—*Ed.*

22. *Va:sif,* or *va:s,* "broomweed" (*Gutierrezia sarothrae*). See Bahr et al. 1994:164. Rea (1997:136–37) has "limber bush" (*Jatropha cardiophylla*).—*Ed.*

sticks they knew of, but he said, "No, I mean the pliant stick." At last, one man brought *vasiv,* and he said, "Yes, this is what I wanted. Bring me also black stone."

They gathered all the black stone they could find, but he said, "No, bring me black stone." At last they brought obsidian, and he said, "Yes, this is what I want." He made a battle-ax. "I will go against the Man Eagle, and in sixteen days if you see a white cloud toward the east you will know that I have succeeded. If you see nothing, you will know that I have been killed." He traveled all night and slept during the daytime. After many days he came to the foot of the mountain and slept. In the morning the eagle came out and circled four times around the mountain to be sure that all was safe. He flew away. Elder Brother sang:

"Up this steep mountain with my sticks I make my ladder."

He threw his sticks against the face of the mountain and they caught there and formed a ladder. As he climbed, he pulled out the rung below him so that the eagle could not see that anyone had climbed the cliff. He found the eagle's wife and said to her, "Your people have sent me to get rid of your husband. Do not grieve. In time he would have killed you, too. If I succeed I will save you and take you back to your home." He made himself into an ant and said, "Will he find me?" "Yes, he looks everywhere." He turned himself into every small animal and still she said, "Yes, he will find you." At last he turned himself into a blue-fly and flew straight up into the air. "Can he catch me?" "No, he cannot rise straight up into the air. If you fly downward he can catch you, but if you fly up you will escape." He said to her, "What does the eagle do when he returns?" "He lies down and goes to sleep." "When he is fast asleep, whistle and call me."

He hid himself under the heart of the lowest body. The eagle came and circled four times around the mountain to see that everything was safe. He came in. His child talked. Eagle said to the child's mother, "Why does it talk? It never did this before." She said, "It is prattling." "Perhaps somebody has been here, and the child is trying to tell me." "You know the mountain is too steep. Children always make noises when they are learning to talk."

Eagle looked to see if anything had come into the cave. He turned over all the dead bodies, but the last one he did not overturn. Eagle lay down and slept. His wife sang:

(a lullaby:) "Sleep, sleep."

The eagle heard her and woke. He said, "There must be somebody here. You never sang before." "There is no one here. You never brought so much meat before. I am happy because of that."

He went to sleep again. She sang. She sang louder and louder, and he did not wake up. At last she whistled. Elder Brother came with his battle-ax and cut off the head of the eagle and the head of the child. In the morning Elder Brother said to Eagle's wife, "Help me sort out the bodies (of Eagle's victims)." They put them in four different piles according to the length of time they had lain there. He said to her, "Heat water and sprinkle it on the pile of fresh bodies." They came to life and their skin was as before. He sprinkled the second pile of bodies, and their skin also was quite dark. He sprinkled the third pile of bodies, and their skin was yellow. He sprinkled the fourth pile of bodies, and their skin was white as bone. When they were all alive, he overturned the water; and it ran down the precipice so that it became a gentle slope. They followed it to the foot of the mountain.

He said to the group that had come alive first, "Where did you come from?" They answered and told him; they said, "We know our homes and the way to return to them."

He asked the group that had come alive second. They also went to their homes.

He asked the third group, and they also knew the way to their homes.

[Origin of Whites]

He asked the fourth group, but they had been dead so long that they could not speak. They made noises: *te'er'er* (laughter). Elder Brother made black paint. He took an eagle feather and stripped the rib bare. He cut it to a fine point and dipped it in the black paint. He gave it to them and said, "This is the way you shall talk to each other." They wanted to stay in this country but he said, "No, I have given you a way to talk to each other. You must go to the east." That is why whatever a white man hears, he can't put it into his mind. He can only remember it when he writes it down. Even when he sings, he has to sing out of a book.

The people that Elder Brother had brought to life made a litter and decorated it. They carried him home on the litter on their shoulders.

Corn Woman

William Blackwater

[Kadagum's Wife]

There was great sickness in that country.[23] All the children died and were buried. Kadagum's[24] children died, all except the youngest; at last this child died also. They buried it. Every morning he and his wife went to the grave and wept there. All day they stayed by the water, and in the evening they came again to weep at the grave. At last the man said, "It is enough. We must do something for our living. It is sad that we have lost our children, but we must live."

His wife answered, "I cannot live in any other way. Work and do whatever is necessary, but I must weep for my lost child. Perhaps someday I will feel differently."

Her husband returned to his fields, but his wife continued to mourn. Sometimes her relatives went with her to the grave to mourn in the morning, and sometimes they went with her in the evening.

Dragonfly Man came to weep with her. He went with her to the grave and went back to his house. Every evening he went to mourn with her, and she was drawn to Dragonfly Man. She went away with him. She lived with him. She stayed with him a little while, but she was crazy; she left him and went to live with another man. She lived with many men. At last she lived with Buzzard. He was a very old man, and she left him. She lived with Duck. She found out that he was not human, and she left him. She lived with Turtle. She found out that he was not human, and she left him. She went toward the east. She came to a village. She lived with White Corn. She lived with Blue Corn. She lived with Yellow Corn. She lived with Red Corn. She lived with All-colors Corn.[25]

Kadagum lived alone at his home. He went to Elder Brother and asked for help to recover his wife. Elder Brother took corn stalks and made a carrying

23. There are few mentions of epidemics in Native American stories of ancient times. This mention is unique to this version of the story. The other version that has been recorded has the woman leave her husband on their wedding night because she really doesn't want to be married to him, not because she can't stand the grief over the death of her children. That other version is in Bahr et al. 1994:111–22.—*Ed.*

24. [The word *kadagum* refers to] A bird about the size of a mockingbird but unidentifiable by the interpreter. [The version of the story mentioned in the previous note agrees that *kadigum* is the name of a bird seldom seen, but the same name appears in a different teller's version of the story of the loss of corn and tobacco. There the word is taken as the name of a tobacco-like plant that, like these birds, is seldom seen and was unfamiliar to the teller (Bahr et al. 1994:99).]

25. Called also prostitute corn, *ko'opot* [I don't know this word—the normal word for prostitute is *ce:paowi,* given as a name for red corn in Rea 1997:348].

basket. He took squash blossoms and made a work basket. He took them to Corn Woman and gave them to her. She forgot all her past life and remembered her husband. Elder Brother led her back. They came a long journey. Elder Brother said, "I will leave you here. Go back to your husband. Whatever people say, pay no attention."

She came close to her husband's house, singing the Corn songs. A man saw her. She was a stranger, and he ran in a circle so that she would pass him again. Again he did not recognize her, and he came back into the village. Her husband came home from his fields at night as usual. He was mourning for her.[26] He went into his house. When it was dark a woman came. He did not recognize her. "What have you come for?" She said, "I have come." "Do you want to spend the night?" "Yes." "I live here alone and do my own cooking. Cook for yourself whatever you wish to eat. When you have finished, sleep on those blankets. I must go to the council." He passed by her to go to the council meeting. She put her hand on him and said, "It is I. I have come back to you." He knew her.[27] She said, "Do not go to the meeting. I can teach you more than they can in the meeting."

The men gathered in the meeting house. They missed him, for he was always the first to arrive, because there was no one to keep him at home. They said, "He must be sick." The man who had seen a woman come into the village said, "I have something to say. I saw a strange woman come into the village. I circled around and looked at her four times, but I did not recognize her." They wondered who it might be. Some said, "Perhaps it is his wife." Others said, "No, she has been gone many years. She may be dead by this time."

A medicine man said, "How shall we find out? We will send a man." He pulled out a rabbit and sent him. Rabbit ran around the house and heard two people talking together on one bed. He could not hear what they said. He came back and reported. The medicine man said, "We have found out that they are talking together in one bed. I will send another man." He pulled out Roadrunner and sent him. Roadrunner ran around the house and heard the man say, "I forgot all about you but you have come back to me." He went back and reported. The medicine man said, "We have found out that it is his wife who has come back to him." It was late at night and they went back to their homes.

After that, Kadagum never went to the council meeting. The men said to each other, "What is it that his wife tells him that keeps him away from the

26. "A man always feel more sorrowful when his wife leaves him than when she dies. He gets over her death, but if she leaves him he always continues to weep."

27. "If a woman leaves her husband, no matter how bad she has been, he is waiting to take her back. Even if he has boasted, 'I am through with her,' if she returns he receives her."

council meeting? All she has to talk about are her dirty ways and all the men she lived with."

At last, one day Kadagum came to the ceremonial house. The man who lived there was alone. He said to him, "This is where you used to sit. You always used to come first. It is good to see you again." He lit the cigarette and gave it to him. He said, "We have missed you. You know we always meet here and talk about what is best to do, and we tell each other the news. What is it that your wife tells you that you would rather stay with her than come to the council?" "Yes, this is the first time I have been here since my wife returned. It is true, she tells me many valuable things and sings songs we never heard before." "Tell me." Just then the others began to come, and the man who lived there said to him, "Come early again tomorrow evening and tell me then."

Next night he came earlier. The man who lived there said to him, "Tell me what we were talking of last night." "My wife has brought back something which will be of great value to us. It is not time yet for her to reveal it." He sang one of the Corn songs. The man who lived there said, "Yes, that is good. It will bring us all kinds of help." Just then the others came.

Again Kadagum did not come to the meetings. They talked about him, and the man who lived there said, "Yes, he talked to me about his wife. I think she has brought us things of great value. He sang me a song, but I do not learn songs well for I am old. Some of you who are young should go to this woman and learn from her." They appointed men to learn the songs. Before they had gone out Kadagum came again. They said, "The man who lives here told us a little about what your wife has brought to us. We should like to hear it." "I have not learned it yet. They are not my songs. If you want to hear them I will bring her here." He went home to bring his wife. The others said, "I don't think it is right for her to come to the council meeting. She is a woman and a prostitute." Some said, "Yes. She has brought us what is of great value."

They were talking back and forth when Kadagum came with his wife. She said to her husband, "How shall I go in?" "Step right in." She changed herself into a duck (*vaatac kopik*)[28] and sat on her husband's shoulder. They saw him come in alone. Those who had wanted him to bring his wife to the ceremonial house said, "We wanted you to bring your wife and you have come alone." He answered, "No, she is with me. Put more wood on the fire and you will see her." They put more wood on the fire, and when it blazed up they saw her sitting beside him as the prostitute corn (all-colors corn). Those who had want-

28. Possibly the ducklike mud hen, or American coot, *vakaig* (Saxton and Saxton 1969:167).—*Ed.*

ed to learn her songs said to her, "Sing for us." The others turned their faces to the wall and lay down.

She began to sing. It was very beautiful. One by one the men who had turned their faces to the wall got up and joined the circle and sang with the rest. Outside it began to rain. She said to them, "These are the songs to bring rain." They believed her. They asked her to sing again next night. Again it rained. Everyone believed her. They said, "Teach us all that you know."

[Corn Man]

She said to them: "In the beginning Earth Doctor called the living creatures. He called wind and clouds, the blackbirds, the woodpeckers, and all the birds that like corn, and he said to them, 'Whenever you find people, use your power.' They started on their journey.

"They came to a high mountain and sent the wind to look for people, but it could not find any. Four times they came to high mountains and sent the wind. It circled all about, but it could not find people. They came to the great water. They crossed it, and on the other side they found corn growing. They made it into a person and gave him bows and arrows and everything that a man needs. They brought him with them toward the west. At every camp they looked for human beings.

"At last they came to Frog Mountain.[29] They sent out the wind and it found a pretty girl and her mother gathering seeds. It came back and told them, 'I have found a pretty girl.' They said to each other, 'It's time to use our power.' They caused rain to fall and went on to Superstition Mountain and camped there. They caused it to rain there also. They gave turquoise to Corn Man and strings of white shell and strings of red coral, and they said to him, 'Take these to the girl and give them to her.' He went down to the foot of the mountain where the girl and her mother were gathering seeds. They had built a fire to roast the pods. In those days they had nothing to eat but desert seeds.

"Corn Man shot an arrow so that it struck close to the girl. She said to herself, 'Where did that arrow come from?' Corn Man came up to recover his arrow, and she said to him, 'What are you doing here?' 'I am hunting. What are you doing here?' 'I am gathering seeds. I have just put some into the fire to roast.' He took the beads from his wrists and from around his neck. He gave them to her and said, 'These are for you. Perhaps what you have put into the fire is ready to eat.' She answered, 'No, I have only just put it in.' He poked the hot ashes with his arrow and said, 'I think it is ready to eat.' They uncovered it and there

29. Mount Lemmon, near Tucson.

were corn and pumpkins and squash all ready to eat. He said to her, 'Come, brush the dust off my back.' She went to him and brushed the dust from his shoulders.[30] The man said to her mother, 'Take all this food to your home. Give it to your husband and tell him to eat. I will bring your daughter to you again.'

"The mother took the food to her husband and gave it to him to eat. She said to him, 'We had buried our seeds in the fire and a man came by. He poked the ashes and all these things were ready to eat in the fire. He gave our daughter valuable necklaces. He wants to take her as his wife. If you do not agree, I will go out and bring her back. If you do, I will go and tell her, and he will bring her himself.'

"Her husband said, 'What shall I say? What he has given us will be a help to our whole people.' His wife went out. She came to Corn Man and her daughter and said, 'You are welcome. My husband agrees.' Corn Man said, 'Go back to your home. Tell all the people to clean their houses and sweep their yards, make everything as clean as they can. On the clean ground set out all the baskets that they have. Make a house for us to live in.' The people did as Corn Man told them. Toward evening Corn Man and his wife started for her home. From the west came clouds and rain. From the clouds fell a rain of corn. It filled all the baskets they had set out and covered the clean ground. Corn Man and his wife came into the village and went to the house that the people had made for them. Corn Man lived there four years and taught the people to plant corn and wheat and beans and pumpkins and squashes.

"That is why we have rain and corn and all these vegetables. The birds who had brought Corn Man (all the birds who like to eat corn) lived there with them for four years. That is why we have all these birds in the cornfields."

[Corn Man and Tobacco Man]

Corn Woman taught them: "There was a medicine man in that village who had a daughter. She was not married. She said to her father, 'I am old. Nobody wants to marry me. Can you help me?' 'Yes, I can help you. But I must kill you first.' 'All right.' Her father killed her and buried her. In a few days a plant grew from her grave. It was tobacco. He said, 'You will not want a husband anymore, but every man will want you.'

"Corn Man and Tobacco Man quarreled. Corn Man said that the people paid most attention to Tobacco; they forgot him, and it was because of him (Corn) that clouds and rain came to them. Tobacco said that the people paid

30. A sign that she was ready to take him as her husband. A woman must not put her hands on any man she does not mean to marry. [In line with that, in "social dancing" (see Bahr, Paul, and Joseph 1997:21–31), unmarried men and women *hold* hands, and that was considered exciting.]

most attention to Corn and that it was because of him (Tobacco) that clouds and rain came to them.

"One day Corn and Tobacco quarreled over *kiinz,* the gambling game. Tobacco said to Corn, 'You are nothing. If it weren't for me you could not live at all. It is I who bring the clouds and the rain, and you come up out of the earth when it is wet. You have no power.' Corn answered and said, 'It is you who are nothing. If it weren't for me you could not live at all. It is I who bring the clouds and the rain. People don't need you. If they do not have me they die, but who would die without tobacco? No one can get along without me, and only a few old men need you.[31] You are nothing.'

"Corn and Tobacco were very angry. They went to their homes and sulked. The people said, 'Which of them should stay in this country?' They talked it over and they said, 'We will put it to the vote. The one that most people want shall stay.' They asked, 'How many are on Corn's side?' Nearly all the people voted for Corn. 'How many are on Tobacco's side?' The old men voted for Tobacco. So Corn won.

"Tobacco knew the vote was against him. He heard them laughing and enjoying themselves and he said, 'They are laughing at me.' He lay down on his bed and sank into the earth. He came out far in the west. A man was living there. At night the man said, 'It is time to go to bed.' Tobacco lay down on his bed and sank into the ground. Again he came out far to the west.

"Corn Man stayed on with the people in the village. There was no rain. The people were suffering from famine. They complained and they said, 'We should not have sent Tobacco away.' Corn was angry because they complained. He wanted to go away. A baby was born in that village and it was Squash. The children played with it and dropped it. It died and they buried it. In a few days a squash vine grew from the grave. Corn went to his home in the east. He lived in the east, and Tobacco lived in the west. In that village there was no more Corn and no more Tobacco. The people said, 'It is our fault. We have sent them away. Now we have no more tobacco and no more corn. Let us find them and bring them back.' They looked everywhere, but they could not find them. At last they said, 'Let us call Dragonfly Medicine Man.' They called him. He looked everywhere in Tobacco's house, but he could not find any trace of him.

"He turned himself into a dragonfly and sank down into the earth. He found the tunnel that Tobacco had made and came out far to the west. A man was living there. Dragonfly said to him, 'Have you seen Tobacco?' He remembered him. He said, 'A man came here long ago. Next morning he was gone.'

31. Tobacco is smoked ceremonially, and its use is limited to old men.

Dragonfly flew up into the air. He dropped down on the ground and sank into the earth. He found the tunnel Tobacco Man had made. He followed it and came up far to the west. He saw Tobacco in that village. He said to him, 'I have come to ask you to return with me.' Tobacco's whole body shook with anger and he said, 'No, I will not come! Why should I go to help those people?'

"Dragonfly returned. He said, 'I have found him, but he would not come with me.' Three times they sent him to Tobacco Man, but he would not come. The fourth time he took four tobacco pods and threw them at Dragonfly. He took tobacco leaves and made four cigarettes. He threw them at Dragonfly and he said, 'Take these back. Leave me in peace. When you want rain, smoke these cigarettes and the clouds will come. When the rain falls, plant the seeds from these pods and they will grow.' This is why, when people are angry, they still throw things at the person they are angry at, and their bodies shake with anger.

"Dragonfly took home the four pods of tobacco seeds and the four cigarettes. He came to the people and he said, 'It is no use to send me again. He is still angry, and we must leave him in peace.' He did not tell the people what Tobacco had given him. He went off into the desert and smoked his cigarettes, and rain came. When the ground was wet, he planted his seeds in the wet earth. Every few days he went out to attend to his field. At last it was ready. He dried the tobacco and smoked it. The people smelled the smoke and they said, 'I smell something. It is like tobacco.' Dragonfly said nothing. They said to him, 'You smell of tobacco.' 'I have been eating greens.' 'No, I smell tobacco.' He told them how he had received tobacco. Next morning all the people ran out to his field. They all took tobacco, and that is how tobacco returned to this country.

"Again the people went out to look for Corn. They found that he lived far to the east, and they appointed Dragonfly to find him. He came to where Corn was living. He said, 'I have come to ask you to return with me.' 'No, I am living here.' Dragonfly talked to him. But he said, 'I tell you, I am not coming.' He broke off the tiny end kernels of the corn and threw them at Dragonfly, and that is why we have small Indian corn and do not have large full ears. Dragonfly returned and said, 'I found Corn, but he would not come with me. He gave me these kernels of corn.' He gave them to the people and they planted them. The corn grew, and that is how corn returned to this country."

[Rain Man and Wind Man]

Corn Woman taught them: "Rain Man and Wind Man lived together. Rain Man was blind and stayed close to home. Wind Man went out every morning to gather seeds for pinole. He went down to the village and played with the people when they gambled. Whenever Rain went out, Wind had to go before him and lead him.

"One day the men were gambling in the village. The medicine man's daughter stood nearby. She would not have anything to do with men, and the people who were gambling said to Wind, 'Do something to this girl and find out why she does not pay any attention to us.' Wind said, 'There will be trouble.' [The people said,] 'We will stand by you whatever happens.' Wind called Little Whirlwind. Whirlwind blew up her skirts. The girl cried out, and her father came and took her home. He knew it was the fault of Wind, and he said to him, 'What have you done? Every morning you take some of the flour that these women have ground, and yet you do this to them. Leave this country or I will kill you.' Wind said to the men who had been gambling, 'I told you there would be trouble, and now it has come. You promised to help me, but none of you said a word for me.'

"Wind returned to his home, and he said to Rain Man, 'The people who were gambling teased me to blow up the skirts of the medicine man's daughter. Now he is going to kill us. We must leave this country.' That night they both left. Nobody knew where they went. There was no wind and only the big-drop rain.[32] The people were hungry.

"They called a council and tried to find the wind and the rain. They appointed four blind medicine men to bring them back to this country. The four medicine men cut divining sticks and prayed in every direction. At last they said, 'We are not sure. We think they have gone to the south.'[33]

"They asked for Kiisop [*gi:supi,* black phoebe]. When they had found him they gave him a downy feather and sent him to the west. He went west and held up his feather. It did not move at all. He returned to the center and went to the north. He held up his feather. It did not move at all. He returned and went to the east. He held up his feather but it did not move. He returned and went to the south. When he had gone a long distance he held up his feather. There was a breath in the feather.

"[Then he set out, and] he came to the land where Wind and Rain had gone. The ground was wet and everything was green. He followed Wind and came to their house. They were asleep on their blankets. He tried to wake them but he could not. For four nights he stayed but he could not wake them. At last they turned in their beds and spoke to him. He said, 'The medicine men have

32. The Pima distinguish between the small-drop rain, which makes the seeds grow, and the big-drop rain, which runs off the hard surface of the earth and does no good to the fields.

33. The medicine men feel a drag upon the divining sticks [feathers] in the direction of the lost person or article.

sent me to ask you to return to the village. The people are hungry and suffering.' 'No, we have left the village. We will not return.' Three times he asked them. The fourth time they answered, 'We will come. Tell the people to strengthen their houses and pile the dirt heavily over the framework.'

"In the morning they started. Rain went slowly and Wind led him. Wind said to Rain, 'Hurry up, we are going home.' The wind blew, and it rained in torrents. The houses leaked, and everything was wet inside the houses. The house of the medicine man leaked in every direction. There was one corner that was dry, and he had put his blanket there. Wind blew the rain in and threw water over his bed. He was angry. He called out, 'Go away from here. You only make trouble.' Wind and Rain went away again. They never came back, and that's why we have hardly any rain in this country."

The Coyote Brothers, Part 1[34]

William Blackwater

Coyote created two brothers and told them to go west and choose a good land for themselves. As they went, they came to a river, and they made themselves rafts on which to cross. The younger brother's raft moved slowly, and the elder brother called to him, "Paddle harder so that your raft will come alongside." The younger brother paddled harder and he came alongside. "A splinter got in my eye. I cannot see." They brought their rafts back to land and washed his eye, but the younger brother was blinded.[35] The elder brother led him back to the village and told Coyote what had happened. Coyote washed his eyes and he could see again. "Now go and choose yourselves a good land."

34. "A true story." [This narrative and the next, also said to be "true," are told as a single uninterrupted story in Russell (1908:230–37). Blackwater evidently considered the two narratives to be distinct.]

35. It was said in the introduction to this book that neighboring mythologies parody each other. The opening of this myth is a beautiful example of that. The Maricopas, a distinct people who lived allied with the Pimas, begin their mythology with two man-gods together on a floating log (Spier 1933:345–46). Those gods are equivalent to the Pimas' Earth Doctor and Elder Brother, who, however, are differently situated and related to each other at the start of Pima mythology. I don't know who parodies whom in that opening situation, but I am sure that the Pimas parody the Maricopas in this text: Pima Coyote-persons replace Maricopa man-gods (characters in fully human form). In effect, the Pimas make fun of the Maricopa opening scene. The parody doesn't stop there: one of the characters tricks the other into becoming blind, by somewhat different means in each story. Then the texts part company, the Maricopa going into the creation of people from man-god molded mud, and the Pima, into a deadly farce about domestic life. This is parody in the broadest sense: the Pimas turn the Maricopa man-godly genesis into canine domestic farce; or, if you wish, the Maricopas "uplift" the Pima canine farce into a genesis. It is impossible to say who wins in such contests, or who made the first move—impossible to guess how it all started. For as far back as these were tribes and neighbors, they probably parodied and reparodied each other.—*Ed.*

The brothers went where Coyote had directed them and they found good land, good trees, good soil, and they built themselves a house. They left that house and built themselves a second house. They left that house and built themselves a third. They left that house and built themselves a fourth house, and they lived in that.

The elder brother said to the younger brother, "Choose which side of the house you will live in." "The north side." "All right. I will sleep on the south side." Next morning the elder brother drew a line through the trees. "Choose which part of the trees will belong to you." "The north part." "All right. I'll take the trees to the south." One tree grew directly on the dividing line, and its fruit grew ripe and weighted down the tree. The elder brother said, "Which side will you take?" "North." "All right. I'll take the south." They ate all day. They went to bed, and the younger brother was sick all night. The elder brother said, "Of course you are sick. The sun shines on my side and ripens the fruit, but yours was not ripe yet."

The brothers lived there a long time and they made gambling sticks (*giinskoot*)[36] and played together. At first they played for fun, but afterward they gambled, and the younger brother lost. He lost his [part of the] house and his land. At last he staked the fruit tree. The elder brother won. The younger brother said, "Now you have everything, and there is nothing for me to do but to die of hunger." "There is another game, and perhaps you will have good luck with that." "What is it?" "Kick-ball."

The elder brother went north and came to a village. "I am looking for the best kick-ball runner." "That is Duck." "I will take him." The younger brother went south and came to Coyote. "I have lost everything, and now I have to play kick-ball for the last game. Who can win for me against Duck?" "Stink Beetle (*tcukokuk*)." They went for Beetle. He said, "When you were talking about me I fell asleep and I dreamed that one of the blue balls fell down by me from above, and I kicked it to the east, and after that I kicked it to the west. By this sign I know that I will win the race."

The day of the race came, and they met to decide upon the race course. Duck's side was the most numerous so they had their way and set the race course around the edge of the whole world, to go east toward the sun and then turn the course to the west. Beetle's side agreed that it would be so. They started toward the east. Duck was already out of sight and Beetle was left far behind. The runners[37] came to a pool of water and they said, "Beetle has lost

36. Stick-dice game.

37. It was the Pima custom for runners to go alongside, and if the ball was kicked wide of the path, they found it and put it back on the race course. In the story these runners are ahead with Duck.

already. Let us stop here and be comfortable." They caught fish and made a fire and cooked and feasted. They were just ready to eat when Stink Beetle came up. "Eat with us, Stink Beetle." Stink Beetle went right on.

The runners ate and had a little sleep and then they started on again. They passed Beetle a little way along and left him out of sight. They came to a pool of water and they caught fish and cooked them and ate. As they were ready to eat, Beetle came up again and they asked him to eat. He went right on, and when they had slept they went on again. A little way along they passed Beetle again and left him out of sight. They came to a third lake and they caught fish and cooked and ate and had a little sleep. Beetle passed them again, and when they went on again they overtook him easily and left him behind. They came to a fourth lake and stopped and caught fish and cooked them and slept a little. Again Beetle passed them.

When they woke up they overtook Beetle again immediately, and Duck laughed as he passed him. Stink Beetle threw his gray scent ahead, and when they came to it Beetle went under very easily, but Duck's party could not get through. At last they found a way and passed Beetle immediately. Stink Beetle threw his blue scent, and he went under easily, but Duck lost a great deal of time because he could not get through. Duck passed Beetle again, and Beetle threw his yellow scent. He could get under easily, but Duck tried and tried and could not find a way through. When he succeeded he passed Beetle again, and Beetle threw his black scent, which was very strong. Duck tried and tried but he had great difficulty getting through. He had just found a way when Beetle crossed the goal line and won the game.

So the elder brother and the younger brother lived together again, and Coyote lived with them. Coyote said, "There is a girl in the village to the north who will not marry any man. Better men than you have paid court to her but she will have none of them. You can go and try your luck if you want to." The two brothers went to the north. The girl was making baskets and paid no attention to them. She had no companion except her pet blackbird. The elder brother said, "I'll shoot that bird." He took his arrow and put it to the bow and killed the blackbird. The girl cried and said, "Why did you kill my pet? It was always with me, and every morning it woke me with its pretty songs." The two brothers started back for their home. The girl pulled the arrow from her pet blackbird and ran after them. She stood at the side of the road and said to the elder brother, "Take your arrow."

They passed on and did not speak to her. She ran a roundabout way and came to the edge of the trail again. "Take your arrow." The elder brother took the arrow and Corn Girl became his wife. The younger brother ran ahead and told Coyote. "I knew that you would win her. She was not hard to get after all."

Again Coyote said to them, "There is a girl in a village to the south who will not marry any man. Better men than you have paid court to her but she will have none of them. You can go try your luck if you want to." The two brothers went to the south. The girl was making baskets and paid no attention to them. She had no companion except her pet woodpecker. The younger brother said, "I'll shoot that bird." He took his arrow and fitted it to his bow and killed the woodpecker. The girl cried and said, "Why did you kill my pet? Every morning it woke me with its tapping." The two brothers started toward their home. The girl pulled the arrow from her pet woodpecker and ran after them. She stood by the side of the road and said to the younger brother, "Take your arrow." They passed on and did not speak to her. She ran a roundabout way and stood on the edge of the trail again. "Take your arrow." The younger brother took the arrow and Itanyi Girl became his wife.[38] Elder Brother ran ahead to tell Coyote. "I knew you would win her. She was not hard to get after all."

The Coyote Brothers, Part 2[39]

William Blackwater

Two hunters lived together with their wives. One day Corn Woman said to the wife of the other hunter, "We have depended for food upon our husbands and we have done nothing." Itanyi Woman answered her, "You were the first to come to this country. Do something, and bring the food that you know." Corn Woman cleared a space of ground and stood in the center and sang:

"I am standing, I am standing.
I know something,
And I will do it."

She shook her clothing and corn fell on the ground. They gathered it in bags and ate it with the meat their husbands brought.

38. [*Itanyi* is] A grass whose seeds were formerly used for food. Not common now, but found in washes. [Russell (1908:73) identifies the plant as "saltbush, *atriplex*." There is no mention of the plant in either of the Saxton and Saxton dictionaries, but Rea (1997:122–23) identifies it as pickleweed, *Allenrolfea occidentalis.* Interestingly, Saxton, Saxton, and Enos (1983:26) give the form *i'ita,* meaning "that-which-has-been-scooped-up," under the entry for the verb *iht* ("to-scoop-dirt-or-seeds"). *I'itañ* would be the imperative form, meaning "scoop-it-up!" It is the perfect meaning for the girl-woman-plant in this story (and sequel) on the origins of marriage and corn.]

39. "A true story."

Corn Woman said to her younger sister, "It is your turn. Do something also." Itanyi Woman said, "I can only sing your song." Itanyi Woman stood up and sang also:

"I am standing, I am standing.
I know something.
And I will do it."

She shook her clothing and *itanyi* seeds fell; they gathered them in bags and ate them with the meat.

Corn Woman ground corn and threw some to Old Man Coyote. He put it in his mouth and he choked. He coughed and coughed, and Corn Woman ran to her husband, "Come quick. Coyote is choking." Her husband ran quickly and threw water in Coyote's face. Coyote laughed and said, "No, I'm not really choking. I'm doing this as an example. From now on when a young man brings home a bride, the old man will always act like this."[40]

Itanyi Woman made a soup of her seeds and gave Coyote a dish. He put a great quantity of the soup in his mouth and rolled on the floor. He groaned and groaned and Itanyi Woman called her husband, "Come quick. Coyote has burned his mouth." Coyote got up and said, "No, I didn't really burn my mouth. I did this as an example. From now on the old man will always act like this (when his son marries)."

The two husbands always went hunting. The younger brother was generous to Coyote and gave him his share of the meat, but the elder brother was stingy. Since then when a man has two sons, one of them is a support to him and the other is not.

One day they were hunting, and toward evening they both killed a deer. The elder brother had a (stone) knife in his sheath and drew it out and skinned the deer he had killed. The younger brother said to him, "May I use your knife now?" The elder brother did not answer him. He packed his venison on his back and set off for home. The younger brother looked everywhere for a knife. He stretched his hand upward and a knife sharpened on two sides came down from above into his hand. He took it and skinned the deer and put the knife in his sheath.

Again the two brothers went hunting, and toward night they both killed. The elder brother's knife was dull and he could not cut. He tried to give it a

40. An old man recently, under these circumstances, put on his wife's shirt instead of his own. He went out to work in his fields and was the laughingstock of the village. Another who was notoriously late in getting out of bed in the morning got up early and began to tinker with his mowing machine (which was in perfect condition). With his hammer he broke several parts of the machine. "He didn't know what he was about; that's all."

better edge. When the younger brother had finished skinning his deer with his new knife, the elder brother said to him, "Let me use your knife and we can go home together." The younger brother did not answer. He packed his venison on his back and set out for home.

The two brothers played *giinskoot*[41] together. At first they played without stakes, but they began to gamble and the younger brother lost. He lost everything and he said, "I will stake my life, and if I win I will win back all my possessions." He lost again and the elder brother killed the younger brother and made a seed bag of his skin.

The younger brother's wife was about to give birth to a child. The elder brother said, "If the baby is a girl I will let it live, but if it is a boy I will kill it." When the child was born it was a boy, but the mother disguised it and passed it for a girl. She took the child and went to another village. She traveled from village to village, living on the leavings of the people.

One day the elder brother was hunting and he brought home his pack of venison. The child followed far behind. A piece of fat dropped from the pack and the child picked it up and took it home to his mother. His mother covered it. The elder brother missed the piece of fat and went to her and said, "I saw the child following me a long way behind and now I have missed a piece of fat."

She gave him the piece of fat the child had brought. The mother wept and said to her child, "If it had not been for your uncle, you would have had all the venison you wanted. He killed your father and left you an orphan so that you have to live on the leavings of other people. Your uncle will try to kill you too, for he suspects now that you are really a boy."

She took him to the mountains to live, and when she went to gather seeds and roots the birds came to the house, so that the boy said to his mother, "Make me a bow and arrows so that I can kill these birds and we will have food." His mother made him a little bow and arrows, and he killed the small birds that came around the house. Again he said to his mother, "What are these little animals that jump along the ground?" She said, "They are rabbits." "Are they good to eat?" "Yes." He killed the rabbits and they ate them. Again he said to his mother, "What are these animals that are bigger than rabbits?" "They are jackrabbits." "Are they good to eat?" "Yes." He killed jackrabbits and they ate those.

One day he went a long way off in the canyon and he saw a deer. He crawled up the streambed within shot of the deer. A hunter was looking for

41. Again, this is the stick-dice game.—*Ed.*

deer in the same canyon and he saw the boy following the streambed on his stomach and he thought, "He must have seen some game." He whistled to the boy, but he held up his hand to warn him to be quiet. The hunter crawled to the spot where the boy was. "There is a deer down there." "Stay here, and I will kill the deer for you. Your bow is not strong enough to kill a deer." The hunter crept on and shot the deer. He dipped the boy's arrow in the deer's blood and said, "Take the venison home to your mother and tell her you killed the deer. I will make you a bow like mine and in four days I will come back to this spot and give it to you."[42]

The child went home to his mother. "I have killed a deer." "No, that is not possible." "Yes, I have killed it." He showed her the arrow dipped in the blood of the animal. "No, it is not possible. Your bow is not strong enough to kill a deer." He took her to the place where the dead deer lay. That night she could not sleep. She thought all the time about the deer. She sang:

"My poor boy killed a deer.
I am an old woman, I made the bow and arrow with which he killed a deer."

In four days the hunter returned to the canyon. He gave the child a bow and arrows. He said to him, "You are not yet strong enough to draw the bow, but I was sorry for you and I wanted to make this for you. I do not expect any return." The child took it back to his mother. "What bow is this?" "It is mine." "No, it is not like yours." "But it is mine." "No, you must have stolen it from someone. You must return it before they miss it." At last the boy said, "Do you remember the deer I killed. I did not shoot that deer. A hunter was hunting in that canyon and he drew his bow and killed it for me. He told me in four days to come back to the same place and he would give me this bow and arrows. He does not want anything in return and I cannot take it back to him."

The child lived on with his mother in that place and he began to kill deer with the bow the hunter had made for him. One day he wounded a deer that escaped with his arrow. A hunter from the village where his uncle lived found the dead deer with the arrow in it. He took the arrow to the meeting of the old men and put it by the fireplace.[43] Nobody in that village claimed it. At last someone said, "There is a boy who used to live in this village. I think he is living in the mountains with his mother. Perhaps this is his arrow." The boy's uncle

42. There is no supernatural element felt in this incident. The hunter is a kind neighbor who knows the mother's story.

43. An old custom.

said, "Give it to me and I will take it to him. Perhaps I will get some venison" (since the boy had a reputation as a good hunter).

The uncle went to the boy's house. "Here is an arrow that was found in a wounded deer. Perhaps it belongs to you. A hunter from our village found it and nobody claimed it." The boy and his mother were eating and they had plenty of venison. They paid no attention at all to his uncle; they went right on eating and did not offer him anything at all. They finished and they put the food away.

The uncle was angry. Next evening he went to the meeting of the old men. He said to the hunter who had found the arrow, "You remember the arrow you found in the wounded deer? I took it to my nephew's house and offered it to him. He did not pay any attention to me. He didn't act as if he saw me." Everybody was laughing at the uncle, because they knew what he had done to the boy's father.

The nephew planned to play *giinskoot* with his uncle. He went to a village and asked a man to go with him. "I want to gamble with my uncle. Will you help me?" They went together, and all the people came to see the boy gamble with his uncle. The boy sat to the east facing west, and the uncle sat to the west facing east. They set out the stakes to play. There was a great stump next to the uncle and on it he had made a face with eyes.[44] The boy said, "Before we play, turn that stump the other way. It is staring at me." "That stump is rooted deep in the earth. I can't turn that stump around." The boy laughed at his uncle because he could not turn the stump. "If I can't turn that stump around you may take all the stakes." "All right." The boy called his gopher to gnaw the roots. He went up to the stump and turned it to face the other direction.

They started to play again. The boy by his power made a nest of young birds.[45] He set them on a bush. "I will take that nest of young quails for my power." "This is not the season for young quails." "Yes, I have chosen them." The uncle laughed at his nephew, and the boy said, "If there is not a nest of young quails, you may take all my stakes." "All right." He went to the bush and brought out the nest and there were young quails in it.

They started to play again. Beside the uncle there was a bowl hollowed in the solid rock (used also for grinding), and the uncle had filled it with water (to cool himself when he became excited in the game). The boy said, "Put that bowl over here by me." "It can't be moved. It is in the solid rock." "If I can't

44. Said to be a sort of mascot.
45. A mascot on his own side.

move the bowl, you may take all the stakes." "All right." He lifted the bowl out of the solid rock and set it down on his side.

Again they started to play. The boy said, "See the new moon. I'll take that for my power." The uncle said, "This isn't the season for the new moon." The boy answered, "If there is not a new moon in the west, you may have all the stakes." "All right." The boy took a curved paring from his fingernail and threw it against the sky. The uncle looked to the west and sure enough, there was the new moon.

The boy sang:

"I am about to shoot my sticks with the corner of my stone."

He hit the sticks and they jumped into the air and turned into butterflies of all colors. "Look, look." Everybody craned their necks to watch the butterflies, and his uncle also. The boy seized him by the hair and killed him. He took his skin and made a seed bag. He took the seed bag that his uncle had made from his father's skin and he soaked it till it was pliable again. He took ribs of the giant cactus and stretched it to shape, and his father spoke to him. "My poor boy, you have worked hard to bring me back to life. It is not possible; my bones are rotted away and I could not walk. There is nothing you can do. But take me down to the stream and throw me in and I will become *tsimitutc* (banded sandpiper?)."[46]

The boy and his mother made their home in that village. There was a place where wild reeds grew, and the people used to go gather them. There were two sisters who went there. One day the boy went out alone and lay in the tall reeds and let the birds come and eat his body. The sisters came by and they said, "I guess that is a dead body." The elder went off, but the younger went over and watched for a long time. As soon as they were alone, the boy came to life and made love to her. "I was pretending to be dead so that I could see you. I am not dead."

They made love all day and toward evening the boy said, "Meet me here again tomorrow." The girl gathered as many reeds as she could to take back to the village with her sister. Next day the two sisters came again. The elder sister said, "That body is nasty," but the younger sister went and watched. The boy came to life and they made love all day. At night the boy said again, "Meet me here tomorrow," and the girl gathered as many reeds as she could.

One day the boy said, "Ask your older sister if you can take my skull home with you." So next day the younger sister said to the elder sister, "Let's take this

46. *Ciwi-cu:c?* If so, "killdeer."—*Ed.*

skull and keep it at our house." "No, it's nasty." But the younger sister took it up and brought it home and set it beside her. At night it came to life and was a handsome man. When the elder sister saw how handsome he was she sat beside him too and he lived with the two sisters.

At night their father heard the girls laughing. "I wonder why they laugh. They never laughed before." When they were out gathering reeds he looked through their house and found the skull. "This must be what they laugh at. They are always laughing." He threw it as far as he could. The girls came home and found the skull was gone. They looked everywhere for it, and at last they found it in the brush and brought it back to live with them. The people of the village talked about these two sisters and they said, "They do not marry. They have a skull for a husband."

One day the crier made proclamation for a hunt, and the skull said to his two wives, "Bring me your father's bow and arrows. I want to go on the hunt." They went to their father and he said to them, "You have a man. I know who that man is. He is the skull that you keep in your house." They begged him for the bow and arrows and he threw them at them. They took them to their husband and he went on the hunt and killed more than all the rest and brought them all to their father.

Again the crier made a proclamation, [calling out] that their village was to race against another village. The skull said to his wives, "Take me to the race course, and set me in position. I want to run in this race. And stake everything you have on our village in this race, for we will win." The people said, "How can a skull win a race? But if he asks, we will take him as a runner."

The runners lined up for the relay race.[47] The runners of the village where the sisters lived were far behind, and the sisters took the skull and placed it at the line for the fourth runner on their side. He ran the length of the course and passed the runner of the other village so that their own village was in the lead. The other runners took up the relay and again the other village was in the lead. When it was the turn of Skull to run again, he outdistanced all the runners on the other side, and again their village was in the lead. He ran four times, and his village won the race.

After this, Skull kept his form as a handsome young man, and he lived with his wives and became a great man. His mother heard of him and came

47. The race course is from half a mile to a mile in length; four runners are stationed at each end for side A, four at each end for side B. Each runner runs the length of the course and touches another member of his team, who runs the course in the opposite direction. When all the runners have run, they repeat in the same order four times.

and lived with his wives in their village. At last there was a drought in his wives' village, and he remembered the country where he had lived with his mother. They all returned to that place and are still living there.[48]

Dove Makes Magic for a Race

William Blackwater

Dove and Chicken Hawk were good runners, and they challenged each other to a race. Everybody staked all their animals and their clothes and their blankets on the game. Dove's party and Chicken Hawk's party sang all night to get power. Dove said, "I wish it were morning already. I wish it were morning already. You would see then, I would beat him." They painted his legs red, and he lay down again. Again he said, "I wish it were morning, I wish it were morning. I would beat him." A little later Dove said again, "I will beat him. You shall see. He will go up and sit in the top of a tree and all his side will be ashamed."

Next morning they ran. Chicken Hawk lost, and all his side cried. Chicken Hawk sat in the top of a tree and wept.

Girl Becomes Star

William Blackwater

A brother and sister lived together. He was a great hunter. All the chiefs (*sivanyi*) from the west, the south, the east, and the north wanted to marry the sister, and they sent Coyote to ask her. She said, "No, I do not want to marry."

The chiefs said, "If that girl will not marry when we ask her, we will send our armies." The girl answered, "Tell them to send their armies. I would rather be dead than consent to marry." Her brother came home from hunting and she told him what message the chiefs had sent. Her brother said, "When the armies come, what shall we do?" She answered, "I will tell you. We will shut ourselves in our house and sink down into the earth. I shall be the morning star. When-

48. In a version related by William Stevens, the beginning of the story is told with hardly more than the statement of the killing of Younger Brother Coyote by his brother the gambler. From the point where the boy kills his first deer to the end of the incident of the unsuccessful resuscitation of the father, the Stevens story parallels the above version. The differences are (1) when the boy throws up his sticks in the *giinskoot* [*gi:ns*] game, thunder strikes his opponent unconscious; his uncle revives and throws, but no thunder sounds, so the nephew takes his life; (2) the father becomes *vaatcpik* (banded duck?) [probably the American coot, or mud hen].

ever the Indians are going on a journey and get up early, I shall be the sign that morning is almost there. When you see me you will remember that I am your sister."

Her brother answered, "I shall go west and become the thunder. When I sound, you will remember that I am your brother."

Coyote went back to the chiefs. They sent the soldiers to kill the girl and her brother. The brother and sister saw them coming and they went into their house and set fire to it. The people thought that they were burned to death in the house, but they sank down into the ground, and she became the morning star and her brother became the thunder.

Girl Becomes Saguaro

William Blackwater

In the villages they were always playing *totka* (woman's game of tied ball) [*toka*]. One of the women would do nothing but play. Finally she left her little girl behind and went on to other villages playing. Her daughter followed her. She had nothing to eat but the refuse people had thrown away. Children at a certain village saw her and they told the people, "Here is a child who is hungry. She is eating the refuse that is thrown away."

The people went out and brought her into the village. Her mother saw her and said, "It is my daughter," and for a little while she took care of her again. Before long the mother went on to still another village to play tied ball and left the little girl behind. The child started out again to find her mother. She came to the village where they were playing and she said to the children of that village, "Show me a tarantula hole." "Why?" "Because I never saw a tarantula hole." They took her with them until they found a tarantula hole. She put her foot over the hole, and she began to sink down into the ground. The children ran to the people and cried out that a child was sinking into the earth. All the mothers looked and saw their own children were safe, and they went on playing. Four times the children called out that a child was sinking. Then the mother said, "Perhaps that is my child." She went to see, and sure enough, it was her daughter. She tried to pull her free but she could not; she sank down into the earth. A giant cactus [saguaro] grew up over that spot.

The people came every day to see the strange plant. At last the giant cactus was tired of having the people come every day, and it sank down into the earth and came up far away near the mountains. Even there the people came to see it, and it sank into the earth again and came up in a deep canyon. Even there the people came to see it, and it sank into the earth again and came up at Carrying Basket Mountain (in the Papago country). It grew there and blossomed and bore fruit. Only the birds could reach it to get at the fruit.

The people said, "What shall we do to get the fruit before the birds eat it all up?" They sent the raven and he broke off the fruit and brought it back to the people. They let it stand till it fermented, and the principal men said, "Drink the fermented juice of the cactus. It will make you crazy. Only whatever you do, do not start any fighting (during the drinking)." The people drank and were made crazy. But some of them drank too much and a fight began. That is why when people drink too much a fight is sure to start.

After they had drunk, they took the seeds of the fruit and put them all into a sack. They gave it to one of the men and told him to scatter the seeds in the mountains. As he was going he met Coyote. "Where are you going?" Coyote answered, "I am going to the village to the drinking." "It is all over." Coyote was sad. "What is in your sack?" "Something." "I want to see it. I want to see it." Coyote asked and asked. At last the man let him have the sack. "Don't open it," he told him.

Coyote took the bag and threw it high up into the air. The seeds blew all about, and that is why cactus grows in every direction. Some of Coyote's seed is still in the ground, and that is why we still see some cactus just beginning to grow.

The Feud[49]

William Blackwater

Editor's Synopsis[50]

A Blind Man's Brother Goes Away. A blind man quarrels with his younger brother, who as a result goes to live in another village.

Marriage of the Blind Man's Nephew to Two Girls from the Blind Man's Village. After a long time, to heal the bitterness, people of the blind man's village send a song ceremony with two young women to the village where the younger brother is now living. The young women dance with the two sons of the younger brother; choosing the younger of these two sons, they marry him.

Back at the Blind Man's Village, the Nephew Is Killed by His Jealous Brother. Learning that his brother has married the two women, the elder son, enraged,

49. There is no other version of this story in the Pima-Papago record.—*Ed.*
50. I have added this to aid the reader of this unusually complicated tale.—*Ed.*

kills the younger. Grief-stricken, the sons' father and mother go far away. But one of the two wives is pregnant; she bears a male child and takes him to her dead husband's parents.

Killing of the Nephew's Jealous Brother. Seeking revenge for her younger son's death, the baby's grandmother disguises herself by blackening her white hair, then goes to her elder son and cuts off his head; later her husband throws their bad son's head in the river. The old woman quarrels with her husband and he goes away; she herself goes away.

Killing of the Nephew's Son's Stepfather. A hunter, unmentioned until now, marries the two widows. The blind man, more or less the chief of the women's home village, sends for the hunter and has him killed.

Killing of the Nephew's Son by the Blind Man. The boy earlier born of one of the women seeks revenge, changes into a large bird, and goes to the blind man's (and his mother's) home village. Sensing danger, the blind man shoots the bird; it is wounded, becomes a boy again, and dies.

The Nephew's Son's Cousin Kills the Blind Man. Meanwhile, the second wife bears the hunter's posthumous son. This boy goes to the blind man's village, where people are dancing. Other people, however, are mourning; the mourners are his relatives. The boy becomes a lizard, steals the villagers' ball, and disappears to the east; later he returns, and with the help of his relatives in the blind man's village he captures the blind man and his wife, brings them home, and burns them alive.

[A Blind Man's Brother Goes Away]

In this village lived two brothers, and the elder of them was blind. They quarreled, and the people sided with the elder brother and blamed the other, so that the younger brother left with his wife and set up his home in another village.

After he had been gone for many years, his brother, who was blind, missed him. He asked the people of his home village and they told him that his brother lived in a village not far from there and that he had two sons. The blind brother said to the people, "Let us send a messenger to say that we will bring the Singing Ceremony (*üdamal*)[51] to their village, so that we can all forget our bitterness."

51. *Eḍa mel,* "inside run," is a dance by specially trained and costumed unmarried young people. Performed for an audience from or at another village, it is a way to show off one's village's finest. The young people "*run*" and dance *inside* a large circle where adult dancing will take place later in the day and through the night. Those adult dancers form a long circular line. They hold hands, and facing inward, they circle and recircle the area where the children or young people had first danced. Both kinds of dancing are to songs, which is why Benedict called this a "singing ceremony."—*Ed.*

The people began practicing for the singing ceremony. When the day came they took with them two pretty girls from their village who were to dance with the sons of the younger brother. The singers began singing in the plaza [dance ground], and these two boys went into their house to paint themselves for the dance. They put bowls of water on the floor and painted themselves. They looked into the water (using it as a mirror) and they were not satisfied; they washed it off and tried again.

At last the younger brother said, "I'm ready," and he went out to dance with the two girls. The elder stayed behind and washed off his paint again and put it on until he was pleased. When he went out to dance, the younger brother was already dancing with the two pretty girls, but when they saw the elder brother with his handsome paint, they left the brother they had been dancing with and they both danced with the elder brother. Now, the elder brother, however, was ugly.[52]

[Marriage of the Blind Man's Nephew to Two Girls from the Blind Man's Village]

When the dance was over the two girls took their husband home with them [back to the village of the blind man], and when they found out how ugly he was, they were angry and they said, "Let us go and take the younger brother instead." They set out for his village [apparently leaving the elder brother behind in the village of the blind man], but on the way there was a great river[53] and they could not cross it. On the other side they saw the younger brother working in his fields. They called to him and said, "We are coming to visit you. How can we get across?" The boy came to the edge of the river and swam it and brought them to his side. They went with him to the house of his father [the brother of the blind man]. The younger brother's father said to the first girl, "Sit down," and she sat down. He said to the second girl, "Sit down," but she remained standing. The father said to his son, "What have you done to her (what relations have you had with her) that she will not sit down?" The younger brother answered, "I have had no relations with her. I swam across the river and brought her across and perhaps I touched her too intimately." His father replied, "That is nothing, she need not be shamed because of that. It is

52. In the *ẹda mel* there shouldn't be this amount of freedom to come and go and change partners. Nor should dancers from the visited village join with the visiting dance corps. Those freedoms are characteristic of the adult "circle" dancing that followed an *ẹda mel*. As it is presented in this episode, the dance has aspects of both dances: the name and special costuming (painting) of the *ẹda mel* and the freedoms of the circle dance.—*Ed.*

53. Mentioned repeatedly in the story, the river seems to separate the two brothers' communities.—*Ed.*

bound to happen at a ford," and he said to the girl again, "Sit down," and she sat down. Last of all the boy too sat down.

[Back at the Blind Man's Village, the Nephew Is Killed by His Jealous Brother]

The parents of the girls [of the blind man's village] missed them and searched for them. The elder brother [whom the girls had rejected] heard of it and learned that they were now living with his brother, and he took with him evil-minded young men and set out for his brother's [and father's and his own old home] village. They came to the river and saw the younger brother working in his fields; they came up to him and killed him, and went back to their own homes. The father of the younger brother said to his wife, "I must leave this place. I cannot stand the sorrow here; we will go away for a time." He called the two girls and said to them, "Look after the fields. When the corn is ripe, harvest and store it." They left and the girls tended the fields. One of the wives was pregnant, and when it was almost time that she should have a child, she said to her sister, "The old people have not returned and I will go and look for them. You are young and do not know what to do; the old woman knows. I will go and stay with them till the baby is born." She left her sister and went out to look for her parents-in-law. She traveled day after day and she was alone in the desert. Her child was born, and she took it up and went on. She had nothing to wrap the child in. When she had gone a little way she saw a hawk dead on the ground, and she stripped off the skin with the soft downy feathers and wrapped the child in the hawk's feathers. She went on searching for her parents-in-law.

They were living in a high place, and they saw something moving in the desert. About nightfall she came to the place where they were. The old man made a cradle for the child and gave it to the mother. Her mother-in-law said to her, "We have been here a long time, but we cannot get over our grief. It is not only that our son is dead; we have learned more. It was our [older] son who left us long ago, it was he himself who came back and killed [our younger son] as he worked in his field. We can never put this sorrow aside in all our lives." The old people continued weeping, and they lived there at that place.

[Killing of the Nephew's Jealous Brother]

The old woman said to her husband and to her daughter-in-law, "This sorrow does not leave us. I am going to visit my son. He may kill me, but I shall go."

Her husband said, "Wait a little and prepare yourself." The old woman's hair was white, and she painted it coal black. When she was ready, she said to her husband, "Meet me in four days," and she set out and came to one of the villages where her son lived. She asked about him, and they said, "There are small villages scattered around here [in the region of the blind man], and he goes from one to the other; we will send for him."

They found him and brought him to her, but he did not recognize his mother because of her hair, and she treated him as a stranger. That night they went to bed in the same room, and his mother said, "I found a cigarette outside; will you smoke it?" Her son took it and smoked, and it put him into a deep sleep. When his mother saw that he was sound asleep she got up and took her knife and cut off his head. She wrapped the head and put it with her things.

Next day she set out to return to her husband. On the day she had appointed, her husband met her in the desert with a lunch. They ate together and she said to him, "It is done; I have killed our enemy." He said to her, "I did not think you would do this thing. I thought you would kill one of those who are at war with us and instead you have killed one of our sons. Now I can never get over this grief." His wife said to him, "Because he killed our son who was our support and our comfort, he was our enemy. I could not get over this sorrow until I had killed him. Now he is dead and we are revenged. Now we will be happy again."

They started home together and came to a stream. The husband said to her, "Give me the head. I have been thinking about what you have said and I know that you are right. I want to look at the head once more." He took it and threw it into the river. She was angry, and they quarreled. He would not go any farther with her; he said, "I am going away; you and our daughter-in-law can go back to the old village."

[Killing of the Nephew's Son's Stepfather]

The old woman went on and came to her daughter-in-law and told her all that had happened. "I am going away, too," the mother-in-law said, and she started toward the east. The daughter-in-law was left alone on the mesa. She took her baby and went back to her sister. She told her all that had happened and they lived together.

In the village where the mother had killed her son [on the blind man's side of the river], there lived a hunter who used to go all over the desert in search of game. One day he came to the house of the two girls and stayed there with them. They missed him in his own village and at last someone discovered that he was living with the two women. They told the blind man and he said, "Tell him to come and see me. He is a friend of mine; I want to talk to him." They sent a messenger.

The hunter said to his wives, "I have been sent for, and I do not know whether it is for good or bad. If it is for good, I will be back soon; if he kills me, stay on this land till the crops are ripe, and harvest and store them."

The hunter came to the blind man, and he said to him, "Sit down. Eat." They ate together, and as they were eating, the men whom he had hired came with their bows and arrows and killed him.

The girls waited for the hunter but he did not come. At last they knew that he had been killed. The little boy grew up, and when he was larger his mother told him what had happened to his father and his grandparents, and he thought, "How can I revenge them? I wonder how many people there are against me."

[Killing of the Nephew's Son by the Blind Man]

He went over to see what the [blind man's] village was like, and when they were having a big dance he made himself into a great bird and flew close over the village. One of the men said, "See the great bird," and all the people stopped dancing and watched the bird. Sometimes it would soar out of sight, and sometimes it would dip down almost among the dancers, and at sundown it flew off to the west. That evening all the old men gathered in the house of the blind man, and one of them said, "Have you heard what we are all talking about? While we were dancing a great bird flew round and round above us, sometimes almost down to the heads of the people. We have never seen a bird like that. Perhaps before you were blind you saw a bird like that and can tell us what it is." The blind man answered, "I have never seen a bird like that. That is not a bird; it is a man. We are going to have trouble. We will have to fight, and it is the spy of the people who will fight us who is looking over our country." "No, it is a real bird; we saw it fly and we are sure."

Next day they danced again, and again the bird came flying round and round over their heads. The third day they danced, and again the bird came just as before. Again on that evening they met in the house of the blind man. "We told you before of the great bird. It comes every day at the same time, and every evening it goes west at sunset." The blind man said, "Yes, you told me before and now you come to tell me again. You would not believe me when I told you first; why should I tell you again? Tomorrow when it comes down again, call me, and I will go out against this bird; perhaps then you will believe me."

The fourth day they danced again and the bird came as before. Some of the people said, "We heard what the old man said, and some of us believed him. Go and get him." They sent a messenger and brought him. The blind man took a hair and enlarged it so that it became a rope. He threw it up in the air and it remained there (in the form of a noose). He called for his bow and arrow and pointed it into the sky. "Is this where the bird is? Is it here?" At last the people shouted, "Yes, it is there," and the blind man shot the arrow and it struck the rope. The blood from the rope sprinkled all the people, and the arrow, falling, hit the great bird and crippled it. It fell, but just as it was about to hit the ground it recovered and flew off. The blind man said, "Follow it. Perhaps you will catch up to it." They followed, but when they came to the big river they could not cross; on the other side they saw the boy, in human form, and they went home again and told the blind man. The boy was terribly wounded; he did not care for the wound properly, and he died.

[The Nephew's Son's Cousin Kills the Blind Man]

Meanwhile the second wife had a child, the son of the hunter, and he grew up also. They told him what had happened to his father and his grandparents. He, too, said to himself, "How shall I revenge them?" He used to go out all over the desert after game, and sometimes he was gone four days at a time. He came to the village [of the blind man] and concealed himself on a mountain overlooking it. The people used to come to the foot of the mountain to gather firewood, and he heard that they were always crying while the people in the village were dancing and enjoying themselves. He watched them many times. At last his mother said to him, "Where do you go? You never used to be gone so often." "Yes, there is a village, and I conceal myself on the mountain nearby and watch the people. In the village they are singing and dancing, but these others come out to the mountain to gather wood and they are always crying." His mother said to him, "Do not go there. That is where your brother[54] was killed. We used to live in that village; the people who come to gather wood,

54. Actually his mother's sister's son. The same Pima word, *we:nag,* would be applied to either brother or cousin.—*Ed.*

and whom you hear weeping, are our relatives, and the rest of the people dance and enjoy themselves."

For a long time he did not return to the mountain. At last he climbed to the same place again, and again he heard the people weeping and gathering firewood at the foot of the mountain. He came down and showed himself to them. They said, "Yes, we are your relatives, and the people in the village are our enemies." The boy said, "I want to go to the village. How shall I get there?" They answered, "There is no way. We are always guarded." The boy said to them, "What do you do with the wood you gather?" "We use it to cook with." "Is there an ash dump (or outdoor fireplace)?" "Yes." "I will make myself into a lizard and fasten myself to this stick of wood. When you get home, throw it on the ash pile."

They knew he was wise, and they took the wood in and threw it on the ash pile (or outdoor fire). When the ashes rose, he went under the earth to the home of the blind man and climbed up the center post. Immediately the blind man knew there was something the matter. He called the people and said to them, "Look carefully. Something is wrong." They turned everything over all through the house, but they could find nothing. "I know there is something here." But the boy was high up in the roof beams and they could not find him. That night as soon as the blind man slept the boy came down the post; he threw dirt in the blind man's face. The blind man said, "I wonder why dirt falls from the roof beams."

The boy told his relatives, "Bring the ball to the dance tomorrow and play with the rest of the village." They came and the people of the village said, "Let's play." They threw it over the roof of the house so that the boy caught it and ran off with it. The blind man cried and said, "This is the boy who was also the great bird. I knew this was going to happen but I had no time to do anything against it. Run after the boy and perhaps you can recover the ball before he gets back to his home."

The people followed, but when they came to the great river, they saw the boy standing in human form on the other side. They could not cross. He held up four fingers to them and went toward the east. The people returned to the blind man and they said, "It was not the boy, for he did not go to his home but toward the east." [The blind man said,] "It was the truth I told you. He held up four fingers, and they are the four days until he will return and fight against us."

In four days the boy came again with all his relatives. They fought against that village and captured the blind man and his wife. Every night the boy and his relatives had dancing, and they made the blind man and his wife dance and sing. They brought them to their home and burned them alive.[55]

Nasia's Twins[56]

William Blackwater and Thomas Vanyiko

[Birth of the Twins]

TV The people (of all the world) lived together [before they went separate ways]. A great shaman became sick, and the people sent to Earth Doctor, and he came to cure him. He instructed the people in curing and in the food that was necessary for the sick.[57] Just before

55. I take this to be a ball-game story (the Pimas' predecessors, the Hohokam, had Mesoamerican-style ball courts), and I see parallels between this story and the old Quiche Mayas' *Popol Vuh*. In the *Popol Vuh* it is two boys who play ball with the lords of the underworld to avenge the lords' killing of their father. Here it is villagers who play by throwing a ball over a blind man's house. (There is no record of such a game among the Pimas, nor perhaps among any native New World people. It is an imagined game.) The game is "against" the blind man who, not seeing, is like an underworld darkness character. The boy's theft of the ball is part of his revenge for the killings of his cousin, father, and uncles—too many characters!

The *Popol Vuh* ball-playing boys burn themselves after they defeat and kill the lords of the underworld. Burnt, they turn into the sun and moon, which is the end of the first, largest part of the *Popol Vuh*. (See Brotherston 1992:215–37 for a discussion of the text as a whole.) In "The Feud," the blind man and his wife are burnt, and the story ends. The decapitation of a young man in the Pima story is an imperfect match for two decapitations in the *Popol Vuh*, first of the boys' father, then of one of the boys. The heads, one thinks, are balls and are like the sun and moon. Another match: in the *Popol Vuh* a mouse climbs in house rafters to gnaw the cords hiding the boys' father's gaming ball, and the boy in "The Feud" hides himself as a lizard in the rafters of the blind man's house.

Thus we have roughly parallel stories with common motifs. The stories are played in different registers: Edenic in the *Popol Vuh*—the passage between cosmic worlds, the miraculous paternity of the twin boys, and their final transformation into the sun and moon—and "post-Edenic" in "The Feud"—the passages across rivers, the marriages, and the absence of cosmic creation at the end. The Pima text lets one see this part of the *Popol Vuh* as a feud between worlds (upper and lower), and the Maya text makes the Pima seem *almost* cosmic.

Because "The Feud" is not cosmic, it could go either in the present chapter or the next. The next chapter's stories concern the Pimas' conflicts with Apaches during a time later than "Eden" but too ancient to connect to individuals living in 1927. "The Feud" lacks Apaches, but like the others it is about mortal conflict between humans, conflict that is set in "secular" or "profane" time as distinct from "cosmic," "pristine," "Edenic," or "sacred" time. One can also say that the more secular stories are "epic" as opposed to "mythic," a distinction that Arthur Hatto (1999) has drawn in a study of a long Mojave text, one of the few incontrovertible epics known from native North America. Although shorter than the Mojave text, "The Feud" and all the stories of the next chapter are, I believe, epic in register (post-Edenic) and content (heroic, treating of marriage and war).

Almost the same can be said of "The Coyote Brothers" and "Nasia's Twins" (the next story in this chapter). These, however, have animals (Coyote, Gopher) in key marital roles; they originate things (corn and wild seeds, gambling games); and they lack feud or war. From myth to epic run various roads.—*Ed.*

56. The songs in this story are sung in Maricopa, and the versions given are the translations offered by the narrators.

57. This is the [origin] of the rites of curing the sick. [A bed of sand is described in the parallel passage in chapter 1. There, Earth Doctor is the sick man; here, someone else is sick and Earth Doctor tries to cure him. As stated earlier, this is really a Maricopa story.]

he died, the great shaman asked them to bring him the bird *giisop* [*gi:supi,* black phoebe]. They brought it and he spread out its tail feathers and said, "There are twelve. There shall be twelve months in the year."

He died, and all the people mourned and the women cut their hair and the birds their tails. Only Dove was absent, and that is why the dove's tail is not trimmed straight across. When they had burned the body of the dead shaman,[58] Earth Doctor and the people and the animals and the birds and the insects decided to leave that place and scatter over the earth. They all went to seek new homes; only Nasia stayed behind. When she was left alone she also set out to find her home—

TV&WB She came to Green River,[59] where grasses and plants and fruit-bearing trees were growing. She thought, "I will make my home here," and she took possession, singing:

"This land will be my land.
These will be my trees;
This will be my water.
Whatever is good to eat will belong to me and I will live here."

The first of every month she bathed in the water of the river and became young again; only at the end of the month was she old. One day she went down to bathe. She lay in the shallow water with her face to the sky and something touched her body. She rose and looked everywhere but she could not find anything. She sang:

"I do not know what has happened."

"Perhaps it was something in the water, or a fish that touched me. Perhaps it was Gopher. Perhaps it was not Gopher after all." And she sang:

"Perhaps it was Gopher.
Perhaps it was not Gopher."

She sat thinking—

58. The origin of the rites of mourning [of the Maricopas and other Yuman tribes—the Pimas didn't cremate].

59. The Verde (Spanish "green") River of today's Arizona. It flows into the Salt near the Salt River Pima-Maricopa Indian Community. Jose Moreno, a Papago, or Tohono O'odham, who told this story to me, said that the woman was called Green Woman and that she stayed young by bathing periodically.—*Ed.*

WB She sang:

"I know now that it was not Gopher.
It was Earth Doctor"—

TV She felt hungry and wanted greens to eat. She turned aside from the road and gathered green thorns.[60]

TV&WB She knew she was pregnant—

WB She sang:

"The trails that I used to travel, I have forgotten already"—

TV&WB She went on and the land became more and more mountainous. She climbed to a high place and sat down. She sang:

"West, south, east, north."

As she named the directions she faced toward them. As she faced the north her first child was born. She sang again:

"West, south, east, north."

As she faced the north again her second child was born.

She said, "I have nothing (with which to take care of these children). What shall I do?" She sang to the sun asking for the gift of a bowl [song not given]. The sun sent down a bowl and she washed the two babies. Again she said, "What shall I do?" She sang to the sun, asking for the gift of cradles [song not given]. The sun sent cradles and all the decorations that go with cradles, and she put the babies in the cradles and made everything right. She said, "What shall I name them?" She sang a naming song:

"(I call him) Parahan;
(I call him) Parahak."

She took them to her home and gathered leaves of the century plant and made a rope and hung a swing for her babies.[61] During the day she left them to gather food, and when she brought the seeds home at night she ground them on a stone nearby. In the day the grasshoppers and crickets came. The elder brother said to the younger, "Have you no power? Can't you do something so that we can sleep in

60. *Soi itka,* a green eaten raw, a little sour; said to be desired by pregnant women. [Compare *s-ho'id-kam i:vag,* "thorny edible-green," eaten raw or boiled (Russell 1908:77). Rea (1997:207–8) identifies this plant as spiny sow-thistle (*Sonchus asper*).]

61. Two ropes are tied at both ends to the beams and are parallel. In the middle, where they sag considerably, a strong cloth is fastened to form a hammock.

peace? They make too much noise." The younger brother killed the grasshoppers and crickets and piled them under the cradle. When their mother came home she saw the pile of dead insects under the cradle and she threw them out. The children cried and cried and she could not comfort them.

The next day when their mother had gone to gather seeds, quails came to the stone where the boys' mother ground her seeds. They were looking for seeds she had dropped. The younger brother said to the elder, "Have you no power? Can't you do something so that we can sleep in peace? They make too much noise." The elder brother killed the quails and piled them under the cradle. When their mother came home, she saw the pile of quails and thought they were dead birds that had been overlooked and that had lain there a long time. She threw them out and the children cried and cried. She could not quiet them. At last she went out and gathered the quails together again and piled them under the swing. Then the children stopped crying. She cooked them and they ate.

Their mother made bows and arrows for the children. They came to her and said, "We saw something in the brush." She said, "It's a wood rat. It's good to eat." The children ran to get their bows, and they killed the wood rat and brought it to their mother. Again they came to her and said, "We saw something in the brush." "It's a rabbit. It's good to eat." The children ran to get their bows, and they killed the rabbit and brought it to their mother. Again they came to her and said, "We saw something in the brush." "It's a jackrabbit. It's good to eat." The children ran and got their bows. They killed the jackrabbit and came and told their mother. "No, it is impossible. Your bows are not strong enough to kill a jackrabbit." "Yes. We did." They went and brought it.[62]

Again they saw something in the brush. "It is a deer; it is very good to eat, but you need strong bows to kill it." The children ran for their old bows and went out and killed the deer. They came back and told their mother. "I don't believe you. Deer are hard to kill, and you aren't strong enough." They took her to the place where the deer lay on the ground. "Go and get flint knives; the hide of the deer is valu-

62. This paragraph follows Vanyiko. Blackwater makes the children afraid of each successive animal: "Their mother said to them, 'Every time I go past the brush I see something come out of it.' The boys took their bows and arrows and went to look. They saw and were frightened and ran to their mother. 'There is nothing to be afraid of; it is something good to eat.' They went back and killed the wood rat." (After this they kill the rabbit, jackrabbit, and deer.)

able, and out of it we will make moccasins and many things. While the boys went in search of sharp stones she filled the wounds of the deer with dirt and called to the boys: "Come and see your deer." She took hold of its tail and twisted it and the deer jumped up alive and ran away.[63] She sang:

"Chase it, boys, chase it."

The boys chased it and the elder got so close that he hooked one of the antlers with his bow, but the antler broke and the deer ran on. The younger brother got so close that he hooked the other antler with his bow, but that antler also broke and the deer escaped—

WB The boys returned to their mother. She had been following their tracks. When they came in sight she turned herself into a stump. The younger brother said, "Was this stump here when we went by before?" The elder brother said, "We'll see. We'll shoot at it and see if it is really a tree." Their mother sang:

"Don't shoot, don't shoot.
I'm your mother."

The boys said to her, "Why did you play this trick on us?" They sang:

"We will shoot anyway."

But their mother changed herself into her old shape and joined them, and they put up their bows and arrows—

TV&WB [Their mother] said to them, "I have told you no one can kill deer with such weak bows and arrows. Hunters will always have to chase deer a long time and over great distances and sometimes lose them in the end." She sang:

"My sons, my sons, you couldn't catch that deer."

The boys were angry at their mother and would not speak to her.

[The Twins' Arrows]

Their mother said to them, "I have pet eagles far in the west, but there are many dangers. I go there sometimes but you could never go." The boys said, "If an old woman like you can go, we surely can go there."

63. This is the origin of the difficulty of deer hunting. It was due to Nasia's spite.

They started and they came to a great flock of nighthawks(?). The elder said, "Perhaps this is the danger our mother told us of. If we go on they will cut us with their wings." They sang:

"(These are) only nighthawks. They cannot harm us."

They went on and came to a great stretch of flowers. Hummingbirds were flying hither and thither over the flowers. The younger said, "Perhaps this is the danger our mother told us of." The elder said, "We know you are hummingbirds. You are nothing but prostitutes, nothing but pretty flower-creatures." He sang:

"(These are) only hummingbirds. They cannot harm us"—

TV They came to a dead bird lying by the side of the road. The younger stopped and picked its feathers and ran with them to his elder brother. "Why did you do that? Don't you know that people will laugh at us and say, 'There were two boys who started after eagle feathers, and they came back with the feathers of a dead bird they found lying along the road'"—

TV&WB They came to the foot of a great mountain and looked up. "I think I saw our birds." "Yes, those were our eagles." The mountain grew higher and higher as they came near it, so that by the power of their mother it almost touched the sky. They sang:

"Maybe we cannot reach our eagles, and we will never get their feathers.
The mountain is too steep for us to climb."

The elder brother said, "Have you no power? Can't you do something before we give up?" The younger brother said, "All right," and he made himself into a gray snake. The elder brother said, "Is that the best you can do? How can you climb this steep mountain without arms and legs? When you are tired you won't be able to hold on and will fall and kill yourself. Then I will have to go back alone and the people will laugh at me and say, 'This boy used to be two; they went after eagles and he came back alone.'" He sang—

WB *"My brother, go on, see what you can do"—*

TV *"See Parahan climbing up"—*

TV&WB The snake crawled up the mountain. It got almost to the top and was tired and fell to the bottom of the mountain dead. His elder brother took him in his arms and held him till he came back to life. When he was alive again he said, "It is your turn to show your power. What can you do?" Then the elder brother made himself into a bit of fluff (as of cotton). "Is that the best you can do? I thought you had more power than that. How can you climb the mountain without hands and feet? When you are tired you won't be able to hold on and you will come all the way down again. Then I will have to go back alone and the people will laugh at me and say, 'This boy used to be two; they went after eagles and he came back alone.'" He sang—

WB *"My brother, go on, see what you can do"*—

TV *"See Parahak climbing up"*—

TV&WB The elder brother got almost to the top of the mountain when his power failed him. Just then a puff of wind came and lifted him the rest of the way and dropped him in the nest of the eagles. At the breath of wind the two eagles flew out of the nest. The elder brother waited in the nest for them to return. The younger brother sang:

"What are you doing up there?
You are not a mountain goat that you live on the tops of the mountains.
You are not the Pleiades that you have your home overhead."

At last the birds came back to their nest. The elder brother took them both, jumped down with them [and dropped dead]. The younger brother ran to where he had landed, and paying no attention to him, he took the larger eagle for his own.[64] When the elder brother came to life again, he said, "This larger bird is my eagle. Don't you know that whenever Mother makes anything for us, she gives me the larger? If she makes food I eat first, and you eat what is left over." So the younger brother gave back the larger eagle and they started for their home. The elder sang:

"These birds are our pets.[65]
The older one is mine and the younger is yours."

Their mother knew of their quarrel, and she sent heavy wind and cold rain. They sang:

64. The larger had a band of white around its neck; the other was dark all over.

65. *Tsoika* [*t-ṣoiga,* "our-pet"], used of a horse or cow that belongs to someone; also used in games to designate one's own marble, counter, etc.

"Perhaps it will rain;
Perhaps the clouds will come up after this pleasant breeze."

The wind blew stronger and the clouds came up. They sang:

"The clouds are coming up."

Again the wind blew stronger and it began to rain. They went on in the rain until dark, and at night they took refuge under a tree; they were cold and crying. They tried to warm the birds, but they could not, and toward morning the younger brother's eagle died of the cold and rain. In the morning they dug a hole and covered the eagle with turquoise beads and placed the younger brother's bow and arrow on top of it and buried it. They sang (a mourning song without words). Again cold rain fell all the next day; they went on and at night took refuge again under a tree. They had only one eagle now and tried to keep it warm, but it died toward morning. They dug a hole and covered it with turquoise beads and the elder brother's bow and arrow and buried it.

They reached home and their mother offered them food. They would not eat, nor speak to her.[66] "Do not mourn for your pets, you will have them again tonight." She went out and came to the grave of the first eagle. She folded back the earth from the four directions and walked (deliberately, setting her feet down with care) four times around the grave. The larger eagle came out of the earth with the beads and the bow and arrow. She went on to the grave of the smaller eagle; she folded back the earth from the four directions and walked four times around the grave. The smaller eagle came out of the earth with the beads and the bow and arrow.

She took them both and went back to her home. She called to her sons but they would not come. She built a fire outside the house and put the birds beside it. As it began to be light, she called again to her sons, "Come out, the birds you left behind have followed you and are here." At last the elder said, "Go and see." The younger brother went out, and there were their two pets; he took the larger, and when the elder came out there was only the smaller eagle left. "Why do you do this? Don't you know that I am the elder and I always have the first of everything? When our mother cooks for us I eat first and you

66. "They knew she had caused all their troubles."

eat what is left." Their mother said, "Yes, you are the younger and should take the smaller eagle." The younger gave up the larger eagle to his brother—

WB The brothers plucked their birds, and their mother said to them, "Now you have feathers (for your arrows), but you have no wood for the arrows. In the west arrow weed grows; it is something that belongs to me." Coyote said, "I know where the arrow weed grows; it is not far from here."

[Their mother] took joints of the arrow weed and fitted them one into the other, and immediately the arrows were ready for use. Coyote said, "That's too easy," and he took joints of the arrow weed and straightened them with an arrow straightener, and he took sinew and tied it and said, "This is the way people will always make arrows." Their mother said, "In the west grows a wood (unidentified) that belongs to me; it is the best for making bows." Coyote said, "I know where it grows; I will go." Coyote went and brought back the top branches. Their mother said, "It is of the lower branches that you will make your bows." She took the wood and immediately the bows were ready for use. Coyote said, "That is too easy." He put the wood under the ashes and shaped and bent it; he prepared sinew for string and attached it to the prepared wood. "This is the way people will always make their bows."

Their mother said, "I will make it that all these arrows will be swift as lightning." Coyote said, "That is too quick." The brothers picked up their bows and arrows and took them toward the west. They stood facing west and they sang and ran a little way and stopped again facing west and raised their bows and arrows to shoot.[67] They lowered them again, but Coyote shot his arrow and they could not see where it had fallen. Again the brothers, facing to the south, raised their bows and arrows and lowered them; they faced to the east and raised their bows and arrows and lowered them; they faced to the north and raised their bows and arrows and lowered them. All of the arrows the brothers shot went true, and their mother went to the places where they fell and gathered them up and gave half to one brother and half to the other. But Coyote's arrows had gone in every direction, and that is why it is always difficult to find arrows after they have been shot—

67. This is hunting ritual, which prescribes three feints before the arrow is released.

[The Two Flutes]

TV The brothers played with their pets. Their mother said to them, "In the east a reed (*vaapk*) [*va:pk*] grows; it is something that belongs to me, and it is best for making flutes." The brothers answered, "We will go and get it." "No, it is very dangerous." "If an old woman like you can go, we can get there safely"—

TV&WB They set the fourth day as the day to start for the reeds. Their mother prepared food for them. They traveled many days and they came to a mountain on which were many mountain goats. The younger brother said, "Perhaps this is the danger our mother spoke of." But the elder brother sang:

"You are nothing but mountain goats.
All you do is stay on the tops of these mountains."

They went on. They came to level desert country and they saw in front of them the mirage of a lake. The younger brother said, "Perhaps that is the danger our mother spoke of." Perhaps now we will be drowned." But the elder brother sang:

"You are nothing but a cheat.
You deceive thirsty men. You are nothing."

They came to several washes and there were many mosquitoes. The younger brother said, "Perhaps these are the dangers our mother told us of. Perhaps we will be wounded." But the elder brother sang—

WB *"You are nothing but mosquitoes.*
All you do is live in marshy places;
All you do is live a day or so.
You are nothing"—

TV&WB They went on. They came to a flock of cranes, each standing on one leg in the water. The younger brother said, "Perhaps these are the dangers Mother told us of. Perhaps they will run us through with their long spears." But the elder brother sang:

"You are nothing but cranes.
All you do is live on fishes and things that live in water;
All you do is stand on one leg.
You are nothing."

They went on. They came to a canyon with steep sides, and when they talked to each other they heard the echo. The younger brother said, "Perhaps this is the danger our mother told us of. There are people all about us." But the elder brother sang—

WB *"You are nothing but bare cliffs.*
All you can do is give back our own voices.
You are nothing"—

TV&WB They went on. They came to a high place and in front of them they saw a red light.[68] "It must be our reeds. We are reaching the place."

When their mother knew that they were coming near the place where the reeds grew, by her power she moved them into the middle of the ocean. The elder brother said, "We must do something to get our reeds. If we go home without them, people will say, 'There are those two boys who went out after reeds and came back without anything.'" The younger brother made himself into—

WB a duck (*vaatcpik*)[69]—

TV a snake—

TV&WB The elder brother said, "I thought you could do better than that. You can't go as far as the reeds under the water. You will lose your breath and die."

The younger brother set out and he came to four beavers that were guarding the reeds. They were of four colors, black, gray, yellow (and one unknown), and he said to them, "Let me pass," and they let him pass. But before he got to where the reeds were, he saw a great red snake wrapped around them and he dropped dead. The elder brother said, "Now see what I can do," and he changed himself—

WB into the same form his brother had taken—

TV into a snake much smaller than his brother,[70] and he set out and came to the four beavers who were guarding the way. He said to them, "Will you let me pass? I want to go to my uncle Snake to get my reeds." They let him pass. He came to the great red snake wrapped

68. The reed is said to be lightning, and the association is close in the minds of the narrators. The role played by the great red snake [which the elder brother will find wrapped around the reeds] is not intelligible without knowing this association.

69. Black with white beak. [Probably the ducklike American coot, *Fulica americana*. Saxton, Saxton, and Enos (1983:62) have *vakaig,* "mud hen"—that is, coot.]

70. At some point around here WB must have rejoined the narrating, but the precise point is not marked in the manuscript.—*Ed.*

around the reeds. He had nothing to cut with. He held his hand to the west and drew down a black knife; he set it to his tongue to see if it was sharp. He held his hand to the south and drew down a blue knife; he held his hand to the east and drew down a white knife; he held his hand to the north and drew down a yellow knife. He held each in turn to his tongue and they were as sharp as possible. He took the black knife and cut off three joints of the reed. The plant grew again immediately to its former size. He threw the knife to the north and took the blue knife. He cut off three joints of the plant. Holding his two cuttings he dropped dead by the side of his brother.

The younger brother paid no attention to him; he took the first cutting of the reed for his own. When his brother came to himself he said, "Why do you do this? Don't you know that I am the older and whatever our mother makes for us I always have the larger?" They quarreled and at last the younger brother gave his first cutting to the elder brother, who said, "I wonder if these are the reeds our mother meant. She will know when we take them to her."

They brought them home to their mother. She said, "These are my reeds," and she dried them and made flutes and decorated them with sunbeams and gave them to her sons. She taught them songs to play and she said, "In the morning before sunrise wake up and try them." [When the time came] she made them face to the north, and they played. "It is very good. In the morning again before sunrise wake up and try your flutes." [That time] she made them face to the west, and they played. "It is very good. Play louder, and in the morning before sunrise try your flutes again." She made them face to the south, and they played. "It is very good. Again in the morning wake before sunrise and try your flutes." She made them face to the east and she said, "Play very loud." They sounded their flutes over the whole world and their mother danced to their music.

[Buzzard's Two Daughters]

In the east at Sawtooth Mountain [on the Gila River Reservation], Yellow Buzzard lived with his two daughters. Every morning they went to bathe at the pool at the foot of the mountain. (That morning) the elder was bathing in the pool and the younger still stood on the bank. She said to her sister, "Come quickly and listen." "What is it?" "There is beautiful music." "Is it a bird?" "No, it is not a bird."

"Come in and bathe." "No, come and listen to the music." She came out and listened. They both heard. It was very beautiful. They went back to their home and dressed themselves and started out to find the music—

TV They came to the home of four men who offered them their music, but it was not the song they had heard—

WB They traveled toward the west and came to the home of Black Lizard. He said to them, "Where are you going?" "We heard beautiful music and we are going to find it." He said, "Perhaps it is mine. I make a fine noise." He brought out mesquite bean cake and offered it to them but they said, "No, we do not want to eat. Let us hear your music." He went to a decaying tree and ran back and forth through a hole in the trunk.[71] The girls listened and said, "No, it was not your song."

They went on, and they came to the home of Squirrel (a small whitish squirrel). He said to them, "Where are you going?" "We heard beautiful music and we are going to find it." "Perhaps it is mine. I have a fine song." He offered them cholla cactus fruit but they said, "No, we do not want to eat. Let us hear your music." He sang his song. "No, it was not yours."

They went on, and they came to the home of Woodpecker and he said, "Where are you going?" "We heard beautiful music and we are going to find it." "Perhaps it is my music." He offered them ants to eat but they said, "No, we do not want to eat. Let us hear your music." He went to a hollow tree and began drumming. "No, it was not your song."

They went on and came to the home of Hawk. "Where are you going?" "We heard beautiful music and we are going to find it." "Perhaps it is my music." He offered them a rabbit to eat but they said, "No, we do not want to eat. Let us hear your music." He whistled, and wood rats came out of their holes and he shot them with his bow and arrow.[72] "No, it is not your music."

They went on and came to the home of Owl. "Where are you going?" "We heard beautiful music and are going to find it." "Perhaps

71. The song of the "black lizard" was said to be made by the rasping of his saw-toothed back against the wood.

72. Wood rats are always hunted with a whistle that causes them to put their heads out of their holes; and hawks have a call that is like the whistle used.

it is my music." He offered them mice to eat, but they refused. He went to the top of a tree. "Whoo-oo-oo." "No, it is not your music."

They went on and came to the home of the elf owls. They were sitting in a row on the branch of a tree. "Perhaps it is our music. Sit up beside us." They sat beside them. The first owl said, "Sit over, cousin." The girls sat over, and the next said, "Sit over, cousin," and the girls got to the end of the row and back again. The elf owls said, "This is our music."[73] "No, it was not your music we were looking for"—
TV&WB They came to footprints on the ground. The younger sister fainted when she saw them. Her sister said, "You never did this before," and she sang:

> *"Perhaps some of those who have claimed to make our beautiful music had power to overcome you."*

They came to the home of the two boys. They were away hunting and their mother was there alone. She said to them, "Where are you going?" "I think we are coming here." They went in. Toward evening she gave them seeds and said, "Take this and prepare food." She sang:

> *"I have nothing prepared for you;*
> *Take this and make food for yourself."*

They took the basket of seeds and carried it four times around the house. When they had finished, the seeds had been turned into flour. They made bread of it.

Toward evening the boys returned to their home. From a distance they saw the girls and they went around the house and came into it without looking at them. Their mother called them to eat, but they went into their beds and lay down without speaking. At night the younger sister went to the bed of the younger brother and the elder sister to the bed of the elder brother. Their mother built a great fire and fed it so that it burned brightly, and she talked all the time to her sons.[74] "Be careful; you do not know who these girls are. Their father is our worst enemy. They have come to destroy us. Perhaps they are menstruating and will destroy you and your bows and arrows and all your powers." The girls played with the two brothers but they lay on their faces and made no move toward them. At last the younger

73. The Pimas say that elf owls' chatter is a constant repetition of the phrase, "Sit over, cousin."

74. This was said to be the custom of a mother who wanted to interfere with her son's marriage to a girl of whom she disapproved.

brother desired the younger sister and he took medicine from under his pillow and threw it in the direction of his mother so that she fell into a deep sleep. Then the younger brother turned over, and after the fire died down he had intercourse with the younger sister. All night the elder brother lay on his face.

In the morning they all rose and went out to bathe. The mother woke and wept, crying, "These girls have run off with my sons." She went out to see where their tracks led, and she saw they led toward the bathing place. "Perhaps they will come back." (At the bathing pool) the girls came out of the water on one side and the boys on the other. The younger brother said to the elder brother, "I will go with these girls." "No, don't you remember what our mother said? They are our enemies." The younger sister said to the elder sister, "Go home if you want to; I will stay with these boys." "What would you do that for? Didn't you hear the old woman talking about us all night?" "I don't care. I will stay." The elder sister dragged the younger sister back to their home in the east, and the elder brother dragged the younger brother back to their home.

The younger brother took no interest in anything anymore. While the elder brother was hunting he lay under a tree and played on his flute. He never caught anything but rabbits, and his brother brought in deer as he always had. The younger brother said, "Come, let us go to the home of these girls." "No, don't you remember what our mother said; she does not want us to marry these girls." "If you will not go, I will go by myself." He made himself ready to go, and the elder brother said to him, "All right. But remember, we will never come back." So they both made ready and their mother wept. "There will be dangers on the way. If your uncles attack you, come home again." They took strings of beads and wound them around the house and said, "If these strings break, you will know that we are dead." They sang:

> *"We're going, we're going, we're going, we're going*
> *To see the girls in the east."*

Their mother sang:

> *"Go on, go on, go on, go on*
> *To find those girls in the east"—*

WB (The next morning they set out.) Turtle was with them, and they said to him, "You had better go back." "No, I want to go with you." "You ought to go back and play on the flute. We might never come back and then you would keep up the flute playing." They sang:

"Play the flute by night and make mad[75] the hearts of the people."

Turtle returned and played the flute. He played at night and a girl came from the east and sat on his lap. He played the second night and a girl came from the south and sat on his lap. He played the third night and a girl came from the west and sat on his lap. He played the fourth night and a girl came from the north and sat on his lap. So Turtle married four wives.

In the west there was a girl who would not marry. Turtle heard of this and he said, "I will go." He sent Coyote ahead of him with many flowers and Coyote threw the flowers over her and came back to Turtle. So Turtle married her and left his four wives.

Turtle got in the habit of marrying in every village, and it turned his head. He died[76] and that is why we are allowed only one wife—

TV&WB They started toward the east and a strong wind came from the west and blew [thorns] of cholla cactus into their faces. The elder said, "These are the dangers our mother spoke of." He sang:

"It is our uncles warning us to go back."

The younger brother said, "No, this is what always happens when people travel in a strange country. These things did not happen while we lived at home with our mother, but we must expect them now."

Their mother wept all the time. At last she said, "What is the use? They will not come back to me now. Perhaps someday they will come. I will not cry anymore."

That night the two boys lay down to sleep. A wolf came up to them; he was wounded and his skin was hanging loose from his head. The elder brother said, "This is what our mother told us of." He sang:

75. The Pima figure is almost equivalent to ours, indicating intoxication, madness, gaiety, and passion in the same term. To us this does not connote religion, but to them this is also the core of the religious notion. [A rare Benedict comment on Dionysianism. I don't know the native word for "make mad" in the song, but to judge from the story context, and if the song were in Pima, the word would probably be *ce:paow-icud,* "to-make-whorish," "to-make-someone-act-like-a-whore." This is a common word in songs. It is normally used in reference to women. (See Bahr, Paul, and Joseph 1997, under the index entry "whore," for more on this.) Here the song reference is to "the people" in general, but the context makes clear that the people in question are women. If the song were in Maricopa, I don't know what the word could be.]

76. The victim of too potent a love charm.

"It is our uncles warning us to go back."

The younger brother said, "No, this is what always happens when people travel in a strange country. Old men have always told tales of things like this that happen to them."

Next night they camped again. A headless hawk dropped into their campfire and burned to death. The elder brother said, "There is no doubt anymore. These are the dangers our mother told us of and we are going to have trouble. Let us go back." He sang:

"The hawks we hear at night are warning us to go back."

The younger brother said, "No, this is what always happens."

They went on and made camp again for the third night. A man's skeleton dropped into their campfire and was burned. "Let us return" [said the elder brother and he sang]:

"It is our uncles warning us to go back."

But the younger brother would not.

They went on and made camp the fourth night. Up in the air they heard a voice singing:

"Parahan, Parahan, return home."

The elder brother wept and said, "Come now, my younger brother." He sang:

"My brother Parahan, come home with me."

But his brother would not agree. The elder sang four songs but his younger brother would not turn back. The elder said, "I will not try any longer," and he sang:

"My brother, I have warned you.
Now we will go on to the end of our journey."

They came to a high place and they saw the home of the two girls on the mountain across the desert. "How will we get there?—for if they see us they will kill us." They caused a whirlwind to come out of the earth and it raised them straight into the air and dropped them into the house of the two girls. Both of the sisters were glad to see them and they stayed there laughing and playing with each other.

Their father heard them enjoying themselves and he said, "Why are my daughters laughing and enjoying themselves? They never did that before." He had a grandchild by another daughter and he sent him to look secretly into the house of his daughters. The child came back crying and said—

WB "There are two men there with eyes like stars"—

TV "There are two men there who shine like stars"—

[Death of the Twins]

TV&WB The father of the two girls sent toward the west for his brave warrior to come and help him kill the two brothers. "My enemies have come into my house, and I want help in killing them." The brave warrior took his club and went to the house of the daughters. The brothers said to him, "Are you there, my friend?" He turned and went back to his home and would not kill them. The father of the girls sent his warriors from the south and the east and the north, and they went to the house of the two girls; and when they saw the brothers they returned to their homes and would not kill them. The father said, "I must look again." He sang:

"I am going to look again for help.
I look in the air."

He came to the Blue Hawks. "Come to my home, come to my home. I need you to help kill my enemy." The Blue Hawks followed all the way to his home, and Bowstring Hawk cut off the top of the [girls'] house with his wings; two Blue Hawks crippled the two brothers; and One-eyed Hawk killed them both. They dragged their bodies to a level place. The girls' father sang:

"I wonder if these are the flute players that I have killed.
Perhaps I made a mistake."

The quails came and sang over their bodies:[77]

"The old woman had handsome boys.
How will she feel now that they are dead?"

Kotat (a woodpecker)[78] came and said, "I am going to tell the old woman." He dropped down into the boys' blood and covered himself with it.[79]

77. Vanyiko explained that the quails were glad because when the brothers were babies they had killed their young.

78. Heard as *ku:ḍaht+* by Herzog (n.d.*c*:7); not further identified.—*Ed.*

79. To use as evidence of his truthfulness. This is regarded as the origin of the red breast of this woodpecker; but it was not made explicit in the narrative.

The people burned the bodies.[80] White Whirlwind came and bent the smoke toward the west until it touched the home of the boys' mother. She saw it and cried, for she knew that her sons were dead. She sang:

"Blue smoke rainbow came from the east and bent to the west.
What was ordained has come to pass."

Woodpecker came flying to tell her of the death of her sons. She sang:

"Why should he come flying with this word?
Does he suppose I do not know what has happened to my sons?"

Woodpecker sang:

"You don't know what has happened to your sons.
They are dead."

He told her, "I fought for them and am covered with blood." She said, "Go back. I don't want you." She took a handful of dirt and threw it after him. "Go home, but you will never be able to get there." The bird flew a little way and sat down on a tree to rest. The ants came and crawled over his feathers and one crawled into his mouth. He swallowed it and it was sweet. He ate all the ants he could find and they bit him inside and he died.

The old woman lived all alone. At night she heard the voices of her sons on the trail from the east. Again she heard them from the west on the trail from the pool where they used to bathe. She heard them come to the door and then their voices died off. She said, "I cannot get rid of this sorrow. I will leave this place." She sang:

"What is the use of living?
I have no children now"—

WB She set fire to her house and threw herself into the flames, but the fire was too hot and she stood aside again. She sang:

"It is my dream.
I knew in my dream that my sons would leave me at last.
It is best to go away from this place."

80. As the Maricopas do, not the Pimas.—*Ed.*

[The Grandson's Revenge][81]

The younger daughter (of Buzzard) was pregnant and it was near the time when she should have a child. Her father sent to her and said, "When your child is born, send me word." He sent continually to give her this message and at last she said, "Why do you send this message to me over and over? I have told you that I will send you word." Her father sent his reply, "It is because you are young and do not know what to do. This is your first child." At last her father said, "I will tell you. It is because if your child is a boy I will kill him, but if it is a girl I will let her live."

At last she called the old women together and said, "It is time for me to bear a child." The old women did everything, but the child was not born. The first day they waited, and the second and the third. On the fourth day toward morning her father lay down and went to sleep. Her sister sat close to her, and she heard singing (from the unborn child):

"I want to come out." (4 times)

She said, "I think it is a boy; I heard him talking. He is hiding because his grandfather means to kill him." The sisters said, "When he is born, we will treat him as a girl." Then the baby was born, and they made him appear as a girl and woke the girls' father. "Come, the baby is born. It is a girl; come and see it." The father said, "Take good care of her. She will be a help to me when she is grown."

The child grew up, and the grandfather brought him dolls and little baskets. He threw them away and would not play with them. His mother said, "Sometimes girls will play with nothing but boys' playthings." So the grandfather brought him bows and arrows and he played with those and would not let anyone else touch them. One day his grandfather was lying on the ground on his blanket and the child was playing nearby. He ran and jumped over his grandfather. Then he climbed a tree directly over him. The grandfather saw that the child was a boy. He said to himself, "My daughters have deceived me," and when they came back again, he said to the child's mother, "Get the child ready. I want to take him to his uncles." His mother

81. The manuscript does not mark a return to both narrators in "duet," but that might have happened, possibly at this point. No further single-speaker passages show in the manuscript, so the remainder is either all Blackwater alone or all Blackwater and Vanyiko together.—*Ed.*

got the boy ready and she said to him, "Your grandfather wants to take you to your uncles, but I am afraid he means to harm you. Nevertheless I must send you."

His grandfather took him to a dangerous country. He called the lions and the bears and the animals that live on flesh. They came and stood crying. The grandfather said to them, "Why do you stand crying? You are able to kill any living thing." "But we can do nothing against this child." The grandfather said, "But this child was born out of heat."[82] "No, we know the truth. This is Rainbow. He is of a great family." They could do nothing. The grandfather and the boy started toward home. When they came to hard ground he took the child by the legs and beat his head on a rock. The grandfather went on home, but before he got there his grandson had come to himself and was already at the village.

His grandfather came in crying, but nobody spoke to him. At last he said, "Why don't you ask why I am mourning? We went to his uncles, and coming home I stopped to get wood. When I came back the boy was gone. Wild animals must have killed him." His daughters said, "The child came home before you and has gone out to play."

Again the grandfather took him with him. When they had come to the wooded country he took a great branch of wood and hit him on the head. The grandfather came in mourning, but his grandson was in the village before him. Again he took his grandson with him. He said to him, "Help me carry this great stick of firewood." The boy sat down and the grandfather lifted the wood onto his shoulder and let it fall. The boy escaped as the wood fell and his grandfather chased him with a club, but the club had no more weight than a cornstalk and the boy was not harmed at all. Again a fourth time the grandfather took him with him and asked him for help in carrying a large stick of firewood. Again he let the wood fall on him, but he escaped. The grandfather ran after him and caught him in his hands to kill him, but his hands had no more strength than a dead man's.

The child went to his mother and said, "Why does my grandfather treat me in this way?" He told her all he had done to him. "Your grandfather planned to kill you before you were born and that is why you have been treated as a girl. I did not tell you before, for there was

82. In the version Herzog obtained from Vanyiko, the phrase is "born in the fire," meaning "born to be roasted, i.e., to be tortured and killed" (n.d.*c*:7).—*Ed.*

nowhere for you to go. Your father's mother lives a long way from here." One day the boy came to his mother and said, "I am going to my grandmother's." "No, it is too far. You would never get there." "Yes, I'm going. I'm afraid of my grandfather." He started off. His mother followed his tracks toward the west and begged him to return but he said, "No," and she tried to hold him by the hand but he vanished into the air. Again she saw him ahead and overtook him and held him, but he vanished as she held him. Four times he vanished into thin air, and she knew she would never see him again. She sang:

"Where are you going?
You don't know your way."

His mother went back to her home and the boy went on. He came to the site of an old campfire and he said to himself, "Perhaps there are people living nearby." He could not find any traces of people. He saw there had been two sleeping places by the fire and he said to himself, "This is the camp of my father and uncle." He took his arrow and shot it into the sleeping place of his father. He drew it out and his father came and sat with him. He took another arrow and shot it into the sleeping place of his uncle and drew it out. His uncle came and sat beside him.

They pushed the logs of the old campfire closer together, and the red coals ignited and burned. They talked all night. Toward morning the two began to sink down into the earth. The boy cried out and tried to stop them; he took hold of his father under the armpits, holding him close. When he held his father, his uncle was sinking, and he ran over and caught hold of his uncle. As soon as he had firm hold of his uncle, he saw his father sinking and ran to him. So he ran from one to the other and they both sank deeper and deeper. As the sun rose both disappeared into the ground. The boy was left alone crying. He sang:

"I will travel by day,
And by night you will sit with me."

He went on, and at night he came to the remains of another campfire. He shot his arrows into the sleeping places of his father and uncle and they came and talked all night with him. In the morning they sank into the ground. So he traveled on, and every night they stayed all night with him. The fourth day he came to the place where his grandmother had burned her house. "I wonder who lived here." He thought of all that his father had told him: "At that house roads meet from the four directions." He looked and found the trails from the east, the south, the west, and the north, but they were old and overgrown. "The land is dead, the roads are dead."

He went toward the west and met Taamtak,[83] who said to him, "Where are you going? I never saw a child here." "I don't know. I am wandering around." "You look like two men I used to know," and he told him of the old woman's two sons and how they played their flutes, and [how] two girls came from the east and they had followed them and been killed. "I am the child of those men." "You are my relative; I am your uncle." They began to cry together and the boy sang:

"Uncle, uncle, uncle
Svaawi."[84]

The man said, "Come to my house. I live nearby. I am going away to gamble but when I come I will find something for you." "No, take me on your back and carry me with you." At last the man consented and when he had put him on his back he felt no weight at all. Taamtak began to gamble, and everything he had [ever] lost he won back again. He won every time he played.

The boy lived with his uncle for a long time and they would go every day to gamble. One day when he was away the boy set out to find his grandmother. He took seeds and dropped them as long as they lasted. When his uncle came back he ran round and round trying to find the boy's tracks, but the blackbirds and quails had eaten the grain and he could find no trace. He sang:

"Birds have spoiled the tracks.
It will take me a long time to trace you."

He searched in wider and wider circles and at last he saw a track going west. He knew the boy was going to his grandmother. He followed in the direction the boy had taken and came to a place where greasewood grew very thick. In one place he could see leaves stirring. He sang:

83. A little gray bird, a winter resident, the size of a sparrow with black stripes over the head [heard as *tamtok* by Herzog (n.d.*c*:7); not further identified].

84. "The bird was the boy's mother's younger brother. The name *Svaawi* sounds in the song when sung, *ceyanawawe*. Vanyiko gives for this: *Cinawawi,* the Maricopa name of this personality" (Herzog n.d.*c*:8).—*Ed.*

"See the greasewood still in motion where my nephew has passed.
Here I will find my nephew."

He went all the way through the growth of greasewood, but he could not find his nephew. He came to great sand dunes. At one place the sand was still spilling down the slopes. He sang:

"See the sand spilling down the slope where my nephew has passed.
Here I will find my nephew."

The boy was far ahead, in level country, and he sang:

"Come on, uncle. I am in front of you."

The boy came to the desert. There was nothing to eat or drink, and when he could no longer endure the thirst he lay down under a bush. Not far behind, his uncle was overcome by thirst and lay down under another bush. Hawk saw the child from the sky and thought, "The child will die and I shall have a good meal off it." He sang:

"I shall have a good meal."

He came down to watch. He said, "This child is my relative. He is the child of Rain (or Cloud)." He brought the rain clouds, and when the large drops fell the boy opened his eyes. He drank and sang:

"These drops of rain came from the sky above and gave me fresh life.
I shall live and not die."

The boy started on. He was nearing the ocean and he came upon the feather of a bluebird (a sign he was approaching). He sang:

"Blue feather, blue feather."

He came to the edge of the ocean. His grandmother lived on the other side and he had no way to cross. He walked along the shore and there were all kinds of birds. He came to Crane and sang:

"Crane, help me to cross this water."

The crane flew up and hovered in the center of the ocean and spread his wings. The reach of his wings was from one shore of the ocean to the other. The boy walked across on the bridge the crane had made. His uncle came to the shore of the ocean and he saw the boy on the other side. The boy spoke again to the crane and asked him to help his uncle. The crane flew up and hovered in the center of the ocean and spread his wings. The uncle started across on the bridge the crane had made, but when he came to the center he looked down and was afraid. Immediately the crane became the size of an ordinary bird, and the uncle fell in the ocean.

Again the boy went toward the west. He came to a pool and stopped to drink. A girl[85] came up for water and she said, "What did you come here for? I never saw a child here before." "You have called me a child and that is what I am. I do not know where I am going. I am going about here and there." "You look like my two sons who were killed in the east." "I am their son." They cried together. She sang:

"My grandchild, my grandchild, you have returned to me."

He sang:

"My grandmother in the west, my grandmother in the west,
I have come to stay with you."

"Come to my house." His grandmother gave him food to eat, and he grew to be a young man. When he was grown he said, "I want to go back to the country of my grandfather." He took some other young men with him and came to the country of his grandfather.

As they were approaching he called Coyote and sent him ahead and said, "Go to the house of my grandfather and bring me secretly the *siikut.*"[86] Coyote went and came back with it. The boy made counters for fifteen, four, and two, and they came into Buzzard's [the grandfather's] village. Buzzard did not recognize his grandson.

The boy asked his grandfather to play *giinskoot.* Buzzard said, "I never play with a boy like you. I play with the old men who are wise and know how. When the game is at its height you would be too young to stand the talk." "You have only a woman's heart. You are making excuses. You are afraid to play with me." So Buzzard played with the boy, and they set out the stakes. Then Buzzard sat down in the seat the boy always took. "That's my place." "I don't care where I

85. Recall that it was said at the start of this story that the grandmother becomes young again at the beginning of every month.—*Ed.*

86. [*Si'iko.*] The *giinskoot* stick with the value of fourteen, the counter next to the highest in value. [For a description of the four sticks, or counters, called *kintskut,* or *giinskoot,* used in the stick-dice game, see Russell 1908:175.]

sit, but I sat down here and I will stay here." "I'll move you." "You can't move me." "I can." "If you can, take all the stakes of this game." The boy picked up Buzzard and moved him to the other position.

They set out more stakes. The boy said, "As I was coming this way I saw a *kootovitc*[87] nest with eggs in it." "No, it is not the season." "Yes. Come and see it, and if there are no eggs I will give you all the stakes." He won again.

The third time they set out the stakes. At Buzzard's side there was a stone hollowed out so that it held water, and Buzzard used to wash his face in it. The boy said, "Better take away the bowl of water." "No, that can't be moved; it has roots." "If I can't move it, you can take all the stakes." "All right." The boy won again.

They quarreled and the boy shot his grandfather four times and killed him. He did not come to himself after he had been killed the fourth time. That is the way he killed his grandfather.

He went back to his grandmother's and called all the living things all over the earth and gave them their different games. He gave them different ways of cooking and different customs. There were a few left, and he said, "I will keep these. There will be other generations and they will need some customs too." So he kept these and that is why every generation has its own ways of cooking and playing games.[88]

87. *Kul-wicigam,* "thrasher."—*Ed.*

88. This story was given in a nonesoteric form by William Stevens. It opened with the coming of the daughters of Buzzard, who have heard the flutes of the two brothers. For a life token, when the brothers follow the girls back to Buzzard's country, they wind up their string of beads four times around [their mother's] house (as also in the fragment "Twin Sons of Rain" ["Rain's Twins," this chapter], told by Clara Ahiel). The strings break when they are killed.

The story of the killing of the brothers by Buzzard differs in the Stevens version. Buzzard first sent a young grandchild who came back reporting that they had eyes like stars; the people of the village, as soon as they saw the eyes, turned back saying, "They are my *wopotcu ikam*" [*wepo cui'igkam*] (said to mean "spirits like myself"). Coyote heard that the people of the village had returned without killing them, and he said, "Why do you set out against them and come back without having done it? I will go and show you what a brave man does."

As soon as Coyote saw their eyes like stars, he said, "They are my *wopotcu ikam,*" and he turned back. Buzzard said, "Let us call Blue Hawk. He is left-handed" (equivalent to being an excellent shot). Blue Hawk agreed. He flew straight up into the air with his club and dropped upon them and killed them.

The child born [later in the story] was disguised as a girl. When the child was grown, he saw the seed bags made of the skin of his fathers, and his mother told him the story of their death. He asked to go to find his grandmother, and he set out, bringing his fathers to life in each camp, as in the story [told by Blackwater and Vanyiko]. He came to his grandmother's house: she was a *maaka* [*ma:kai,* "medicine woman"] and recognized him. On his fourth question she declared herself and they wept together. (Stevens stated that this was the form in which it was told to children.)

Cloud's Twins[89]

William Blackwater

There lived in the village a girl who would have nothing to do with men. One day she was sitting making mats of *vaav*[90] reeds, and she spread her mat and lay down to rest. There were a few clouds in the sky, and presently a light big-drop rain began to fall. Two drops fell on the girl's body, and it was not long before the people noticed that she was pregnant. They talked about her: "You are nothing but a loose woman. You have been with men." She had always said she would never marry.

When the time came for her to have a child, she had twin boys. People talked among themselves wondering who their father was, and they said, "We will all meet in the girl's village and put the babies in the center of the circle to find out who their father is." But the children did not go to any man. They made another circle, but still the babies would not go to any man. Someone made them a present of a little fawn, and it grew up with the children and was very tame.

When the children were old enough to play with other boys, they heard them call their fathers *vaav, maam,*[91] and they said to their mother, "Who is our *vaav,* our *maam?* We don't know these things." She said to them, "Yes, you have a father, but he does not live in this village. He is Cloud, and he lives far to the east." When they had grown to be big boys, they came again to their mother and said, "You told us that our father lives far to the east. We want to go find him." "No, it is too far. You could not go so far." "Yes, we have made up our minds to go." "Very well. But if you cannot get there, come back again."

They started and came to the country of the east. There were four houses there; the first was Black Cloud's, the second was Red Cloud's, the third was Gray Cloud's, and the fourth was White Cloud's. They went to the house of Black Cloud. He came out and said to them, "What have you come for?" "Our mother told us that our father lived in the country of the east and that his name was

89. The version given by Russell (1908:239) begins, "When the Hohokam dwelt on the Gila River. . . ." Yet this idea of a girl impregnated from the sky is prominent in the mythology of the Yavapais, Apaches, and Navajos. For the Pimas it is a minor motif, and "extra" to the creations and miracles that they tell in the rafter.—*Ed.*

90. Possibly *va:pk,* "cane," "reed," as earlier in "Nasia's Twins." *Vaav,* in a later paragraph, is a different word meaning "father," as stated.—*Ed.*

91. Each sib [or clan, in ordinary English] has its own term for "father." [In the rafter, "Passage to Earth's Surface" section, the sibs are called "companies."]

Cloud. Perhaps you are our father." "My name is Cloud but I have no children. I am not your father. There is another man next door, whose name is Red Cloud."

They went to Red Cloud. "What have you come for?" "Our mother told us that our father lived in the east and that his name was Cloud. Perhaps you are our father." "My name is Cloud but I have no children. There is another man next door whose name is Gray Cloud."

They went to Gray Cloud. "What have you come for?" "Our mother told us that our father lived in the east and that his name was Cloud. Perhaps you are our father." "My name is Cloud but I have no children. There is another man next door whose name is White Cloud and he travels far and wide. Perhaps he is your father."

They went to White Cloud. "What have you come for?" "Our mother told us that our father lived in the east and that his name was Cloud. Perhaps you are our father." "My name is Cloud. You can stay with me."

One day White Cloud said to them, "I do not know yet whether you are my children. What can you do?" The younger stood up and made a clap of thunder; the elder stood up and made a long rumble of thunder. "Yes, I think you are my children. Tonight I will put you outside and if you live until morning I will know beyond any doubt." They went outside and it was very cold. In the morning when he called them to eat, they were as well as ever. "Yes," he said, "you are my children." He took good care of them and gave them whatever they needed. The wind was their uncle and was always taking them wherever he went. At last the boys said, "We think we have stayed long enough. We want to go back to our mother." "All right. If anyone asks you where you have been, do not answer them. Wait till I have said the word."

The twin boys returned to their home. Everyone asked them, "Where have you been?" They did not say a word. Over and over people asked, "Where have you been?" At last the boys said, "We have waited long enough." They told the whole story; all the people came to a meeting and they told them. The clouds came up in the sky and thunder came in a great clap. It killed the twin boys.

Rain's Twins

William Stevens

Rain had two sons. They lived with their mother and did not know their father. One day they were playing and they saw the great black clouds overhead. They ran to their mother and said, "See, mother! Look at the great black cloud." She knew it was their father. They went outdoors again and the cloud was gone. They ran back to their mother. "Mother, the cloud went away." "I guess it went home."

The children thought about what their mother had said, and one of them said to the other, "Let us ask her about his home. We want to know where his home is." Next day the big black clouds came up and they ran to their mother and said, "That big black cloud has come again. Where does it live?" "Yes, it has a home. It is your father." When they knew this, they always watched for the cloud and wondered about his home. At last they went to their mother and said, "We are going to our father's home." "No, it is too far. You will never get there." Yes, we are going. Prepare food for us."

They set out. Every day the clouds came up in the east and guided them. At last they came to a mountain and they saw a house at its foot. They said, "It is our father's house." They went toward it and a man came out. He had a bow and arrows and a shield and a club, and he lifted his bow to shoot. The younger hesitated, but the elder brother said, "Do not hesitate or he will shoot us." They went on and the man stepped back. Four times they came on and each time he stepped back. He said to them, "Where did you come from? I have never seen children here before. What did you come for?" "We are looking for our father. We heard that he lived here." "No, he does not live in this house. Over there is another house." They went to the second house. "No, he does not live in this house. I am your uncle. Your father lives in the house you just came from."

Four times they went back and forth. At last the man in the first house said, "Yes, I am your father. If you are really my children, stand and make yourselves known." He showed them a narrow plank on which to stand, and the elder said to the younger, "Go and stand there and make yourself known." "No, you are the older." They disputed four times, and at last the elder stood on the narrow plank and made a great clap of thunder. Four times he made the thunderclap. It hit his father and he lay dead. When he came to himself he said, "Yes, you are my son." The elder said to the younger, "Stand up and make yourself known, too." The younger brother stood on the plank and made a blinding flash of lightning. Four times he made lightning. It hit his father and he lay dead. When he came to himself he said, "You are my son." They lived there with their father and their uncle the wind.

After a while the boys wanted to go back to see their mother. "All right." Their father gave them a mule and said, "If anyone meets you and wants to talk, pass right by. The first four persons you meet you must not speak to." They got on the mule and started home. They saw clouds rise in the east, and they watched them appear and disappear.

The first person they met they did not speak a word to. The second person they met they did not speak a word to. The third person they met they did not speak a word to. At last they met a fourth person and there was no cloud visible in the whole sky. They thought, "Our father can't see us." The younger said, "You go ahead and talk." "No, you." The man said, "Where are you coming from? Children never come here." The elder brother was just about to answer him when a tiny bit of cloud appeared in the east, and the lightning struck out of that cloud and killed them. Rain took them back to his home and has kept them ever since, and the elder is the crack of thunder and the younger is the flash of lightning.

Rain's Twins[92]

Clara Ahiel

Old woman Itanyi[93] lived by herself on Mount Kwakwada with her baby grandsons and gathered seeds for them. She put her children in a swing and went off every morning. The children cried. Grasshopper and Cricket came and said, "We are your relations," and they sang them a lullaby:

> *"Go to sleep.*
> *Go to sleep."*

The children killed them both and piled them up. Their grandmother came home and she saw the grasshopper and cricket dead.

Next day quails came. They said, "We are your relatives," and they sang them a lullaby (no words). The children killed them and piled them up. Their grandmother came home and threw them out. The children cried and cried. At last she went out and picked up the quails and cooked and ate them and the children were satisfied.

92. Despite the "rain" of the title, this story has less in common with William Stevens's "Rain's Twins" than with Blackwater's "Nasia's Twins" (the pile of quail, the bows and arrows made by the old woman, the life token). Evidently it is a short piece of the Nasia tale.—*Ed.*

93. *Itanyi*, "saltbush" (*Atriplex* sp.). See note 38, this chapter, for more on this plant name. *Kwakwada*, "twins, of twins," later in this sentence, could be the plural form of *kuadi*, "twin," a Mexican Spanish word borrowed from Nahuatl. Compare Santamaría 1978 (*cuate, cuata*). See Saxton, Saxton, and Enos 1983:108 for the spelling of *kuadi*.—*Ed.*

The children grew up. Their grandmother made them bows and arrows, and she said, "Shoot east." They shot east. "Shoot west." They shot west. "Shoot north." They shot north. "Shoot south." They shot south. She gave them all [of the] directions so they would be great hunters. She told them to keep away from women or they would lose their power.

(Later, when they had gone, she strung string back and forth in the house as a life token.)[94]

94. That is, so long as the strings do not break she knows the boys are still alive. The boys in "Nasia's Twins" do the same.—*Ed.*

3

PIECES AFTERWARD, ON WAR

Introduction

Donald Bahr

The origin of the Apaches and the origin of the Pimas' hostility toward them are both given in the main "rafter" text of chapter 1. It is said that the hostility began as a way to assure death, and it was occasioned by parents taking sides over children's disputes. The stories to be told in this chapter, like those of the previous one, don't involve Elder Brother or Earth Doctor (although the Apache origin and origin of hostilities did involve Elder Brother). But the absence of those gods didn't render the previous chapter's stories post-Edenic. In fact, I consider all of the previous chapter's stories to be of the same primordial or Edenic or ancient (the words are equivalent) time period as the rafter. Why then do I judge the present stories to fall not only after the rafter but also after Eden?

There are two reasons. The first is implicit and deals with a change in mood between the rafter stories and the four stories of this chapter. The second is explicit and deals with statements made in different versions of one of the four stories. First the implicit reason. The rafter ends with war, namely, the conquest of the Hohokam, but really all the way through both that text and the "pieces left out," including the part about the conquest, one gets the feeling that a lone person out walking was in no danger of being killed in a chance encounter with a member of an enemy tribe. (In chapter 2, for example, consider Corn Man or Kadagum's wife.) Apaches, the Pimas' main historic enemies, were *created* in rafter times, just as whites were, but like whites they are not active through the remainder of that text or the pieces left out. Eden was effectively Apache-free.

The Ho'ok and the Man Eagle were threats to lone Edenic travelers, but Apaches were not. Eden had an expansive, literally a young world, feel. True, this period ended with a conquest of the Hohokam, who had killed Elder Brother, but that conquest was gloriously, imperiously unlike the reality of the less ancient, Apache-riven times that are the subject of this chapter. In the conquest, the advancing Pimas won every battle, but in the time of the stories of this chapter, no Pima was safe away from the village alone. I suppose there were Pimas in 1927 who thought exactly that: the tribe had experienced a glorious conquest of the Hohokam, and then came the hard times.

Second, the statements made in the specific text "Koolhaa," or "The Orphan Boy." This is a text that is given in short form in the rafter and longer form in the present chapter. We saw other examples of such rafter attachment/detachment in the last chapter. Here the problem is a bit more complex, because the names of the characters are not identical in the two versions, the rafter version stops sooner than the text in this chapter, and most importantly, the rafter version is set entirely in the time of the Edenic imperial conquest, whereas the present chapter's version is set entirely in Apache hard times.

The discrepancies would be unbridgeable if we had no other versions of the story, but we do have three: those of Thin Leather (Russell 1908:227–30), Juan Smith (Bahr et al. 1994:258–60), and the Papago, or Tohono O'odham, narrator Juan Dolores (Saxton and Saxton 1973:169–74). When they are considered, it is clear that the full form of the story has two generations of war victims. The names and ethnic affiliations of the victims, and the affiliations of the killers, are given in the following list. The decisive information is this: (1) the ethnic affiliation of the second victim, in the four texts that have such a victim, is Pima in the text of this chapter, Hohokam (captured and raised by the Pimas) in three texts, and Apache (captured and raised by the Pimas) in one; (2) the name of this victim, when given (three texts), is always the same—Kakanyip, or Kakampe as Benedict spelled it; and (3) the victim's killer, when stated, is always Apache.

What does this information tell us? First, that Pima narrators don't always agree. This should surprise no one. And second, that most versions of the story (three of five) bridge from a glorious Hohokam conquest (the second victim is a Hohokam captured and raised by the Pimas) to Apache hard times.[1] That the "Apaches" come after the "Hohokam" in the Pima sense of the past should again surprise no one. What is surprising, or at least fortunate, is that we have a story that makes the transition.

The Information[2]

Name and Affiliation of the First Person to Be Killed

WB: Decorated Feathers Medicine Man (Hohokam)
TV&WB: Sohani Maaka (Pima)
TL: Tcotcuk Tatai Siwan (Hohokam)
S: Tcotcuk Tatai Siwan (Hohokam)
D: Two Whirlwinds (Pima)

Affiliation of First Victim's Killers

WB: Pima
TV&WB: Apache
TL: Pima
S: Pima
D: Apache

Name and Affiliation of the Second Person to Be Killed

WB: Name unstated (a Hohokam who was captured and raised by the Papagos is mentioned, but he is not named, nor does the story tell his fate)
TV&WB: Kakampe (Pima)
TL: Kakanyip (Hohokam captured and raised by the Papagos)
S: Kakanyip (Hohokam—the name is given but the story doesn't tell his fate)
D: Name unstated (Apache captured by the Pimas)

Affiliation of Second Victim's Killers

WB: Name unstated (no second killing in this version)

1. Actually one of three "votes" for the Apaches as killers is from a text that considers the victim's affiliation to be pure Pima. But the overall picture is still that of a transition from glorious times to a time beset by raiders.

2. The sources for the texts are: WB, "The Rafter Hauled," this volume; TV&WB, the next text; TL (Thin Leather), Russell 1908:227–30; S (Juan Smith), Bahr et al. 1994:258–60; and D (Juan Dolores), Saxton and Saxton 1973:169–74.

TV&WB: Apache
TL: Apache
S: Name unstated (no second killing in this version)
D: Apache

Now, if the Apache war stories generally come after the Edenic time of the rafter, do any of them tell events of recent memory, or are they all about a time that we might call "late ancientness"—not as ancient as Eden but ancient in some sense? They are the latter, that is, they are about events to which no Pima of 1927 could trace personal knowledge. In 1927 there were many veterans of Apache wars: first-hand knowledge. Those people also knew of events from their parents and grandparents: second- and third-hand knowledge. Such was the recent past of 1927, the past traceable through known people to the events being told about. For Pimas and most other people without written records—oral society peoples—this past goes back just about a hundred years.[3]

The Pimas had a kind of written record, really a memory aid, in the form of "calendar sticks." These were four- or five-foot-long saguaro cactus ribs with lines cut into them to show years and with sign marks representing important events of each year. No numbers were used. What was shown was a sequence of years from a starting place (such as a meteor shower) to "now." The sticks were sometimes passed from parent to child, but those that are known went back no more than eighty years. (Russell pictured and gave the tellings from some [1908:36–66].)

There are Apache episodes in the calendar sticks, but the events of the stories of this chapter are not among them. If the chapter's stories were broadly known, as the Koolhaa story surely was, then they would be like the rest of the stories of this book: common knowledge, believed to be true, and not traceable to a first teller. This makes them "late ancient," belonging to a period that ended sometime around a hundred years before the "now" of 1927.

We can now see the importance of the orphan boy story. It carries the Pimas' sense of their past for two generations beyond Hohokam times. If the Hohokam ended around A.D. 1450, as most archaeologists think (Haury 1976), then the orphan boy story would date to about 1500, a good three hundred years before the earliest year on an early-twentieth-century calendar stick. That is a long gap!

3. For a discussion of this, see Bahr n.d.*a* on the "floating gap."

The orphan boy story (in some versions) attaches late ancientness to the Hohokam, but the other three stories of this chapter fall entirely into the long, mostly unnarrated "late ancient gap." These stories are about war, but the enemies are all Apaches. There are no Hohokam. The Pimas didn't connect these stories to individuals of 1927. One of the stories, "Eagle Hawk Man," was told by the Papagos, or Tohono O'odham, as well as the Pimas. Another, "An Old Woman's Grandson Rescues His Mother," resembles an Edenic or rafter story of the Yavapais. (The boy hero kills a series of monsters; he is raised by his grandmother because his mother has been captured by enemies; but in this version the hero saves his mother, whereas in the Yavapai version he never sees her again [Gifford 1933:353–64]). The last story, "The Survivors," is very short and melancholy and, one supposes, could be any tribe's story.

One expects to hear about the witch, the flood, and the Hohokam from the Pimas. One does not expect to hear these more secular war stories, which again are not about Apache fights of near-at-hand memory but about older and, one might say, "mythic" or "epic" fights. This collection has more of them than any Pima or Papago collection published before. That is an aspect of the fullness, or completeness, of this collection.

Koolhaa (or, The Orphan Boy)

William Blackwater and Thomas Vanyiko[4]

[Death on the Salt]

WB A Papago[5] lived with his wife and child [a little boy], near the joining of the Salt and the Gila River—

TV The people were living along the Salt River Valley. To the east Sohani Maaka[6] lived alone with his wife and a little boy they had captured from the Apaches—

4. Benedict said that Oliver Wellington also contributed to this text, but his contribution was "very short and is used only when it adds to the others." Only one portion from Wellington is marked in her typescript.—*Ed.*

5. Called Decorated Feathers Medicine Man in Blackwater's short version from the rafter. In both, as well as in two others previously published (Russell 1908:228–30; Saxton and Saxton 1973:169–88), the main character in the story, the orphan, regardless of his father's affiliation (Hohokam or Papago), is a Papago, or Tohono O'odham.—*Ed.*

6. *Ma:kai,* "medicine man, shaman." The name S'óhañi (Herzog n.d.*c*), also written Sohañ (Russell) and Suhañ (Saxton and Saxton), seems to lack a Pima meaning. This is unusual for the names in Pima stories, but this story has several such. A simple explanation would be that the names—really the *characters*—originated in another language and tribe. I can't prove this, however.—*Ed.*

TV&WB They were always in danger from the Apaches. One night the shaman knew the Apaches were coming against them. He called the little boy and said to him, "The Apaches are coming tonight. Take my medicine box and hide in the field. You are small and they will not find you. If I am killed, take my medicine box and go to the village. Perhaps they will take care of you." The boy took the box and hid in the field. Toward morning the Apaches came and they fought all day against the shaman—

TV Toward the middle of the afternoon they killed Sohani Maaka. The Apaches said, "Why did it take so long to kill him? He should have died from his wounds long ago." They cut open his body and over his heart they found a hawk feather. They took it home with them[7]—

[The Orphan Adopted]

TV&WB The boy took the medicine box and went to the village. Two Whirlwinds Shaman took pity on him and adopted him as his own son.

Two Whirlwinds Shaman had a daughter—

WB&OW named Koolhaa[8]—

TV&WB She was about the age of the little boy—

WB whose name was Kakampe—

TV&WB When they were grown, Two Whirlwinds wanted to keep the boy with him because he was a good hunter and a good worker in the fields. He gave his daughter to him and they were married—

WB One day after it had rained for many days, they were out of meat and Kakampe wanted to go hunting. His wife said, "No. It is dangerous. Wait until the rain is over." But her husband insisted—

TV&WB He went hunting into the Apache country and the Apaches overtook him and killed him. They cut up his body and scattered the pieces, and looped his intestines all over the brush. In the evening his wife waited for him—

7. Sohani Maaka is connected especially with power over the wind, associated with the hawk feather. Since the Apaches took the feather back to their own country, this explains the prevailing direction of the wind [—according to Vanyiko. But in Blackwater's words, "The medicine box was taken to Casa Grande, and it is for this reason that the winds blow from the direction of Casa Grande," that is, from Papago country, as stated in Blackwater's short rafter version].

8. Written "Kold Ha'akam" by Russell, "Pu:l Ha'akam" by Saxton and Saxton. The first word lacks a known Pima meaning; the second means "jar-having."—*Ed.*

WB Two Whirlwinds called together the old men. He said, "My son-in-law is missing. He always comes back from hunting before dark, but today he has not returned. I am troubled. Has anyone seen my son-in-law?" They answered, "No, we have not seen him. Perhaps he has killed some large animal and is still busy skinning and packing it home. Let us wait a little." They sat and waited. The father-in-law was troubled and he sang:

"Sorrow fell upon me from above and covered me"—

TV Kakampe's wife said, "Where did he go? He has not come home. Perhaps he is dead." And she sang:

"I see the lights of Apache campfires"—

WB The people began to weep with them, and the father-in-law said, "I know that something is wrong. Go home and eat and come again. We will go to seek him." They went home and ate—

TV [Then they] went out to the mountains, following his tracks. They came to the place where he had been killed. They gathered the pieces of his body where they had been scattered, and his intestines that were looped all over the brush, and they made a pyre and burned them. They dug a hole, and in it they put his ashes and bones. They returned to the camp and brought his wife. She sat in the ashes and wept, singing:

"You, my poor Apache husband,
They have cut you in pieces and scattered your body"—

TV&WB They returned to their village after the burning—

WB In four days the father-in-law called together the old men. He said, "I have called you for a purpose. I think this trouble that has come upon us will continue as long as we live in this valley. Shall we not leave this place and go to the south?" They talked among themselves—

[A New Orphan]

TV They said, "If we stay here, the Apaches will come against us and destroy us, and there will be no end to our trouble. In four days we will leave this country and find another."

On the fourth day they set out for the south. They camped the first night along the Gila Valley near the Little Buttes. Again [Kakampe's] wife mourned him, singing:

"Sadness has come upon us
And sorrow overwhelms us."

They went on the next day and camped, and at this place Two Whirlwinds Shaman stopped with his people [and they settled there], and his daughter bore a child—

WB at Aankap,[9] below Casa Grande—

TV The [rest of the] people continued to the south. They camped at night, and at this place Two Arrow Feathers Shaman stayed with his people. Next day [those who had not yet settled] went on again and they camped at night. At this place Blue Deer Shaman remained with his people. The last of the people went on under Owl Shaman, and at night they camped and remained in that place and lived there—

WB At Aankap Koolhaa's son grew to be a little boy, and he heard the children call their fathers *vaav, maam.* He came to his mother and he said, "What do these boys mean? Who is it that I should call *maam?* Who is it that I should call *vaav?*"[10] His mother took the child in her arms and embraced him and wept—

TV&WB He used to go hunting with the men. One day he went with them, and one of the hunters took the young birds of the thrasher[11] and threw them at him. "Take these to your mother and eat them this evening." He ran with them to his mother and threw them at her feet. She said, "What is this?" "A man stuck them in my belt and said, 'Take these to your mother and you'll have something to eat.'" His mother cried and took him in her arms and said, "My poor boy, these are good for nothing." She told him how his father had been killed and why he had to take the leavings of other people. When the boy heard, he cried and went to his uncle—

TV he went to Buzzard Shaman—

[The New Orphan Rises]

TV&WB who said to him [or, whom he asked], "What is it these Apaches are like? Are they like cholla cactus, covered with thorns? Are they like giant cactus growing each by itself?" "No, they are just

9. *A:ngam,* "willow-place," today's Papago, or Tohono O'odham, village of Anegam.—*Ed.*

10. Each sib has its own name for "father," as was discussed in connection with the rafter story.—*Ed.*

11. *Ko'otovitc* [must be *kul-wicigam,* "curved-bill thrasher"], an inedible species. [As explained by Oliver Wellington,] Koolhaa had many suitors and refused them all. One of these was angry and threw the useless birds down before her son, saying, "Even if your mother will not have me, see, I give you these birds."

like us; they are men." Then he told his uncle what his mother had told him. His uncle said, "Tonight come to the meeting of the old men. I will call the war chief. He gave him a cigarette and said, "Bring this to the meeting and when you have been there a long time, pass it, holding it close to the ground, until it has been all around the circle. When it comes to you again, stick it into the ground."

He went to the meeting. They said, "This is the council of the old men. Children should run home." But his uncle said, "Let us bring in the orphan boy. I think he has something to tell us." He waited till the men had talked. Then he lit his cigarette and passed it (with a low sweeping motion) to the person sitting next to him, and when it had come back to him after going around the whole circle, he stuck it into the ground beside him. He stood and said—

WB ***"I was a poor child.***
With my hands folded upon my stomach I came into your houses.
When you gave me something to eat, I burned my mouth (in my haste).[12]
When you went hunting, I followed behind.
You stuck in my belt the young of the thrasher. I thought it was good to eat and I ran with it to my mother.
She saw it and turned her back to me weeping;
She told me, "It is not good to eat,"
And she turned again and told me of the enemy who had killed my father.
I was cut to the heart. I could not bear it.
I went to men of importance
And they pitied me and appointed days for me.
On the fourth day I went to the land of the Apache.
The first night I lay and slept without fear;
The second night I lay and slept without fear;
And on the next day I came to the country of the Apache.
The Apache land was covered with drunkenness,
The Apache mountains were covered with drunkenness.[13]

12. Only a person so hungry as to disregard all etiquette would eat food before he had allowed it to cool.
13. "The country swam before his eyes as if he were drunk."

And I thought of the words of my mother, how she had told
me that the country of the Apache was full of danger.
I grasped tight my club and my shield.
I came to a stone and I sat upon it.
Around me the land was littered with the fragments of bones,
and with broken arrows.
I went on again and came to a spring in the country of
the Apache.
With the black paint of my face I covered the waters.[14]
Again I came to a spring in the country of the Apache.
With the clipped hair of my head I covered the waters.
Beside the waters stood [my own] skull.
I lifted it and drank my blood,
And I strengthened myself.
When I had drunk I spoke intoxicated words.

I sent out Gray Coyote to spy on the enemy.
He returned, saying, "I have seen the fires of the enemy."
Then were my warriors as wild beasts and as birds of prey,
And they ran against the enemy and killed them without effort.
I heaped around my enemy all that was theirs, and gathered
it into my hand.
I turned myself, and behind me the trees I had brushed were still
in motion,
And the water I had stirred (in drinking) was still in motion,
And the stones I had stumbled over were still rolling.
I returned to my village, and I gathered my warriors beside the
water hole.
I chose a fast runner and sent him ahead to bring the news of
my victory.
When they heard, the sick and the old lost their weakness.
They rose and came together rejoicing."

After he had spoken, the old men sat in silence. He was only a child and he had spoken well. His uncle said, "The speech of the child has made me dumb." They rolled native tobacco and smoked. They talked together whether they should name a war path and take the child

14. In this and the following, to spoil the water.

with them. They appointed the war path and smoked together. The boy spoke again[15] and said:

> ***"The earth is covered with beasts of prey.***
> ***The sun rises, but its light is covered;***
> ***The night comes, but there is no darkness.***
>
> ***I gathered my bones for firewood,[16]***
> ***And with the bright light of my fire the whole earth was painted.***
> ***The mountains were colored with crimson light.***
> ***Of the skin of my head I made sandals;***
> ***And from my intestines a belt, and girded my loins.***
> ***I satisfied my hunger with the excrements of my bowels;***
> ***I took a rib from my body and made of it a fire stick.***
> ***I took it in my hands and set out over the whole earth, over all the hills and forests;***
> ***In the shelter of the trees I traveled,***
> ***Seeking everywhere what I did not find.***
> ***I came to a great plain and I fell prone upon my face and slept there.***
> ***There my brother came to me, face to face.[17]***
> ***I threw out my arms to embrace him,***
> ***But they closed empty on my own breast.***
> ***My face was streaked with my tears***
> ***And my hair was untended (in grief).***
> ***I raised myself and I said,***
> ***'I will go to the east,***
> ***I will seek out Nasia, the shaman.'***
> ***I groped for her through the darkness,***
> ***And I was not sure I had found her.***
> ***I spoke to her and I said, '(Help me,) you who use the bows of the Apache for the frame of your carrying basket;***

15. Vanyiko knew only the first of the two Orphan Boy recitatives.

16. Imagery in which the warrior-visionary gathers strength from his own body parts recurs in the parallel passage in Lloyd 1911:194–95 and in the first of the two Orphan Boy speeches, just given ("drank my blood").—*Ed.*

17. In a different story, from which this speech seems to have been adapted, the hero has a brother who reappears in a vision after having been killed by the Apaches (Lloyd 1911:193–204).—*Ed.*

The arrows of the Apache for the shoulder pad;
The arrow shafts of the Apache for the netting hook;
The bowstring of the Apache for the string of the net;
The hair of the Apache for the cord (to bind the net to the frame of the basket);
The blood of the Apache to paint beautiful patterns upon your carrying basket.'
In these words I spoke to her, and she gave me her powers.

I said, 'I will go to the zenith,
And I will seek out the Downy Nest Shaman.'
I came to him, and I spoke, saying, '(Help me,) you who use the arrows of the Apache for the ribs of your house;
The arrows of the Apache for the withes laid crosswise;
The bowstrings of the Apache for cord to make them fast;
The hair of the Apache for the thatch of your roof.'
He set me in the midst of his house, and he gave me a cigarette.
I blew out the smoke, and it curled in many colors.[18]
He gave me his powers, and I slung them under one arm and went on.

I cried, 'I will go to the south, to Driftwood Shaman,'
And I cried to him for help.
I came to him and I said, '(Help me,) you who make the bow of the Apache as the rainbow,
The arrows of the Apache as the reedy desert grass;
The arrowheads of the Apache as soft downy feathers;
The poison of the Apache as the sacred green scum on standing water.'
In these words I spoke to him, and he gave me his powers;
I slung them under one arm, and I went on.

I said, 'I will return again to Nasia, the shaman,'
And I cried to her for help.
I came to her and I said, '(Help me,) you who flatten the bows of the Apache for headbands;[19]

18. Clouds.
19. Worn by the men, especially in gaming. They were braided of corn husk and colored.

***Who use the arrows of the Apache for the sticks of the* kints**
***game, and the blood of the Apache to paint their markings;*[20]**
Who make of the Apache hair your girdle.'
With these words I spoke to her, and she gave me her powers;
I slung them under one arm, and I returned with strength"—

TV&WB After he had spoken they set four days of preparation for the war path. When the days were finished they started for the country of the Apaches. The orphan boy went ahead with one of the scouts to spy out the country. They came to a group of Apache children. The children saw them and ran back and told their parents. His comrade said to the orphan boy, "What shall we do? The children will tell their fathers and mothers and they will overtake us and kill us. It is a long way back to our camp. The orphan boy said to the other, "Make yourself into a coyote and scratch out our tracks. I will make myself into a crow and fly up onto that great rock and caw at them." He turned himself into a crow and the other turned himself into a coyote and scratched out their tracks.

The Apaches came. They could find nothing but the tracks of a coyote. They said, "Perhaps it was a coyote the children saw, or perhaps they were frightened by that crow sitting on the mountain." They went back to their homes. The two scouts changed themselves back into their own forms and returned to the camp.

They said to the war party, "We are close to the enemy. Let us fall upon them while they are unprepared." They overcame them, and the orphan boy and the scout who was with him killed the first Apaches—
WB They saved alive one of the strong men of the Apaches and bound him. They brought him to the orphan boy and they said, "See, this is what an Apache looks like." He answered, "Now I see," and he seized the war club of the Apache and killed him. He took his knife and cut off his head. He pulled out his intestines and looped them over the brush. He cut his body in small pieces and scattered them over the ground—
TV&WB In the village his mother knew he had overcome the enemy. All the people wondered why she dressed in her finest costume and was happy. She sang[21]—

20. This is another reference to *gi:ns,* the stick-dice game. The sticks are variously marked, sometimes with red paint (Culin 1907:148–51).—*Ed.*

21. These are all victory songs after the taking of the scalp.

WB *"The shaman has a brave heart that can withstand ridicule.*

Though in this spot I may be killed and my body scattered over the ground, it does not matter.

This deed of my son will go down in the memory of men.
Everyone will know of it"—

TV&WB *"The Apaches, the Apaches. They have killed you*
And have strung your intestines over the brush"—

TV *"My poor son. Good fortune came to you,*
And your name spreads over the land.

The Apaches are killed.
I give the cries of victory all alone.[22]

Listen, people; hear the war cries,
It is coming near"[23]—

WB The people began to talk about her, and they said, "She has become a prostitute."[24] But she sang again:

> *"My poor son, you will have good luck and come home bringing the bows and arrows of the enemy and the scalps of the enemy."*

The war party gathered the bows and arrows of the Apaches and took their scalps. They started for their own country. The orphan boy said, "When I give the war whoop, throw the bows and arrows and the scalps of the Apaches into the air."[25] He gave the war cry four times and they threw the bows and arrows and the scalps of the Apaches into the air. It began to rain and they sang:

> *"I am giving the war whoop, and the bows and arrows and scalps of the Apaches are hurled into the air."*

They stopped at night. The ground was green from the rains. They cut the grass and called it Hoed Ground—

TV&WB They came through the Gila Valley and came to Little Buttes. They set up three stones as pot rests (*tci ton*) [*cetto*] and they

22. The whole village is quiet except for her shouts, for she alone knows what has happened.

23. A victorious war party sends a messenger in advance calling out at intervals the names of those who have killed Apaches.

24. Because she is so happy.

25. Rain magic.

put the scalps on them;[26] and ever since, the place has been called Apache Pot Rest—

WB [They sang:]

"I am standing in this land, and out of it grows a feather.
I am standing, giving a war cry"—

TV&WB They came to level ground and stopped there. One of them had a single leg of an Apache and he made marks with it on the rock; and ever since, that place has been called Apache Running Foot—

WB They came near their own village, giving the whoops of victory and singing their own names. They gave the orphan boy his name and sang:

"Paataankap."

All the Apache children that they had captured they gave to [Koolhaa,] the mother of Paataankap.[27] She brought them up in that village. The Apaches set out to avenge themselves upon this village. When they came near they saw that they were outnumbered and fell back—

[Then Sinks]

TV&WB Four times Paataankap went into the Apache country and overcame the enemy. His mother gathered all the scalps he had brought and put them into a large olla. She covered it and took it to the mountains. She left it there and sang:

"In this round windbreak you will stay.
You will not leave it to return to your friends and relatives"—

WB Because of these war paths of Paataankap there are no longer so many Apache in the San Carlos country; and when the Pima go there to hunt, they are not molested—

TV Paataankap made his home in this village with his mother and died there. For this reason it is called Aankap—

WB He came back from his last war party. He was sick and they tried in every way to cure him. He went over all the mountains seeking strength, but he could not get strength from the mountains. He returned to his home and died there. The shamans met together and

26. While they camped for the night.
27. *Paat,* "bad, ugly"; Aankap, name of village. [Generally heard and interpreted as Paḍ A:ngam, "Bad Willow-place." See Bahr et al. 1994:235, 322n1.]

they said, "It is because he killed so many enemies. We must have a ceremony to take away the danger when one has killed an enemy." They instituted the purification ceremony, and that is why when a man has taken a scalp we hold a sixteen-day ceremony to purify him.

Eagle Hawk Man[28]

Thomas Vanyiko and William Blackwater

[The Hawk Meeting / Vanyiko]

In the Land of the Macaws (near Fort McDowell) a young man made himself a running course around Red Mountain. He ran there for three mornings. On the fourth morning he heard a great wind behind him. It passed through his body in the form of an eagle and left him for dead. When he came to himself, he ran on again. He heard the noise behind him again. It passed through his body in the form of a hawk and left him for dead. When he came to himself Eagle and Hawk were before him. They set him on his feet, and Eagle gave him the stone of the medicine man (square flint knife) and Hawk gave him a flint hawk fetish. They said to him, "Keep these always and take good care of them." He took them to his home and made a bag for them. He always wore it wherever he went.

[The Hawk Meeting / Blackwater]

In the Land of Macaws (near Fort McDowell) a man lived with his two sons. Every morning and evening they practiced running. One night the younger son had a dream. He was to make a running course around the mountain (Red Mountain) and run there every morning for four days. "If anything happens there, it will be important for you, but perhaps nothing will happen." He made the course and ran there the first day, but nothing happened. He ran there the

28. This is a well-known song cycle, with the narrative strung loosely on the songs. The story [connects] sets of songs that are used for war, for the cactus-wine drinking, etc. [In a version told by the Papago, or Tohono O'odham, narrator Juan Dolores (Saxton and Saxton 1973:189–209), the hero is a war orphan called Hawk Meeter whose early life parallels that of Paataankap in the previous story. Blackwater and Vanyiko omit those matters but tell a fuller version of the adult years. In both versions the hero cruelly sits out a battle in which a rival, Decorated Headdress, is killed—though this event is much clearer in the Dolores version than in the ones Benedict took down. In any case, Eagle Hawk Man the cruelest hero I know of in all of Native American literature. Overall, the Dolores version gives fewer songs than Blackwater and Vanyiko's, but some of them are the same as in the present version—and Dolores gives the native language text.]

second day, but nothing happened. He ran there the third day, but nothing happened. He ran there the fourth day and he heard a loud noise behind him. He did not look behind. He was hit from behind and knocked down so that he died; when he came to himself, he was holding a flint thunder stone in one hand, and in the other, a flint hawk fetish.[29] He put the stones in his medicine bag and he sang:

"I ran, and a bird passed through me.
It is Eagle Hawk."

[The Isolation / Vanyiko]

The people saw that he had something valuable, and they built him a house of cactus ribs, and they set the doors to the west and to the south, to the east and to the north. He stayed in his house and practiced the powers he had received. He sang:

"My house of cactus ribs,
From the western door Eagle comes out and flies back and forth.

My house of cactus ribs,
From the western door Hawk comes out and flies back and forth."[30]

[The Isolation / Blackwater]

He took the form of a great game bird and lived with the large birds. He came seldom to his own people and then sometimes as a child, sometimes as a young man, and sometimes as a hawk. The people did not know what he looked like. One day someone saw him on a steep cliff painting his shield. He ran to the village, and they all ran out to see Hawk Man. Song:

"Why do the people come running to see me?
I have lived in their village a long time.
Why do the people come running to see me?"

That was the first time the people saw Hawk Man.

29. It is tabu to look behind. The flint thunder stone is the chipped knife, about six inches long and almost as wide, that figures in sacred paraphernalia.

30. The medicine man himself took these forms.

[Against Painted Headdress / Vanyiko][31]

The people made war against the Apaches, and Hawk Man heard of it. He sang:

"My first expedition against the enemy.
I must go over all the stiff-feathered earth;
I must go over all the downy-feathered earth."[32]

He sang again:

"Word (of this expedition) has swept on to the Apaches.
Their women and children wept."

When the people had already set forth, Hawk Man overtook them while wearing a headdress of raven feathers. They sang:

"From a great distance you brought these feathers and came to us."

The war party was about to separate, and both [divisions] went to Hawk Man and begged him to come with them. He sang:

"You asked me to go in both directions, and my heart is still.[33]
With black eagle feathers you asked me to go in both directions;
With black hawk feathers you asked me to go in both directions."

They contended which party he should go with. He sang:

"The people have lost their heads about me.
They saw my wing-end claws and they have lost their heads about me."

The two parties went on and he lingered behind. They fought, and the Apaches outnumbered the Pimas and drove them back. Decorated Headdress[34] was their leader, and he retreated with them. The people said, "We should send word back to Hawk Man that the Apaches have defeated us." They chose a messenger and sent him to Hawk Man with the message, "The Apaches are driving us back, and Decorated Headdress with us." Hawk Man sang:

"Decorated Headdress, you say you are brave.
When you come near the lodgings of your enemies, you cry like a woman, you cry like a child."

31. [The songs included in this section were] sung especially at the purification ceremonies after taking a scalp.

32. The stiff feathers of the earth are of course the trees, [and] the downy feathers the clouds that hang across the mountains. These were more than figures of speech to the narrator: "The trees *are* the feathers of the earth; the mists on the mountains *are* downy feathers."

33. "As a brave man I do not jump to a decision or get excited. I wait."

34. Undoubtedly O'oi Wonamin, "Painted (or Striped) Headdress." In the Juan Dolores version the decorations were stripes of blood, one for each of the enemies the man had killed (Saxton and Saxton 1973:200).—*Ed.*

Then Hawk Man went against the enemy and drove them back and the people followed. They overcame the Apaches.

Again Hawk Man lingered behind, and the Apaches cut him off from his people. They said, "Now he will be killed." Hawk Man stood in the center of his enemies, and he sang:

"In this land of Tcu Kakoltk,[35]
With my song I take the shape of a yellow snake."

He took the shape of a yellow snake and passed through his enemies. He became a hawk and rose into the air, descending upon the Apaches and killing them in every direction.

The people returned home victorious. As they were on the way they saw dust rising in a canyon. They were afraid and went to Hawk Man. He sang:

"Red beasts act drunk,
Going hither and thither."

[With His Brother / Blackwater]

The people went to war against the Apaches. Hawk Man took his tiny shield and club, and his brother saw them and laughed. He said, "Why do you carry these? They are too light to be of any use." Hawk Man said, "Let me alone. I will try them. I will stand here while you shoot at me, and after that I will hit you with my little club." "No, that would be murder. I would kill you." They argued, but Hawk Man insisted, and his brother shot at him. Every arrow glanced off his tiny shield and none of them did any hurt. Then Hawk Man came up to his brother with his tiny club and knocked him on the head so that he fell down dead.

The people were ready to start against the enemy, and Hawk Man said, "Go on, I will stay with him till he recovers and bring him along." When his brother came to himself he carried him after the rest.[36] His brother never laughed at Hawk Man after this, and all the people knew what powers he had.

That evening the war party sang for power against the enemy. One of the warriors wore a headdress of white feathers. The whirlwind came and lifted the headdress in the air. All the people cried, "How shall we get the war bonnet back again?" Hawk Man said, "I will get it back." He changed himself into a hawk and rose in the air, bringing down the white feathers. This was the second time the people had seen him take the shape of a hawk.

35. Could be Cew Gakoḍk, "Long Crooked (or Bent)," presumably a mountain.—*Ed.*
36. The songs that accompany these incidents were not recorded.

Again the people went against the Apaches, and the Apaches outnumbered them and chased them. The old men were weak and fell to the rear and they said, "We have heard so much of this Hawk Man. Can he do nothing to save us?" Hawk Man held his hands above his head and a gourd rattle fell at his feet. He picked it up and used it to accompany his song. He held the Apaches spellbound, so that they were not able to come forward another step.

There was a leader of that war party who wore the feather headdress of a warrior who had killed an Apache. Hawk Man sang a song against him:

"You are not a warrior who has killed an Apache.
You cry like a woman, you cry like a child."

That leader's father was killed on the war party, and his son threw down his headdress and never tried to avenge his father at all.

As they were going to make war, on the march they heard a noise at night. They were frightened and cried out for Hawk Man. He sang:

"There is nothing to be afraid of.
You have acted like children."

[The Wine Drinking / Vanyiko]

His (ceremonial) father (in the scalp-purification ceremony) made cactus wine and called all the people together to drink. They made him sit down at a place (*va'aki*) of the principal men. He sang:

"You seated me with much talk (ritual formality),
You spread hangings like the wind for me to sit upon.
You spread clouds around me."[37]

His father gave him a cup to drink from. He sang:

"One cupful he gave to me.
It made me drunk and I talked much."[38]

He gave him a second cup, and he sang (same, but substitute "two"). He gave him a third cup, and he sang (same, but substitute "three"). He gave him a fourth cup, and he sang:

37. The ceremonial names for the paraphernalia of the cactus-wine ceremony symbolize rain that will follow the ceremony.

38. This song and the following one starting "I am not drunk" must be the sources of the song lines in Benedict's passage on Dionysian drunkenness that I quoted in this book's introduction. If so, then she changed the songs more than she should have from this version to the Dionysian passage—for example, by deleting the line "I am not drunk." Still, one can see this entire sequence here as about a drunk man fighting off stupor, an image that in the introduction I attributed to Benedict, not to the Pimas. It would be a masked sentiment in this text, however. On the surface, the text is about a man too tough to get drunk.—*Ed.*

"Four cupfuls he gave me.
I am about to lie down overcome."

A medicine man [the ceremonial father] said, "I will give you my power." He breathed into his mouth. Hawk Man sang:

"I am not drunk. I am not drunk.
You breathed red wine into me.
I will never be drunk."[39]

And he sang:

"I drank with the quail and with drunkenness.
He painted my face with his black paint.
I drank with the nighthawk and with drunkenness.
He painted my face with his white paint."[40]

And he sang:

"Drunkenness overcame me.
When I came to myself, I saw first the new moon.
When the moon darkens in the zenith (May),
My blossoms begin to come out.
When the (new) moon rises before sunrise (July),
My fruit ripens.[41]

The wine works within me.
The foam works within me.
A hole appears in the foam and it clarifies."[42]

[The Wine Drinking / Blackwater]

Blue Medicine Man made the wine ceremony at Casa Grande and invited Hawk Man. Everybody watched for his coming. Whoever came, they said,

39. Nevertheless, the narrator insisted that the power the old man had given him [Hawk Man] was not the power to resist being overcome by drink, but the power of bravery in battle. Power to be a good runner, a good gambler, was also given in this way.

40. The black face paint is symbolic of the warrior going out on the warpath; the white, of the warrior after having killed an Apache.

41. I give the explanation as the narrator gave it. In explaining the first line he said, "When the sun sets with the moon still in the zenith, and the sky around the moon darkens," but he was aware that the seasons are not told by any position of the moon.

42. This is the figure for the sense of vision that follows the haze of a certain stage of wine drinking. [That's true to Benedict's definition of Dionysianism, and it is a valid reading of this song, which is probably the source of her phrase, quoted in the introduction, "[the Dionysian] mingling of clouded vision and insight."]

"Perhaps it is he," but he did not come till late in the evening. The people crowded about him so that he could scarcely move. He sang:

"The people of this pueblo have heard of me.
They are anxious to see and hear me.
The people of this pueblo have heard of me."

Blue Medicine Man made him sit down on the seat of the principal men. When they passed the cup they brought it to him, but he refused.[43] He sang:

"From the house of Blue Medicine Man the drink comes.
It comes round the circle and is passed to me."

At last he drank. The first singer had started his songs, and when it was the turn of Hawk Man he sang the songs of the wine drinking.

Blue Medicine Man said, "I will give him my power. Open your mouth." Hawk Man laughed because he thought he had more power than Blue Medicine Man, and he sang:

"Red wine was breathed into me,
But it cannot make me drunk."

When the wine had been passed to all the principal men and the singers, they brought it out for the people to take to their homes to drink. The men took Hawk Man to all the houses where they were drinking, and in every house they offered him wine. The people watched to see if he was strong.[44] Sometimes it seemed as if he was about to be overcome by the drink, but he sang:

"I am Eagle and I am Hawk.
I can never be overcome by drink.
I travel over the valleys and over the mountains and I never fall."

[The End / Vanyiko]

Hawk Man traveled over all the earth. He was known everywhere. He sang:

"I go west. You hear the thunder of the eagle.
I go east. You hear the thunder of the hawk.
I go everywhere.
Everywhere I hear my name.

I am Eagle Man. I go over all the earth.
I am Hawk Man. I go over all the mountains."

43. To show that he was not too eager.
44. One of the recognized tests of the strong man.

The people turned against Hawk Man. They said, "He thinks himself a great man. When he kills an enemy, he does it all by himself. Why doesn't he share with us?"

Hawk Man sang:

"The people say that I kill my enemy all alone.
I do it with my bow and with my arrows of wild reed."

The people took up their bows and arrows to shoot Hawk Man. He took the form of a hawk and escaped from them. He covered himself with the mirage. He sang:

"With the mirage I covered myself.
Their arrows passed through it (harmlessly)."

He went to the country of the large birds and lived with the eagles and the hawks. He seldom came to the country of his own people. He sang:

"I go with the birds,
With all kinds of birds."

The large birds welcomed him to their country. They said, "He is a bird like ourselves," and Hawk Man sang:

"Morning is coming and in it all kinds of birds gather.
In it my name is spoken."

His own people did not even know what he looked like anymore. Some said, "He is nothing but a woman, and has the form of a child (small, with hair that has grown only to his shoulders)." He sang:

"They call me a woman.
They call me a child.
I am more than that.
When I see fires at the edge of the world,[45] *I go there.*
When I see fires on the tops of the mountains, I go there.

I do not want to marry.
I am afraid of women."

His people still tried to kill Hawk Man, but he said, "They will not kill me. I will die anyway." He grew weaker and weaker. For four years he was sick. He sang:

45. Fires of the distant enemy, that is, the Apache.

"I am growing thinner and thinner.
I will not live long.
My life is a narrow strip."

He called his brother and gave him his medicine man's fetishes and his power to become an eagle and a hawk. He died and his brother took his power.

His brother led an expedition into the Apache country. They were outnumbered and the Apaches pursued them. The old men were behind. A song [from the brother]:

"The old men are crying for help.
Hawk Man will come to their rescue."

Hawk Man's brother lifted up his hand and received a gourd rattle from the sun. He sang and accompanied himself with the rattle:

"The Hawk Man has made the enemy retreat."

He kept the power of Hawk Man.

[The End / Blackwater]

The people turned against Hawk Man. He always chose a small party to go with him against the Apaches (about ten men). The people said, "Why does he keep it secret? Let him tell us all and we will all go with him." Hawk Man was sad when he saw that the people had turned against him. He knew what the people said against him. He sang:

"The people are talking against me.
They call me a woman and a child."

The people tried to kill him and he defended himself. He sang:

"My shield, my pretty shield, is scratched with arrow points,
And my club, my pretty club, is stained with blood."

He went to live with the great birds. He seldom came to his own people. He had never married so he had nothing to stay at home for. He lived with the game birds.

His people still tried to kill him. At last he went to his father and said, "Tell the people not to try to kill me any longer. If they wait I will die soon anyway." His father went to the council of the old men and told them, "Do not try to kill him. He will die soon anyway." Song:

"You say I do things for my own glory,
And therefore you seek to kill me.
But I do things for your good."

For four years Hawk Man was sick. He grew thinner and thinner. Above Casa Grande at Kwahatatk[46] they had a cactus-wine ceremony and he went there. He sang:

"My soul is passing.
I will die soon."

He died there, and as he was about to die he called his brother and gave him his medicine man's thunder stone and his hawk fetish. He died and his brother had his power.

His brother came to the next wine ceremony at Kwahatatk, bringing his power, but he was overcome by the drink. He fell down and broke the hawk fetish.

An Old Woman's Grandson Rescues His Mother

Clara Ahiel

An old woman lived with one grandson. His father had been killed by the Apaches and his skin made into a seed bag; they had captured his mother and burned her with torches. His grandmother did not tell her grandson (so that he would not be made sad). She said to him, "Never go far from home; it is very dangerous. Over there lives a *nai'uabik*[47] who will swallow you." The boy remembered what his grandmother had said and when she had gone out for seeds he went out. There were two trees with red berries that belonged to the *nai'uabik,* and the boy ate one of their berries and the *nai'uabik* came and swallowed him. He took out a bottle and broke it. With the edge of the glass he cut the monster's stomach. He cut all its organs and at last he came to its heart and the monster died. He came out of its stomach and went home to his grandmother. "I killed the *nai'uabik.*" "That is impossible. Nobody can kill Nai'uabik. Nobody can go near him." "Yes, I killed him." He took his grandmother to the place where the monster lay, and sure enough, it was dead.

46. Perhaps Kuhadk, a village on today's Papago, or Tohono O'odham, Reservation.—*Ed.*

47. No doubt the aquatic monster whose name is usually spelled *ñe:big.* See Bahr et al. 1994:244, 323n7, on this creature in Pima mythology. The present episode, new to the written record, is about the same as one attributed to the man-god Elder Brother by the Papagos of Quitovac, Sonora, Mexico. For those people, the killing of such a monster is the founding event of a ceremony called the *wi:gita.* In the present story, no ceremony results from the killing. The Pimas had their version of the *wi:gita* ceremony, however. There are notes by Benedict on it under "Notes on the Navitcu" in chapter 5 of this volume; there is a speech about the Navitcu, an important character in the ceremony, in the same chapter; and there is a story about this character in the Navitcu section of the rafter.—*Ed.*

In the morning his grandmother said to him. "Do not go away from home. It is very dangerous. Over there lives a very tall man who whips children." His grandmother went out to gather seeds and the boy took food and went where the tall man lived. He took food with him and a club. The giant came out of his house and the little boy whirled his club around his head and killed the giant. He went home to his grandmother. "I killed the giant." "That is impossible. Nobody can kill the giant." "Yes, I killed him." He took her to the place where he lay, and sure enough, the giant was dead.

Next morning his grandmother said, "Don't go away from home. It is very dangerous." She went out to gather seeds. Bluebird came to the house. "Let's go to the ruin and get nuts." Bluebird was lazy and didn't gather nuts, but he ate the nuts the boy gathered. The boy saw this and bluebird laughed. He went again and stole nuts from the boy's pile. The boy was angry. He took a stick and threw it at the bird so that it broke both his legs. "Now I'm dying. Use your power to cure me." The boy rubbed dirt from his neck and rubbed it on Bluebird's legs. They knit together and were straight as before. Bluebird was glad and he said, "I will tell you something. Long ago the Apaches killed your father and made a seed bag out of his skin. They tortured your mother and took her captive."

The boy cried bitterly and went home and lay down on his bed. His grandmother came in. "What is the matter?" "Someone told me something that makes me very sad." "Yes, that is why I never told you." "I know now. The Apaches killed my father and tortured my mother and took her captive. She is still alive. Make food for me; I will go against the Apaches." His grandmother wept. "It is dangerous. The Apaches will take you too and kill you." "Make food for me. I will go."

He went a four days' journey. At last he climbed a mountain in the Apache country and sat down on the top to take his bearings. Down below there was an Apache village and there he saw his mother. He changed himself into a snake and went down the mountain. He came to two old Apache men. He knocked them down and shook their bones out of their skins. He put on the skin of one of them and went into the Apache village. The Apaches said, "Why is that old man so happy? What is he dancing about?" He kept on till he came to his mother. She had just filled her carrying basket with seeds and she knelt down to lift it on her back. She said, "What is the matter that I can't lift my carrying basket?" She got up and looked and there was her son holding it [from] behind. They fell on each other's neck and wept. "Oh, my poor son, the

Apaches will take you and kill you." "You cannot send me away. I will change myself into a dove and you will carry me in your carrying basket." He turned himself into a dove and sat in her carrying basket.

She took him home to her (Apache) children, and she said to them, "You must be very careful of the little dove so that he will grow up to be your pet." But her children were rough with the little bird and threw it against the wall. Her husband said, "This is not the season for young doves. Perhaps it is dangerous (*mainshakatoñ*)."[48] He called a medicine man and he said, "Yes, something will happen."

The Apaches came together from all the villages and they formed a great circle and put the bird in the midst. The medicine man took it to twist its neck, but it flew out of his hands and turned into a great eagle and flew down and killed all the Apaches. Only his mother was left alive. He took the seed bag that had been made from the skin of his father and put it in the stream. It spoke to him and said, "It is no use. My body was cut in pieces with a hatchet. You will have to leave me as I am." The boy threw himself and his mother into the stream and they were drowned.

The Survivors

William Blackwater

There was a famine and all the people had to eat was *giak* (a desert root).[49] While they were out gathering it, the Apaches came and killed them all. Only one boy was left, and he mourned all the time, crying in the shelter of the bushes. He was afraid the Apaches would come again. He tried to go hunting. The Apaches had killed all the birds, too. There was only one quail left. The boy and the quail lived together. One day the quail was gone a long time and the boy set out to find her. He lost his way and died. Now the quail was all alone.

48. Word of undetermined origin. The part from the "sh" forward seems suspiciously like the way a Pima would pronounce the Spanish-origin word "Sacaton," the name of the Agency headquarters—"ṣa ka ton," with accent on the "ton." Normal Pima puts its accent on the first syllable of a word, not the last; and the normal way to say "dangerous" is *sta-e:bidam*. Benedict glossed the word she wrote down as "manitou," the Algonquian term for "sacred, spiritlike."—*Ed.*

49. Russell (1908:74) and Rea (1997:289–90) have *kiak,* a kind of amaranth whose seeds are used.—*Ed.*

4

COYOTE TALES

Introduction

Donald Bahr

When Pimas volunteer today to tell a traditional story, either among themselves or to outsiders, this is the kind of story they are likely to tell: "The Coyote and the Quail" (present here as "Coyote Eats His Own Bowels"), "Why Dogs Sniff Each Other's Behinds" (not here), and a few others. These are short, funny, usually cruel stories, but the cruelty doesn't matter because the victim is Coyote, who always comes back for more. The present large collection, mostly from Blackwater, should please Pimas because it contains stories no longer current; and it is good for the record because these stories are missing from most other collections.

Coyote is a trickster and survivor, and so it is appropriate that these stories are the last kind we come to and that they may be the last to die—or, let us say, they are the only kind that can't die. But in reading them, please keep in mind that a mythology or telling of ancientness with nothing but this kind of story would not be much of a mythology. These stories are like the fun house at the fair. The rest of the mythology is the rest of the fair—the rides, races, stock show, implement displays, games, and food booths.

Coyote Marries the Hunter's Wives

William Blackwater

A hunter had four wives who were all beautiful, and Coyote desired them. He took a deer's head[1] and put it under a rock ledge in a deep canyon. He went

1. One of those prepared as a hunter's headdress.

to the hunter and said, "I have seen a deer in this canyon. I want you to kill it for me." The hunter prepared himself and they went together to the canyon. They did not see the deer. "Perhaps it has gone onto that rock ledge right down below." Coyote crawled to the edge of the cliff. "Perhaps it is way under the ledge." The hunter hung way over to look and Coyote gave him a push. He fell to the bottom and was killed. Coyote climbed down and changed clothes with the hunter.

He got to the hunter's house after dark. His wives had set out food for the evening meal and they gave Coyote the hunter's spoon. Coyote sat down to eat. He didn't know how to use the spoon, but when they were looking he pretended to be using it, and when they looked away he lapped the beans with his tongue. One of them saw him and she said, "That is not our husband," and she warned the other wives so that they thought, "Perhaps this man is not our husband."

They went to bed,[2] and Coyote lay with two girls on either side of him. He was tired, and he went to sleep and slept heavily. His wives got up and took rolls of deer hide and put them in their places. They took water in their ollas, and pinole, and went out to follow their husband's tracks in the moonlight. Coyote was hot with the rolls of skin on each side of him. "Move over, you're too hot." They did not stir. He pushed hard and discovered that the rolls were empty.

His wives followed their husband's tracks to the edge of the cliff. They could not find traces any farther. They leaned over the edge and down below they saw their husband's body.

Song (one of the rain songs):

"Hi e lu[3]
White Coyote made a blue deer and set it under the edge of the cliff.
Hi e lu
And put blue mist upon it (to deceive) our husband;
Mourning we have come here.
Hi e lu

2. In another version [I haven't seen it] the elder wife says to Coyote at bedtime, "You never sleep in the house with us. You sleep in the outhouse." Coyote begs to sleep with them, but in vain, and as soon as he has gone they set out to follow their husband's trail.

3. A phrase like this is usually connected to "Corn songs." Such songs are often included in stories on the origin of corn such as those told by Blackwater in chapter 2. (There Blackwater mentions songs but doesn't sing any.) See Bahr et al. 1994:305–7 (a long endnote, numbered 6) on the types of these songs and their signature phrases.—*Ed.*

And put brown mist upon it (to deceive) our husband;
Mourning we have come here.
Hi e lu
White Coyote made a blue deer and set it under the edge of the cliff.
Hi e lu."

In the morning Coyote got up and followed them. He came to the cliff and saw that their tracks led straight on, and he knew they were not coming home. He followed them, and they saw him far behind.[4] Song:

"You black Coyote, you threw our husband over the cliff.
You gray-eyed Coyote, you threw our husband over the cliff."

They flew up as birds, and when he got to that spot he could not find where their tracks went. He ran round in a circle trying to pick up their tracks; he ran in larger and larger circles, but still he could not find them. He ran back to the spot where he had lost them and began again. He heard someone laugh, but he could see no one. He looked in every direction. He looked up in the air and saw his wives. "Take me up where you are." "I don't think we can." "Oh yes." They took off their belts and threw them to him. He tied them together and fastened them around his waist. "Don't talk till we get you up." They pulled him up. Coyote looked at them. "When I get where you are I'll put my arms around you," he said. The wives dropped him, and he fell to the ground. "Pull me up again." "No." He took his bow and arrow and shot at them, and he hit one in the leg. They all flew up into the sky and became the Pleiades.

Coyote took the leg to a shaman and said, "Make me a woman out of this leg."[5] The shaman took it and made a woman. "Now I have done what you asked me to do. Don't touch her for eight days."

They started home. They made camp the first night and lay down with the brush between them. Coyote could not sleep. "Where I lie, there are ants. Let me sleep on your side." "No, you must not." "Yes, I can't sleep here." Coyote came over and lay down beside her. As soon as he touched her she was nothing but the leg again. He took it up and went back to the shaman. He was crying. "Make it a woman again." "No, I made it for you once and you did not do as I told you to." He took it up and threw it away. Coyote went home crying.

4. In the other version, he comes in sight as they are eating their morning meal. They call on Spider to take them up, and when Coyote gets to the place where he had seen them, he stops first to eat up everything they had left behind. (Laughter.) He hears his wives laughing at his greed.

5. This whole incident is omitted in the other version.

Red Racer Snake and Coyote

William Blackwater

Coyote and Red Racer Snake went hunting. They said to each other, "Where do you live?" Snake said, "I live nearby but we have never met before. In four days come to visit me and bring your friends. We will have a talk."

In four days Coyote called his friends and said, "Let us go to visit Red Racer."

Red Racer invited them into his house. "Here you are. I am sorry I have nothing to eat. We will talk, and you will have to eat when you go back to your own homes." While they were talking, Red Racer was making a bow. He said to his wife, "Build a big fire." When it had burned down he said to her, "Spread out the ashes. I do not want to send my visitors away hungry." He got up and laid the bow in the ashes. He lay down beside it and said to his wife, "Rake the ashes over me." Pretty soon he got up and came out holding his bow. He sat talking for a long time, then he said to his wife, "Don't forget what is in your fire." She uncovered the fire and there was squash, hot melons, green corn. Red Racer took these and gave them to his guests. They ate and ate. At last even Coyote said, "We had better be going home. Come and visit me in four days and bring your friends."

After four days Red Racer said, "Let us go to Coyote and have more talk."

Coyote invited them into his house. "Here you are. I am sorry I have nothing to eat. We will talk, and you will have to eat when you go back to your own homes." "All right." Coyote made arrows, and he said to his wife, "Make a big fire." When it had burned down, he said, "Spread out the ashes." He put an arrow in the ashes and lay down beside it. He said to his wife, "Cover me over with the hot ashes." His friends waited and waited, but Coyote did not come out.

Red Racer said to Coyote's wife, "Don't forget what's in your fire." They called him four times but there was no answer. They found him burned to death, and his friends went back to their homes hungry. His wife took Coyote's body into the house and shut the door. She stood facing the east and sang. He came to life and laughed. "Why are you laughing? You killed yourself and I brought you back to life." "No, I had company, and I have just woken up."

Turtle and Coyote

William Stevens

Turtle wanted meat, and he went out and sat on the trail of the deer. Pretty soon the deer came and they saw something white on the path. They heard something singing:

"Lots of deer, lots of deer,
Slender legs and yellow eyes and funny-looking faces." (laughter)

One of the deer stopped. "What is that? One of you go and smash it." A deer went and tried to step on Turtle's head. Turtle drew in his head, and the deer's hoof slipped on Turtle's shell. His leg broke and he died. The other deer saw that he had fallen. "What is the matter. Why does he want to lie down by that ugly creature?" They heard again:

"Lots of deer, lots of deer,
Slender legs and yellow eyes and funny-looking faces."

"That other deer lies down and does nothing. Some of you go and smash it." A second deer went up and tried to step on Turtle, but his hoof slipped on the shell and he broke his leg and died. When the other deer saw that the second deer lay down beside the ugly animal, they circled closer around Turtle and saw the two deer lying there dead. They ran off, and Turtle got out his carrying net and took the two deer home.

Turtle dressed his venison and set it to cook. Coyote smelled it and he came to Turtle's house. "Where did you get it?" Turtle said, "When I want venison I go out to the trail of the deer and lie in the middle of the path. When they step on me they fall down and die." He gave Coyote meat to eat, and Coyote said, "In four days come to visit me."

Coyote went to his home. He said to his wife, "Mend my carrying net for me," and he took it out and lay down on the trail of the deer. He sang:

"Lots of deer, lots of deer,
Slender legs and yellow eyes and funny-looking faces."

Sure enough the deer came. "One of you go and smash it." One of the deer went to where Coyote was lying and stepped on him and killed him. All the deer came up and trampled him into the dirt.

In four days Turtle went to Coyote's [house]. He found Coyote's wife. "Where is the old man?" "He took his carrying net and went out to get deer."

Turtle laughed. "I'm going back home." Coyote's wife went out to look for Coyote Man and she found him trampled into the earth. She put Coyote in the carrying net and brought him home and called the neighbors. They laughed at what had happened, and they burned his body.

Coyote and Frog

Clara Ahiel

Little Frog was sitting under the cottonwood leaves. Coyote came by. Little Frog sang:

"Big tail, sharp ears, little mouth.
Homely-looking thing."

Coyote was angry and he tried to find where the song came from. He couldn't find anybody at all. He went on a little way and there he heard the song again:

"Big tail, sharp ears, little mouth.
Homely-looking thing."

Coyote came back and looked everywhere again, but he couldn't find anything. He went on again. He had gone a little way when he heard it again:

"Big tail, sharp ears, little mouth.
Homely-looking thing."

He took a stick and turned everything over. At last he saw Frog. "Was it you who was singing that song?" Frog didn't say a word. "I'll tell you what I'm going to do. I'm going to chew you up." "If you do, my brother will come and kill you." "I don't believe you at all. I've eaten frogs before and nothing happened." "My brother will kill you." "Who is your brother?" "Water is my brother." "No, I don't believe you at all." Coyote jumped on Little Frog and ate him right down.

Coyote went on his way. His path got muddy and he laughed. Pretty soon he had to climb up to the branches of a cottonwood. The water kept rising. Coyote cried and climbed higher up in the cottonwood tree. At last he was at the very top of the tree and the water began to go down. Storks came with food in their baskets and they said to Coyote, "Friend, come down and share our food with us." "No, the water is too deep." "No, we are standing on the ground." Coyote jumped down and was drowned.

Deer Planter

William Stevens

Long ago a man wondered what he knew (what he could do that would be of benefit to him). He gathered deer droppings and planted them in his field. He fenced it and made a gate. On the fourth day he saw little deer beginning to come up from the ground. In another four days the field was full of little fawns. In another four days they had grown as large as young deer when they leave their mother, and in four days more they were full-grown does and male deer.

"Now I have really done something. After this I'll never have to work hard; I'll always have plenty of meat. Now I will kill the first one." He killed it and put it in the pot. As it was cooking, up came Coyote. "Hu! Here comes Coyote again."

Coyote smelled the venison and he was very happy. "Well, you are here. I'll invite myself." He sat down and ate. When he had eaten he said, "Where did you get the deer? I will get some, too, and in four days you will come to my house to eat."

The man told him that he had planted deer dung in his field and in four days deer had grown from the seed he had planted. "Now I don't have to go hunting and I can have venison whenever I want it." Coyote said, "How can it be? I thought nothing grew except from grain and grass seeds." "No, deer grow, too." "I will go home now. Whenever you kill another, I will come over to help you eat it."

Coyote went home. He said to his wife, "Help me to build up a fence." They made a fence and he gathered deer droppings and planted them. Next day he went to look. There was not a sign of little deer. He went back next day. "That man must have told me a lie. Maybe he went hunting and told me this story to make fun of me." The third day he went again. There was nothing at all. He took a digging stick and dug, but even the dung was gone. He said to himself, "That man must have known what I'd do and he came and dug up the dung and planted it in his own field. They're growing over there." Again he went the fourth day (saying), "Perhaps I ought to have waited till the fourth day." There were little deer coming up all over his field. He ran to his wife. "My little plants came up. My little plants came up. Pretty soon we'll have plenty of meat."

When the deer were full-grown he said to his wife, "Gather plenty of wood. I'm going to kill one of our deer." The old woman gathered plenty of wood, and he brought the deer. He said, "I'm going to invite my friend." He went to his house and invited him. [Later] they ate together [at Coyote's house]. Coyote said to him, "Don't go home yet. Don't go home yet. We'll have another before you go." By this time the deer were well grown and wild and harder to catch. Some of them jumped over the fence. He called his wife, "Come and help! Come and help! The deer are getting away." His friend had already gone home.

His wife came out and she caught hold of the deer Coyote was chasing. He ran after the others but they had all got away. "There's one deer left." The deer was dragging the old woman in every direction around and around. "Hold on! Hold on! I'll be there." But just as he got there, the old woman's hold gave way, and the deer escaped. Coyote ran, but he could not get it. He chased it for days and days. "Someday I'll get you. You have that rope around your neck."

At last he sat down under a tree. "I'm hungry and thirsty. I can't go any farther. I'll go home." He was half dead and all scratched from the brush. The end of his tail and the tops of his ears had been torn off.

When he got near home, his wife saw him coming. She picked up her things and ran; she was afraid of the scarecrow. She did not know him at all. He wanted something to eat and he missed his wife. He followed her and when the old woman saw him on the trail she was more frightened than ever. "He's coming after me." Coyote called to her, "Wait, I am your husband." "No. My husband was a good-looking man." Coyote called to the neighbors and said, "I am the one who planted deer. They escaped and I chased them and I am all torn by the brush." They believed him, and his wife went home with him.

She said, "What shall I do to make your hair grow again?" She gathered gum and tried to stick hair on his back. His friend heard (what had happened), and he killed one of his deer and gave the skin to Coyote. He drew it over his body and stuck it on with its blood. Coyote said to his wife, "Come, we will try again. We'll build a better fence." They built the fence and planted the dung, but nothing grew.

Lion and Coyote Rope Horses

William Blackwater

Coyote could not kill anything. He hunted and hunted. He was thin and starving. He met Lion. Mountain Lion said, "You look thin. Can't you get anything to eat? Come with me and I will give you plenty to eat." "All right. I'll go with you."

They went together. Mountain Lion took a rope and made a noose. He laid it on the trail that horses took. He took the other end of the rope and hid himself in the brush. Horses came by and one of them caught his foot in the noose. Mountain Lion held the rope and threw him. When he had killed him he said to Coyote, "Eat this horse. I will go on now, but by the time you have eaten this horse, I will be back again."

While Coyote was eating the horse, another coyote came by. (The first) Coyote said to him, "You look thin. Can't you find food?" "No." "Come with me. You'll have plenty to eat." He took him to the trail the horses followed. He made a noose just like Mountain Lion's and laid it on the trail. He took the other end of the rope and hid in the brush. The horses came by, and one of them caught his foot in the noose. Coyote tried to kill him but the horse kicked and ran. Coyote was caught in the rope and was dragged along behind. His friend followed. First he found Coyote's right leg, then he found his left leg, his right arm, his left arm. At last he found his body. He reached the horse and there was only Coyote's head on the end of the rope.

Coyote Is Pursued by Lion

William Blackwater

The turkeys were holding a rain ceremony, and they sang:

"Our feathers bring the clouds and it will rain." (repeat)

They danced around a pole. Coyote came by. "Let me sing too." They gave him a turkey feather to put in his hair. They gave him a place in the line just where the pole would fall. They sang and sang, and at last the tree fell, right on Coyote's tail. He was pinned down. They laughed and laughed, and they went home.

It was raining,[6] and Coyote was crying all alone in the pouring rain. Lion came by. "What is the matter?" "The turkeys' pole fell on my tail." "What will you give me if I set you free?" "I will give you my ears." "I've got ears." "I'll give you my tail." "I've got a tail." "What can I give you?" "Something I haven't got myself." "All right. Help me to get free, and I'll find something you haven't got."

6. Because they had just had the rain ceremony.

Lion freed him. "Just let me run on ahead and I'll get the present." He ran on. He left a chip[7] on the path and he told it, "When Lion calls me, answer him." The chip answered Lion. At last Lion got impatient, and he came along the trail and found the chip. He set out in pursuit of Coyote.

Coyote had run as fast as he could and had come to an old man. "Hide me in your knee. Lion is after me." "All right."

Lion came. "Have you seen Coyote?" "My knee has been so sore I haven't seen anything." "Let me see your knee." Lion pressed the swelling on the old man's knee, and out jumped Coyote. He ran as fast as he could, and he came to an old woman. "Hide me in your cheek. Lion is after me." "All right."

Lion came. "Have you seen Coyote?" "I have had such a toothache, I haven't seen anything." "Let me see your tooth." Lion pressed the swelling, and out jumped Coyote. He ran as fast as he could, and he came to Badger. "Help me. Lion is after me." "All right. I'll help you somehow."

Lion came. "Have you seen Coyote?" "Yes, he's right here. What do you want with him?" "I want to give him something." "Come in if you want him." Lion came in. Badger discharged his odor and killed him.

Badger and Coyote skinned Lion and made a quiver out of his skin. Badger said to Coyote, "Take the quiver and go straight home. On the way, even if you see a ripe saguaro, do not eat it. Don't eat anything till you get to your home."

Coyote set out. He came to the first giant cactus and did not eat it. He came to the second and did not eat it. He came to a grove of mesquite trees. He was very hungry. He said to himself, "They look so good. They are ripe and sweet. I guess I'll eat a little." He hung his quiver of arrows on the bush and climbed up. He began to eat the mesquite. The beans cracked and made a little noise. Then he heard a little louder noise. There was his quiver come alive again. Poor Coyote!

Coyote and the Turkeys

William Blackwater

The turkeys went out to cut pine trees. They took their axes and set to work. Coyote came by. He said, "Give me an ax and I'll help you."

"No. When the trees fall, you would get caught under them. You are not quick enough."

7. Translated, "a small piece of wood," but whether the double meaning exists only in English I do not know.

"Yes, I am quick." He jumped about one way and then another to show how quick he was. They gave him an ax. He took it and cut down a pine tree. Sure enough, the tree fell on Coyote's tail. He was caught under the branches. He broke off the smaller branches, but he could not get his tail free. At last a turkey came by.

"Come and help me lift this branch so that I can get free." Turkey helped him. Coyote said, "Now, go along to my house and tell my wife to cook and eat you. Tell her to leave your head for me to eat when I come home tonight."

"All right." Turkey went. He got to Coyote's house. His wife was there. Turkey said to her, "I met Coyote. He told me to tell you to boil his bows and arrows and his shoes and have them ready for him to eat when he gets home tonight." Coyote's wife gathered together his bows and arrows and his shoes and boiled them. Turkey went off.

That evening Coyote came home. He said, "Where is the turkey's head?" He was hungry.

Coyote's wife said, "Here is your evening meal. Turkey told me to boil your bows and arrows and your shoes." Coyote was angry. He said, "I'll get even with Turkey." He set off to find him. He followed his tracks to a well. They stopped there. He looked down into the water, and there was Turkey. He dived in. The well was deep. He came out. He took a stone under each arm and dived to the bottom. He walked along the stones under the water but he could not find Turkey. He came up. He was exhausted. Turkey laughed. Coyote looked up. There was Turkey sitting on a dead branch that hung over the well.

Coyote went to call the beavers. He said to them, "Gnaw through that branch." When they were halfway through, Coyote said, "That's enough." He thought he could break down the branch when they had gnawed that much. The beavers went home. Coyote tried and tried to break down the branch, but he could not. He went back again to the beavers. "Come and help me again."

"No. You said it was enough. We won't come to help you again."

So Turkey was saved.

Coyote and Buzzard

William Blackwater

Coyote and Buzzard were friends. Coyote went to Buzzard's house and boasted of his travels. "There is no creature living that I haven't seen. I've been over the tops of mountains and all through the deserts in every direction." "Yes,"

Buzzard said, "but I've seen all those, and I've seen more, too. No person living has seen so much as I have. Up above the sky there is another world, and nothing down here is so beautiful as that is." They were always talking.

They went out together and killed their enemies. Buzzard killed one and Coyote killed the next. They said, "Now we must choose our ceremonial fathers for the purification ceremony." Coyote chose and said, "I will take White Whirlwind." Buzzard chose and said, "I will take Red Whirlwind."

After four days they were purified. Buzzard said, "Our fathers have been working for us, and we have done nothing for them. We must go out and kill deer." They went out together, and Buzzard caused it to be very hot so that Coyote and the deer were overcome and Buzzard got a deer for his ceremonial father.

Then Coyote said, "I must get something for my ceremonial father," and he caused it to be very cold so that Buzzard and the deer were overcome and Coyote got a deer for his ceremonial father.

Buzzard and Coyote lived together and every evening Buzzard would leave and be gone all night. "Where do you go all the time?" Coyote said. "You leave me all alone, I have nobody to talk to." "I told you before. I go to the world above. I have Earth Flower,[8] and it makes me restless so that I can't help traveling." "Take me along with you. I want to have Earth Flower." "No, I don't think you could stand it. I have to be gone a long time to get Earth Flower." "Yes, I can stand it. I go all over the desert and I am not worn out." "Maybe. Get on my back, but don't open your eyes."

Coyote got on Buzzard's back and held tight, and they came to the country of the sky. There was the mountain (where Earth Flower grew) and Buzzard said, "Go up the mountain now. I cannot go up with you. Do not look around; keep your eyes straight ahead."

Coyote started, but before he got very far he looked around. As soon as his eyes were no longer straight ahead, he began to wander all over the mountain back and forth. He cried out for Buzzard but there was no answer. Coyote was terrified. He ran about wildly, and in his fright he jumped right off the mountain of the sky. He fell and fell, days and days and months and months, maybe it was years. When he got to earth his bones were already picked white and dry.

Buzzard lived alone. One night at the meeting of the old men a hunter said, "I went a long long way from here, and I came on human bones. They were white and dry and had been there a long time. Who is it who has been missed?" They counted over everyone but no one was missing.

8. A lichen. If carried in the pocket it gives irresistible wanderlust. [It is also said to be an aphrodisiac.]

Next night they talked of it again, and Buzzard said, "I will tell you what I think. A man lived with me once and one night I took him with me to the sky, and I lost him there." Next night Buzzard stayed at home and began his songs. He sang till morning, but Coyote did not come to life. Next night he sang again. The third night at midnight he heard a howl. Toward morning he heard it again. Again toward dawn he heard the same howl, and just as the sun was peeping over the horizon, up came Coyote (laughter). He came back and lived with Buzzard again.

Coyote was always going out in the evening and staying till morning. Buzzard said, "Where do you go? You leave me all alone, I have nobody to talk to." "Yes. You know you took me to the sky and I got Earth Flower. Now I am restless and I can't help traveling all the time." "Let me see Earth Flower." "No, I can't take it out (of the medicine bag)." "Yes, I want to see if it is just like mine." "No, I can't show it to anyone."

They wrestled, and Buzzard got the bag and opened it. There was nothing in it at all.

Coyote and Buzzard (and the Apaches)

Oliver Wellington

Old Woman Tcukovaki (quail)[9] lived with her two granddaughters (son's daughters), and Old Woman Kwahaduk (long-legged ant)[10] lived with her two granddaughters. They went out to gather wild wheat (*ââk*),[11] and the Apaches came and took them prisoners. They killed all the party of quails that were with them except one man. He came home crying. All the old men were together in council and they said, "Someone is coming crying. Perhaps it is one of the quails. What is the matter?" "All the quails have been killed, and Tcukovaki's grandchildren and Kwahaduk's grandchildren have been taken captive. Who will carry the news?"

Roadrunner said, "I will carry the news." He went to Old Woman Tcukovaki and he said, "Your grandchildren have been taken by the Apaches, and all the people that were with them were killed." Tcukovaki cried for her grandchildren:

9. The old woman's name, Tcukovaki, is not the word for "quail" (*kakaicu*).—*Ed.*

10. *Kuadagi,* "harvester ant."—*Ed.*

11. Probably *o:ki,* "unidentified plant" (Saxton and Saxton 1969:172), which is probably the same as what Rea (1997:384) wrote as *awkivik,* "unidentified taxon."—*Ed.*

"Son's daughters, son's daughters.
Vanum, Nâânât (names of girls)."

Roadrunner went to Old Woman Kwahaduk and he said, "Your grandchildren have been taken captive by the Apaches, and all the people who were with them were killed." Kwahaduk wept for her children:

"Poor me, poor me.
I have long legs and one intestine that coils up inside me.
Poor me, poor me."

Tcukovaki said, "If anyone goes against the Apaches and rescues my granddaughters, he shall marry them."

Coyote heard and he said, "I will go. I will rescue the quail girls." He set out, but the Apaches saw him and killed him and he never came back.

Buzzard said, "I will go. I will rescue the girls." He went up to the birds' country, and from there he saw the quail girls gathering wild wheat seeds for the Apaches. He flew down to them and spread his wings. He said to the older girl, "Sit on my back and I will take you to your home." He said to the younger girl, "I will come back for you. Tell the Apaches that your sister was lost gathering wild wheat seeds."

He brought the older sister to Old Woman Tcukovaki and he said, "Younger Daughter is left behind. I must go back and get her."

The Apaches kept close guard over Younger Sister after her sister was lost; they would not let her out of their sight. They let her go only after water. One day as she was going out to get water she looked up and saw Buzzard. He flew down. She set her olla down just where she was and got on Buzzard's back. He took her back to her home. He said to her grandmother, "Now I will marry the quail girls. We must have a big dance so that I can marry them." Old Woman Tcukovaki had a big dance and Buzzard married the quail girls.[12]

Coyote and the Crows

William Blackwater

The crows did not like the color of their feathers. They took out their feathers and threw them into hot water. Then they bathed in cold water and stayed there all day. [They sang:]

12. After the narrator had finished the tale he added, "Coyote tried to rescue the second girl, too. After Buzzard had brought home the first girl, Coyote's friend (that is, another coyote; the first had been killed) set out to rescue the girl who was still held by the Apaches. He ran into the Apaches who were trying to track the first girl who had disappeared, and he was killed."

"We are making our feathers all colors." (repeat)

New little feathers came out all over them and they were coal black. They were very beautiful.

Coyote came by. "How pretty you look! What did you do to get that color? Let me be that color, too." "We pulled out all our feathers and put them in boiling water. Then we bathed in cold water and stayed in all day." Coyote took off his skin; there was nothing left but raw flesh. "Get into the cold water." Coyote went in. "Now you must sing." They taught him:

"We are making our feathers all colors." (repeat)

Coyote sang, and he stayed there all day. In the evening no feathers came out. The crows laughed and laughed, and they flew away.

Coyote came out of the water. He was cold and almost dead. He got as far as a hollow tree. Roadrunner came by. "That's a funny-looking coyote over there." Coyote said, "Yes, I wanted to look like the crows with their new feathers. They pulled out their feathers and bathed in cold water all day, and by night they had beautiful black feathers. I guess I won't live any longer. I'll die right here. There is only one hope; if you could go to Lightning and ask him for fire, I could warm myself."

Roadrunner went to Lightning. Lightning gave him one coal. He brought it back, but it went out before they had lit the tinder. "Go again."

Roadrunner went again, but Lightning was angry that he had wasted his first gift, and he tried to kill him. Roadrunner dodged and got back to Coyote. "Lightning is angry and will not give me another." Coyote died there in the hollow tree.

Bluebird and Coyote

William Blackwater

In the beginning Bluebird was dirty gray. He came to a pool of water. It was a beautiful blue. "If I dive into the water, perhaps my feathers will turn blue like the water." He dived in. He came out. His feathers were gray as before. He thought to himself, "If I pull out all my feathers and dive in, perhaps when they come in again they will be blue like the blue pool." He pulled out all his feathers and dived in. He sang:

"Blue waters, blue waters, I dive in and turn blue."

He came out. He was still gray. Four times he dived into the pool and sang his song. When he came out the fourth time he was as blue as the blue water.

Coyote came by. He said, "What are you singing?" "I wasn't singing anything." "Yes, I heard you." "What did you hear?" "I heard, 'Blue waters, blue waters,' but I couldn't hear the rest." "If you heard that, I'll sing it all for you. I didn't like my gray feathers, and I thought that if I dived into the pool they would come in blue. So I sang:

'Blue waters, blue waters, I dive in and turn blue.'"

Coyote said, "Help me to turn blue, too."

Now, at that time Coyote was very beautiful; he had heavy soft fur. Bluebird and Coyote set to work and pulled out all his hair. Bluebird taught him the song and told him to dive four times.

"Blue waters, blue waters, I dive in and turn blue."

When he came out the fourth time his hair was as blue as the blue pool. Bluebird said, "It is time to go home. Remember this: don't sing the song again for four years."

Coyote promised. He set off for his home. He was humming as he went along. At first he left out some of the words. He liked that song, and he sang more and more of it till he sang the whole song through with all the words. He stumbled in a prairie dog's burrow at the top of a hill and rolled over and over to the foot. When he picked himself up, his hair was coarse and scraggly. He was a dirty sandy color. He looked just as coyotes do now.

Coyote Eats His Own Bowels

Clara Ahiel

There was no rain, and the quails went up to the mountains to find a place to drink. [They sang:]

"We are dying of thirst.
We must find water."

They found a drinking place. Coyote had been there, too, and he had drunk and was lying fast asleep. They pulled out his bowels and filled him up with stones. They piled the guts in the baskets that they had on their heads and set off. They came to a place where trees grew and they camped in the shade and roasted Coyote's guts.

Coyote woke up. He started to run, and the stones rattled. He turned round and round and round, but he could not see where the noise came from. He came to where the quails were cooking. "I smell something very good." He ran up. "Where did you get that nice fat?" "An eagle came by and killed a calf, and he gave us the guts. Come and eat with us." Coyote was very happy. "How good this is." He ate and ate.

When he could not eat any more he said, "I'm through. I must go on now." When he had gone a little way the quails began calling, "Coyote was eating his own bowels."

Coyote heard them calling. "What?" "Nothing. Somebody was calling behind those hills."

Again they called, "Coyote was eating his own bowels." "What?" "Nothing. Somebody was shouting."

A third time they called, "Coyote was eating his own bowels." "What?"

They called a fourth time, "Coyote was eating his own bowels." Coyote heard, and he came running. "I will kill you all." He set fire to the bushes, and all the quails flew into the air.

They made a quail of cholla cactus, covered it with quail feathers, and put it with them in their hole. Coyote came running. He came to the first quail.

"I am not the one."

He came to the second.

"I am not the one."

He came to the third.

"I am not the one."

He came to the fourth.

"I am not the one."

Finally he came to the last one of all, and it did not answer when he spoke to it. Coyote fell on it and tore it to pieces and ate it. It was cholla cactus and Coyote died.

The Mesquite Tree

William Blackwater

In the village there was a beautiful girl who would have nothing to do with men. They came from all the villages to ask her to marry them but she would not. At last a young man from the east made up his mind that he would win the girl who refused all her suitors. He went to her village and paid court to her, but she would have nothing to do with him. She sent him away.

He said to her, "Before I go, let me stay one night with you." "No. Why should you stay a night with me?" He asked four times, and at last she said, "Very well. But do not bother me."

The young man made a full-sized doll and he slept with the doll. In the morning he left and went to his home. The girl buried the doll and it became a mesquite tree; it grew till it was a large tree. The people heard of this tree and they came to see it. It began to blossom, and at last the beans came on the tree. All the people were forbidden to touch the tree.

At last Coyote came to see the tree and fell on the beans and ate them all. He was so full he couldn't move. When the people came, they saw Coyote lying there and they whipped him. He vomited and scattered the mesquite beans all over the ground. That's why the mesquites grow in every direction.

War of the Coyotes against the Sun

Thomas Vanyiko

There were coyotes. It rained and was cold and they could not hunt. They were starving to death and they could only stay in their homes. At last it stopped raining. They took counsel and said, "We are going to kill the sun. It is his fault that we have been cold and hungry." They all got ready to go to war with the sun.

They went to the east till they came to the high mountain the sun comes up behind. They camped at the foot and said, "In the morning when the sun rises, we will climb up and kill it." As soon as it began to grow light, they started up the mountain. At dawn they got to the top. There was the sun way, way off in the sky. They couldn't reach it at all.

Next morning they tried again, but it was just the same. Again the next morning they climbed the mountain, but it was no different. At last, the fourth morning, the sun was tired of seeing the coyotes, and he threw down his spears and bruised them black and blue, and sent out his heat and singed them. So that is why Coyote's face looks black and singed.

5

ORATORY

Introduction

Donald Bahr

With the end of the previous chapter we exhaust the kinds of stories about ancientness that an expert Pima would know. Blackwater was the most prominent teller in each chapter except the first, so we can say that the book represents his expertise, supplemented mightily by Vanyiko's and somewhat by that of Ahiel, Stevens, Wellington, and Kisto. We don't know whether Blackwater told every story he knew, or how many of those the others knew—no doubt some of them, and some he didn't give.

The whole is not fixed, even for one person. One will know some stories well and others poorly. If stories are not exercised by being told, they weaken just as muscles do. A person may not know exactly how many stories he or she knows—few people would count them. There is an order to them, however, an organizing line running through them, a "rafter," the main telling of ancientness. This was the telling that people traditionally tried to hear over several of the longest nights of the winter.

The previous chapters show how short the whole of the rafter was. There are texts that come after it and others that could have been in but were left out from the rafter that Vanyiko and Blackwater constructed for Benedict. Vanyiko took the lead in that, which is why there is so much of Blackwater in the next chapter. And there are the war and Coyote chapters, moving and amusing, respectively, but not part of the rafter.

Our present concern is, What do orations add to prose stories? The answer is that they add certainty; they are the memorized words of the ancients. Four such speeches are given in the earlier chapters, two in the rafter and two in the war story of Koolhaa. More could have been included, because their connection to events and characters in the prose stories is clear. Instead, the others are placed in this chapter because Benedict kept them separate from those stories, because sometimes the connection to a particular story is tenuous, and because seven of the speeches have no known connection to any story in the previous chapters. The sequence of speeches in this chapter follows that gradation, and the footnotes describe the connections or the lack thereof.

This gradation of connections is further evidence of the openness of the Pima-told past. Oratory brings their home-told prose stories out of doors. The orations were delivered in loud voice at ceremonies for war, rainmaking (or just the onset of the summer rainy season), harvests, intervillage dance presentations, and for what Benedict called "thanksgiving" (probably the same events as the dance presentations). One can say that all these events needed public speaking: to focus the participants, to pray with (because gods and spirits were involved), and to celebrate with. Thus the oratory had a life and goals of its own. It was not wholly bound to the prose-based telling of ancientness, nor was the latter terribly needful of oratory. *Sometimes* the two converged.

All of the orations, being memorized, came from ancientness, that is, from original speakers whose precise connection to present individuals was unknown. Thus, what the gradation means is that some of these orated ancient speakers have firm places in the prose tellings and others totally lack them: anonymous gods, gods awaiting stories. One can't say which is the tail and which is the dog, the oratory or the prose. Both were centers of gravity. Between them were the plain people. Thus, when both literatures were strong, the children were awakened each morning by a grandparent saying something like an oration, as my friend Lloyd Paul of the Salt River Pimas recalled:

Eḍa añ uḍali, *ha-we:m ki: g ñ-kekel* *ñ-ba:b c ñ-hu'ul, ñ-tatal,*	*When I was a child,* *living with my old-timers,* *my grandfather and my* *grandmother, my uncle,*
mat am o i ma:si c am o wa:m g *ñ-hu'ul, ab o cei mans am o* *wamik am o i'icud g kakawiyu,*	*when it would dawn and my* *grandmother got up, she would* *say for me to get up and water* *the horses,*

hekaj matṣ hab-a ta:tam hegam kakawiyu mac a:cim a ta:tam, mat hekid am o tonam wo i: g ṣu:dagi, hab-a ta:tam hegam kakawiyu c am gegoki.	*because the horses feel like we feel, [when] they're thirsty [they'll want to] drink water, so feel the horses as they stand [in the dawn].*
"Wamgiñ, wamgiñ, wamgiñ" bo cei—nt abṣ am i s-ap iñ-ce'ehe.	*"Get up, get up, get up," she says, as I cover myself better.*
Hegai ep, mat am b o ñ-a:gas, e:p, matp o ha'icu ñ-ab uliñkad, kunts g we:m ki:kam o bei, c ab a'al ab o ñ-amjeḍ im wuwha, k wuḍ ep wo ñ-cikpankad e:p, hegai.	*This too, she'd declaim to me, too, that I'll have good luck, I'll get a wife, and there'll be children from me, and that will be my work, too, that-one.*
Am a woho, mant hekid am i hema bei g we:m ki:kam, am s-mai mo o ki am a woho hab kaij g ñ-hu'ul,	*It's true, I did get a wife, then I knew it was true what my grandmother had said,*
mo wuḍ ñ-cikpan hegai mat g a'al o ho-gegos—ha'icu a ga:gid i eḍa, hekihu hi eḍa mo g kuagi o gagda, c am a hekaj ki:dag.	*that it is my job that the children get fed—look for something around here, back then it was firewood [to sell], and with that to get a living.*
O idañ am gawul cu'ig ahawa i:dañ, mo ha'icu e'eṣa, mañ nakogahim c am ha-ge'eda g ñ-a'alga.	*Or then [when it was my turn] it was a little different, to plant something [be a commercial farmer], so I did it and raised my children.*
Kutp i:dañ has am o wuad, am i ge'eda e:pai mat—pi heḍai atp hab o a'aga mo ob ñ-a:ga c am i s-hotam ñ-wa:maigid.	*And now they do somehow [to live], of course they [children] grow up, too, and—no one tells them as I was told so I would get up in a hurry.*
Ñe:, añ hema ṣoiga, k hab s-koiyato kawiyu.	*Look, [as a boy] I had a horse, a buckskin horse.*
Pi ṣa'i taccu g wijina, ep g piliñ. Ñt abṣ an o dahiwa k am o—hasko ha'ap añ taccu mant am o him—mat o hi:.	*It didn't need a rope, or a bridle. I just sit on it and—whatever side I want to go, I go—and he goes.*

Nt am o i nagya am ha'ap, s-o:mko e:p, o o'ogig hegai, am o im ha'ap o hi:, hegai kawiyu.	*I'll just hang off on that side, right side, or the left side of him, and that's the way he'll go, that horse.*
Pi ṣa'i taccu g pilñ. Am on i ṣa:mud hegam kakawiu, matp hebai o i meḍ g ṣu:dagi, gam hu i ha-ṣa:muñ k am o i'ic.	*It didn't need a bridle. I would drive the horses, [to] wherever the [irrigation] water had run, drive them there and water them.*
Mo i huḍ, atp uḍ ep ñ-cikpan, a huḍ hab ep o ñ-ju:, e:p, no pi wuḍ a cikpan hegai. B o ñ-a:g g ñ-hu'ul maṣ wuḍ a cikpan hegai.	*It [the sun] would set, it was also my work, it would set and I'd do it again, also, because it's a job. My grandmother told me it's a job.*
Ñ am b o ñ-wua c am a ha-ñu:kud g kakawiyu. Eḍa heki hu ṣ mu'i g ṣoṣoiga, t am a woho hab e-wua, c hab o gegikwa g ki:jig, mat hema am o nako k am o i'ic.	*I did that and took care of the horses. Then at that time there were many horses, and it was true, they would stand at the gate, then someone would manage to make them drink.*

Those are Paul's memories of his grandmother's wake-up calls seventy years ago.[1] The idea of finding a woman and getting children is key to the mythology; the practical emphasis on feeding them (likewise the horses) belongs to the oratory. Thus, note how many of the speeches in this section tell thrilling adventures through most of their length, and then end with something like:

I gathered my harvest and stored it.
And my young boys shall eat of it and have good health,
And my young girls shall eat of it and have good health,
And my old men shall eat of it and prolong their days,
And my old women shall eat of it and prolong their days.

This, from the very first speech that follows, is Dionysus at home.

1. My thanks to him for giving some Pima-language text to this book.

SPEECHES TIED BY CHARACTER OR EVENT TO THE NARRATIVES OF ANCIENT TIMES

Rain Ceremony [Mockingbird Speech][2]

William Blackwater or Thomas Vanyiko

[Making Firm the Earth]

In the beginning earth had no firmness.

In the west Black Mockingbird Shaman heard me and answered
my cry.
He covered the earth with his flying;
Upon each tree, upon each mountain he rested.
He finished his work;
He said to the earth, "Remain fixed," but it would not.
Black Mockingbird Shaman, you failed.
But you left with us your black winds, black clouds.
When we ask, you will give us what we desire.
In the south Blue Mockingbird Shaman heard me and answered
my cry.
He covered the earth with his flying;
Upon each tree, upon each mountain he rested.
He finished his work;
He said to the earth, "Remain fixed," but it would not.
Blue Mockingbird Shaman, you failed.
But you left us your blue winds, blue clouds.
When we ask, you will give us what we desire.
In the east White Mockingbird Shaman heard me and answered
my cry.
He covered the earth with his flying;
Upon each tree, upon each mountain he rested.
He finished his work;
He said to the earth, "Remain fixed," but it would not.

2. "A speech of Elder Brother." [The typescript doesn't say who spoke this text, Blackwater or Vanyiko. It refers to a passage in the rafter that Benedict attributed to both narrators. On scene were both Earth Doctor and Elder Brother.]

White Mockingbird Shaman, you failed.
But you left us your white winds, white clouds.
When we ask, you will give us what we desire.
In the north Yellow Mockingbird Shaman heard me and answered my cry.
He covered the earth with his flying;
Upon each tree, upon each mountain he rested.
He finished his work;
He said to the earth, "Remain fixed," but it would not.
Yellow Mockingbird Shaman, you failed.
But you left us your yellow winds, yellow clouds.
When we ask, you will give us what we desire.

Up above the Shaman of the Downy Nest[3] *heard me and answered my cry.*
He smoothed the earth and the hills
And overturned the mountains and the trees.
He finished his work, and the earth stood firm.

Down below Gray Spider Shaman heard me and answered my cry.
He bound the trees together as fagots are bound.
He encircled firmly the edges of the world.
He spun in the west the black carpet
And set upon it the black palace,[4]
And the earth stood firm.

He spun in the south the blue carpet
And set upon it the blue palace,
And the earth stood firm.

He spun to the east the white carpet
And set upon it the white palace,
And the earth stood firm.

3. This is the bird *kootavitc,* "thrasher."

4. A rim of trees is imagined growing around the world edges; therefore it is the whole world Spider binds as a fagot. The carpet, or "hanging," is an old native textile, symbol for clouds, which are here pictured as carpets of the sky. "Palace" translates *va'aki,* the stone [or adobe] cities of the ancient people; here and in the next several lines these "palaces" are figures for clouds, and also have ceremonial reference.

He spun in the north the yellow carpet
And set upon it the yellow palace,
And the earth stood firm.

[Spreading the Heavens]

In the west Black Measuring Worm Shaman heard me
and answered my cry.
He touched the earth four times in his coming.
He broke into four segments and stood up the four crotched posts
(of my dwelling).
In the south Blue Measuring Worm Shaman heard me and answered
my cry.
He touched the earth four times in his coming.
He broke into two segments and stood up the horizontal beams
(of my dwelling).

In the east White Measuring Worm Shaman heard me and answered
my cry.
He touched the earth four times in his coming.
He broke into ten segments and stood up the straight cross poles
(of my roof).

In the north Yellow Measuring Worm Shaman heard me and
answered my cry.
He touched the earth four times in his coming.
He broke into many small fragments and stood up the outer ribs
(of the house dome).

Down below Yellow Gopher heard me and answered my cry.
He brought brush and covered the framework of my dwelling.
He made four gopher mounds about my dwelling, to the west,
to the south, to the east, to the north.
And he brought the fine earth of the gopher mound and packed
it upon the framework of my dwelling.
He finished his work.
And with my power I blew the smoke from my cigarette;
It rose and formed white clouds over the dome,
And rain came from the clouds and sprinkled the land.

[Reaping the Harvest]

In the land I planted seeds,
And they grew big stalks, broad leaves, beautiful flowers, perfect seeds.
I gathered my harvest and stored it.
And my young boys shall eat of it and have good health,
And my young girls shall eat of it and have good health,
And my old men shall eat of it and prolong their days,
And my old women shall eat of it and prolong their days.

Navitcu[5]

Probably spoken by William Blackwater

Hear now the words that make the stalk of the heart to blossom
and our steps to reel.

For I made him from a stick of driftwood;
With the breath of the sun I gave him life.
With the beauty of the dawn I painted his face.[6]
And with the last shadows of the darkness I marked lines upon it.
From the wing feathers of the great birds I made his headdress,
and the butterflies lit, fanning their wings among the feathers.
From the rainbow I made his bow, and from the Milky Way his arrow.
I gave him gray fog as a mantle upon his shoulders, and strong
wind as a girdle about his waist.

Notes on the Navitcu

Ruth Benedict, from statements by William Blackwater

In the fall a round [circular] house or windbreak was built for a harvest ceremony (which is still held among the Papago [the *wi:gita*]). The people model

5. See the Navitcu section of chapter 1 for this character in the context of the telling of ancient times. The story at that point was by Blackwater, who was also Benedict's source for the notes following this text. Thus, this speech was probably from him.—*Ed.*

6. As with red clay, before the pattern is applied [to a pot?]. [According to Russell (1908:108, 266), the decorated wooden Navitcu mask was worn by a medicine man in the treatment of disease; Navitcu medicine men also claimed the power to bring rain. On the origin of the mask, see the Navitcu section of chapter 1.]

clay fruit, grain, ears of corn, melons, whatever is scarce at the time, and in the morning they bring these to the ceremonial house.

The singing begins in the evening. The Navitcu, perhaps sixteen of them, go about from house to house acting as clowns and begging for something to eat. They sing all night in the round house, with the imitation fruit piled in heaps about them. Each village sits by itself and sings different songs as its turn comes. They may be rain songs, for instance.

In the morning they all come out of the round house carrying the modeled fruit, corn, etc. They do not sing then.

It is the business of the Navitcu to see that everybody has something to eat. Each family eats together.

[Written later by hand: There was] cactus liquor drinking.

The Mountain Goat: A Rain Recitative

Thomas Vanyiko

In the beginning the winds lived and the clouds lived,
And all the creatures of the earth learned to walk upon the earth and to give their cries,
And human beings learned to work and to know their dreams.

Then trouble came upon the earth, and everything was taken from the people.
They came to the medicine man to ask the cause of their trouble.

And the medicine man took his medicine bag[7] and laid it before him.
He took a necklace of white shell beads and he stretched it along the back of the bag.
He took the outside tail feathers of the eagle and he laid horns at the head of the bag.
He took the middle tail feathers of the eagle and laid a tail for his grandson.
He took bits of iron[8] from his bag and laid hoofs for his grandson.
He took sleigh bells[9] from his medicine bag and laid eyes for his grandson.

7. Throughout, the medicine bag is given its ritualistic name, "grandson."

8. Meteoric iron is commonly found in medicine bags, it is said.

9. Sleigh bells, *kakpapol* [*kaksipul*], are necessary accoutrements for the Pima as they are for the Yaqui. [They are brass jingles, worn by the ceremonial clown dancers called *pako'ola*.]

He took downy feathers from his medicine bag and made hair for
his grandson.
He took his sacred square flint knife from his medicine bag and
made a heart for his grandson.
He took downy feathers from his medicine bag and made lungs
for his grandson.

He set his grandson down facing the west, and black lightning
came from his body.
He sat him down facing the south, and blue lightning came from
his body.
He sat him down facing the east, and white lightning came from
his body.
He sat him down facing the north, and red lightning came from
his body.
And his grandson lived, and was a mountain goat.

He shook himself and from him rose the fog,[10]
He shook himself and from him rose the clouds,
He shook himself and from him fell the rain.
He jumped from peak to peak of the mountains and into the
great water to the west.
There he made his home.
Whoever asks, it is he who brings the rain to answer him.[11]

The Mountain Goat

William Blackwater

In the beginning when the earth was made,
The winds across it were alive, and the clouds above it.
But man forgot his dreams,
The creatures of the earth forgot their manner of walking and
their cries,

10. The speaker explained that it was the dust rising from his shaggy coat that formed the fog and the clouds.

11. Later, reviewing Benedict's rendition, Vanyiko told Herzog that the last three lines, "He jumped . . . to answer him," were an explanation, not part of the speech itself. The version he gave to Herzog ends with the same six lines Benedict obtained from Blackwater: "I put my seed . . . old women may eat of it and lengthen their days" (Herzog n.d.*b*).—*Ed.*

The birds forgot their flying and their song,
And trouble came upon the earth.

They came to the medicine man and cried for help.
He called his medicine bag[12] *and of him made a mountain goat for his people.*
Of the downy feathers of the macaw he made his hair,
Of the outer tail feathers of the eagle he made his horns,
And with the wind he twisted them.
Of the middle tail feathers of the eagle he made his tail.
Of the sacred square flint knife he made his nose.
Of sleigh bells he made his eyes.
Of pieces of iron he made his hoofs.
Of his sacred crystal he made his heart.
Of a string of blue beads he made his intestines.
Of a string of white beads he made his fat.

I took it and turned its head to the west;
It breathed, and from its nostrils came forth red lightning.
I turned its head to the south, and from its nostrils came forth blue lightning.
I turned its head to the east, and from its nostrils came forth white lightning.
I turned its head to the north, and from its nostrils came forth red lightning.
It breathed and formed white clouds, and rain came and sprinkled the earth.
I put my seed in the earth,
And the plants grew, big stalks, broad leaves, pretty flowers, healthy plants, perfect seed,
That my young boys may eat of it and have good health,
That my young girls may eat of it and have good health,
That my old men may eat of it and lengthen their days,
That my old women may eat of it and lengthen their days.

12. As in [Vanyiko's] version, this is called "grandson" throughout.

Notes on Rain Speeches and Rainmaking

Ruth Benedict, from statements by Thomas Vanyiko and William Blackwater

In drought any man will go to a medicine man (*maaka*) [*ma:kai*] and ask for a ceremony. The medicine man goes to a man who knows the Mountain Goat speech (or other rain recitatives) and the people gather for a night ceremony. About the middle of the night the speaker will recite the rain recitative, and afterward they will sing some rain songs. There is no preliminary fast for any of those who take part, and no altar is set up. The ceremony may be repeated the following night.

"If a mountain goat is killed, for four days there will be rain or cold weather. To bring either of these one can take a mountain goat horn and throw it up into the air."

Rain or War speeches can be used for curing. Curing incident: An old man was bitten by a rattlesnake and was in great pain. A friend came and told him, "It was only a little worm that bit you." He went through a rain speech, and the old man said, "I forgot all my pain, and when he had finished I was cured."

Speech of Elder Brother, after His Resurrection[13]

William Blackwater

My earth is weakened and my mountains are crumbling.
Four times I was shot and left for dead.
I put my hands upon the earth and raised myself.
I looked over the whole land.
Toward the west lay my green snake (river),
And I followed it and cut arrow weed.
***I made four* aamina.[14]**
About me was darkness.
I stretched my hand into the darkness
And took my cigarette and lit and smoked.

13. This is Blackwater's version of a speech given by Vanyiko in chapter 1, the "His Resurrection" section. Benedict noted that the speech was used in rain and curing ceremonies. It was also used for war.—*Ed.*

14. "Counting sticks." For more on *o'omina,* see the "His Resurrection" section of the rafter.—*Ed.*

I blew the smoke down on the earth and I smiled.
On the Black Mountain I put my hands.
I took the sacred crystal and put it on the ground.
Toward the west I put my hand and drew down the black fog;
With it I covered my sacred crystal.
Toward the south I put my hand and drew down the blue-green fog;
With it I covered my sacred crystal.
Toward the east I put my hand and drew down the white fog;
With it I covered my sacred crystal.
Toward the north I put my hand and drew down the yellow fog;
With it I covered my sacred crystal.
Upon it the power of my enemies was gathered into one compass,
And I took it into my hand.

When I had done this, I took four steps toward the east.
I took one step and stumbled upon Yellow Buzzard Medicine Man.
I took the second step and stumbled upon the Speaker.
I took the third step and stumbled upon the Brave Man.
I took the fourth step and stumbled upon the Industrious Man.
Toward the east I followed the shining road and came to a spring.
In it I dipped my hand and strengthened myself.
Upon the flowers around it I laid my hand and strengthened myself.
I came to Mount Vaakamoiakut[15] *and from it I laid my hand and strengthened myself.*
I came to the sun and followed the sun to the west.
The trail of the sun was beautiful with beads, with flowers, with feathers.
All these I overturned.
I followed the sun toward the west and came to the Talking Tree.
From its branches I cut four aamina *to replace the* aamina *of arrow weed.*
From the middle branch I took wood and made a war club.
From its knothole I made a water vessel.
I stripped the bark of the tree and decorated it with the rays of the sun
And put it upon my head as a headdress.

15. Ba'ag Muakud, "Eagle Killing-place."—*Ed.*

I followed the sun toward the west and came to a spring.
I knelt down to drink.
I followed the sun toward the west and came to a mountain.
Down that mountain I slid to Earth Doctor
And fell before his feet as a stone.
A strong wind came from the west and blew me to the east
And dropped me again at the feet of Earth Doctor.
A strong wind came from the south and blew me to the north
And dropped me again at the feet of Earth Doctor.
A strong wind came from the east and blew me to the west
And dropped me again at the feet of Earth Doctor.
A strong wind came from the north and blew me to the south
And dropped me again at the feet of Earth Doctor.
A strong wind came from below and blew me to the heavens
And dropped me again at the feet of Earth Doctor.

I spoke to Earth Doctor and said,
"I have come to ask for the thing that I desire."
"What is it that you desire?"
"I desire to destroy the people of the earth.
The people of the earth are many."
"How is it that there are so many people on the earth?
I will send and see how many people are living there."
He sent Gopher, his pet.
He came to the Black Spring and planted kokpotk.[16]
He covered the surface of the water with the feathers of the Raven.
He came to the Blue-Green Spring and planted kawak.[17]
He covered the surface of the water with the feathers of the bluebird.
He came to the Red Spring and planted frog spittle.
He covered the surface of the water with the feathers of the macaw.
He came to the White Spring and planted bulrushes.
He covered the surface of the water with the downy feathers of the eagle.

Gopher came up from the east and saw that the people were many.
He saw pueblos over all the earth.

16. Bulrushes. See also the "His Resurrection" section of the rafter.—*Ed.*
17. Cattails. See the "His Resurrection" section of the rafter.—*Ed.*

He saw that it would be hard for the enemy to approach them
(without betraying themselves).

Darkness was above me,
And I put my hand into the darkness and took my cigarette and lit it.
I blew the smoke to where my Gray Owl sat, and I sent him over
the earth.
He went to the enemy and weakened them.
I set him by the fire of Earth Doctor.
I blew my smoke to where my Dwarf Owl **(kukowol)**[18] *sat,*
And I sent him over the earth.
He went to the enemy and weakened them.
I blew my smoke to where my Burrowing Owl sat,
And I sent him over the earth.
He went to the enemy and weakened them.
I blew my smoke to where my Roadrunner sat,
And I sent him over the earth.
He went to the enemy and weakened them.

War Ritual: Speech of Elder Brother [from an unknown time][19]

Thomas Vanyiko

Toward the west I cried for help to the people of that country,
And they pitied me and answered my cry.
They shook the earth as they came into my country.

Toward the south I cried for help to the people of that country,
And they pitied me and answered my cry.
They shook the earth as they came into my country.

Toward the east I cried for help to the people of that country,
And they pitied me and answered my cry.
They shook the earth as they came into my country.

18. *Kokoho.—Ed.*
19. I don't know what in the telling of ancientness this speech could refer to.—*Ed.*

Toward the north I cried for help to the people of that country,
And they pitied me and answered my cry.
They shook the earth as they came into my country.

I cried to Yellow Spider Shaman[20] *of the north,*
And he spun his thread.
Four times he bound the heart of my enemy
And the hands of my enemy,
And he threw him aside as a thing of nothing.

I set out toward that place[21]
And I swam the four waters.
Beyond the four waters
I found the shaman of my enemy.
All about him day shone untroubled
And the light of the night was undisturbed.[22]

Beside him grew the wild reed in which was his strength;
Its plume waved in the air.
With fear I put out my hand and plucked it,
And with it I scattered his food,
With it I scattered his fire,
With it I sprinkled his drinking water upon the sand.
He lay there suspecting nothing,
All over him his blanket the colors of the sunlight.[23]
My warriors were as animals that hunt one another, and as birds of prey;
They overcame the enemy and all the powers of the enemy.
Then at that victory the brush was trampled,
And the clouds appeared over the mountains.

20. Yellow is the color associated with concealment from the enemy. The yellow light makes it impossible to distinguish [things] at a distance.

21. That is, where the enemy is. This describes the spiritual journey in which the shaman overcomes the spiritual power of the enemy.

22. A stock figure to indicate peace.

23. Herzog (n.d.*b*) wrote: "The Apache used to have blankets of rags and pieces of skin sown together. The rays of the sun would break at these uneven places and glitter early in the morning. The enemy lies there unsuspecting, enjoys this play [of light], and draws his blanket around him to sleep some more—although the Pima [warriors] are close."—*Ed.*

I looked back, and behold! the white whirlwind in the east, its top bent to the west;
I looked back, and behold! the black whirlwind in the west, its top bent to the east.
I went under the white whirlwind carrying my dead enemy,
And under the black whirlwind with a captive child.
I came to my house, and the roads branched;
The captive child stared down each crossroad.
But I brought him to the house of the shaman.
The power of the shaman lay beside him inert,
And the deed of my victory stirred it up.
The clouds of the shaman lay beside him inert,
And the deed of my victory raised them up to the sky;
From the sky the raindrops fell sprinkling the earth.

In the earth I planted my seeds and they grew,
Big stalks, broad leaves, pretty blossoms, perfect seed.
From the plants I gathered the harvest and stored it away,
And the young boys shall eat of it and have perfect health,
And the young girls shall eat of it and have perfect health,
The old men shall eat of it and shall lengthen their days,
And the old women shall eat of it and shall lengthen their days.

Speech of Elder Brother [from an unknown time][24]

Thomas Vanyiko

This earth I am walking upon is not my work,
Nor the trees, nor the mountains, nor the fowls of the air, nor the creatures of the ground, nor the human beings.
To them (human beings) was understanding given,
And I am one among them.

The underworld is my work.
The world above is four,[25]

24. I don't know what in the telling of ancientness this speech could refer to.—*Ed.*

25. Referring to the four layers in which the world is conceived, as also the heavens, in the line below. [Herzog (n.d.*b*) wrote: "The four layers of the earth refer to the four creations of the earth, three of which covered the previous creation."]

And the heavens above are four.
With my crystal cane I bored through the earth even to [Stone Ax Mountain],[26]
And there I received my power to withstand cold,
My power to withstand thirst,
To be alert, to be a good shot.

At noon in the shadow of the tree I lay down to rest.
Many a day has passed,
And many a morning and evening has gone,
And they brought me good health.[27]

Prophecy of Elder Brother [from an unknown time][28]

Thomas Vanyiko

I go to my own home, being already without life,
And my people shall follow me when their time is come.

Love the land and make no trouble.
Plant seeds in the ground and reap harvest of them.
The running streams are the veins of the earth,
And the gold, the silver, the iron in the mountains are the bones of the earth.
She is alive and not dead.

It is not you who will kill her.[29]
From the east will come her murderers.

26. The symbolism of "cane" was constantly insisted upon. The narrator gave as an example, "I have my cane," meaning "I have been elected to office." "Cane," he said, meant "power, wisdom." [Hatviñ Du'ag, "Stone-ax Mountain," is a purely mythical mountain (Herzog n.d.*b*:2).]

27. Only the last stanza of this recitative refers to the story of Elder Brother. [It is not clear how this speech fits into the telling of ancient history. The opening lines say the world is not Elder Brother's "work," which is true to the prose narrative: Earth Doctor made the world. But the next stanza says the underworld *is* Elder Brother's "work." No other text says this.]

28. "Not used in curing or war ritual." [This speech can be imagined as having been spoken either at the time that Elder Brother was about to lead the Pimas from the underworld to make war against the Hohokam or at the time that he left them to look after themselves, when the conquest had been completed.]

29. On the question of gender, see note 6, chapter 1.—*Ed.*

You may be ignorant, but you will be content;
Until at last you will see that day
When they will kill the earth.

After these things I shall bring light to you again,
And you shall see and know.

War Recitative [Oration][30]

Thomas Vanyiko

Over my head sadness was tied in fast knots,
And I lifted my hand and untied them.

In the cuttings of my hair I was entangled,
And over the dry bones I stumbled,[31]
And I came to the great shaman.
His wife and his son wept with me, and he gave me good fortune against my enemies.
I slung it under my arm[32] *and I went out of that house.*

In the cuttings of my hair I was entangled,
And over the dry bones I stumbled.
I came to the Orator.
His wife and his child wept with me, and he gave me power to withstand cold and to withstand thirst.
I slung it over my arm and went out of that house.

In the cuttings of my hair I was entangled,
And over the dry bones I stumbled.
I came to the War Chief.
His wife and his child wept with me, and he gave me my strong desire.
I slung it under my arm and went out of that house.

30. The mention of Nasia in this speech ties it to that ancient character, but there is no mention in the known narratives about Nasia of the events of this speech.—*Ed.*

31. He was so weak with grief that the long hair cut in mourning was a snare to make him stumble, and he could not lift his feet over so small an obstacle as dry bones.

32. As a medicine bag is carried.

In the cuttings of my hair I was entangled,
And over the dry bones I stumbled.
And I came to the Brave.
His wife and his son wept with me, and he gave me black paint for my face and power over darkness.
I slung it under my arm and went out of that house.

I turned to the east and I came to the woman Nasia, and I cried for help.
I said to her, "(Help me,) you who have the bows of the Apache for the ribs of your house,
The strings of their bows to tie the cross-ribs of your house."
She gave them to me, and I slung them under my arm and went out of that house.

Again I returned to the woman Nasia, and I cried for help.
I said to her, "(Help me,) you who use the Apache quiver for the fringe to decorate the stick with which you prop your burden basket."
She gave it to me, and I slung it under my arm and went out of that house.

Again I returned to the woman Nasia, and I cried for help.
I said to her, "(Help me,) you who use the Apache arrows for the shoulder pad under the burden basket."
She gave them to me, and I slung them under my arm and went ut of that house.

Again I returned to the woman Nasia, and I cried for help.
I said to her, "(Help me,) you who use the arrow-points of the
Apache for the netting hook of your burden basket."
She gave them to me, and I slung them under my arm and went out of that house.

Again I returned to the woman Nasia, and I cried for help.
I said to her, "(Help me,) you who use the power (blood) of the
Apache to paint patterns on the net of your burden basket."
She gave it to me, and I slung it under my arm and went out of that house.

I took all these and went out against my enemy.
I killed many, that I might bring happiness to my people.

Nasia Speaks[33]

William Blackwater

I came to you not knowing the road;
On the hills I stumbled,
I stumbled over stumps and over stones.
I came, and behold! your house of stone;
Your people around you were at peace,
Your wife was at peace;
I went into your house of stone, and all that you possessed was uncovered,[34]
Your water was uncovered.

Welcome to the Aaduma [*Eḍa Mel*] Ceremony[35]

Thomas Vanyiko

You have come, my friend; you stand upon my land.
Look about everywhere and see for yourself how poor it is.
It is covered with broken pieces of pottery.[36]
It is covered with hair, cut in mourning.

In the east is a shining pueblo.
In it lives a great shaman.
It is covered with winds and clouds and is difficult to approach.
I went up to it from the right hand and looked in at the crack, and a medicine man sat there with his back to me.[37]

33. Nasia is a character from ancient times, but the events of this speech are not explained in the known narratives on her.—*Ed.*

34. A picture indicating security.

35. See "The Feud" for this kind of ceremony, but the events in that story don't correspond to the events in this speech, which is one that could be used at any such ceremony. The same is true of the next speech, which is also for *eḍa mel.*—*Ed.*

36. Broken in mourning ceremonies.

37. A figure for long drought.

I spoke to him and I said:
"Look about and see how poor my land is;
Your mountains are crumbling down.
At the foot of the mountains the crawling things have forgotten their running and forgotten their cries.
Your trees are nothing but sticks (leafless).
In them the birds have forgotten their flying and forgotten their cries.
Your washes are covered with accumulations.[38]
In them the fishes are dead and have forgotten their swimming."

He turned his face to me and said, "Go home: you will receive all that you desire."

I returned and came to my first camping place.
And there the wind blew from the east and crossed the earth to the west.
From there, black shadows came, and black clouds covered the earth.
In them came black birds sprinkling black seeds over the land;
In them came blue birds sprinkling blue seeds over the land;
In them came red birds sprinkling red seeds over the land;
In them came white birds sprinkling white seeds over the land,
And left the world bright with many colors.

You have brought your wind.
You have brought your clouds.
You have brought your rain and covered the earth.
In it your boy and your girl will play all day long (i.e., in the ceremony) and there will be happiness in the land.

Welcome to the Aaduma [Eḍa Mel] Ceremony

William Blackwater

Your desire, my friend, has been fulfilled.
You have come, you stand upon my land.

38. *Tâhâkut,* spider webs, etc. [*ta:nhadag,* "trash"], which show water does not [or has not recently] run there.

Look around and see how poor it is.
It is filled with sickness,
It is littered with potsherds,
It is strewn with cuttings of hair.

The roads of my land are old,
And the houses of my country are about to fall.
My mountains are old and crumbling.
My streams are covered with accumulations.

The people of my land have forgotten their dreams.
The beasts of the field have forgotten their cries.
The birds of the air have forgotten their flying and their songs.

I turned to the shaman of the west and cried for help.
He pitied me and sent his wind to cover all the land.
After the wind, came the black clouds and covered the land.
After the black clouds, came the black birds and scattered the black seeds from their wings, from the west to the east.
After them came the blue birds and scattered the blue seeds from their wings everywhere over the land.
After them came the red birds and scattered the red seeds from their wings over the hills and the forests.
After them came the birds of all colors and scattered the seeds of many colors from their wings along the washes,
And white drops of rain came from above and sprinkled the land.

And in the land I planted my seed, and it grew,
Big stalks, broad leaves, pretty blossoms, perfect seed.
From the plants I gathered the harvest and stored it away,
And the young boys shall eat of it and have perfect health,
And the young girls shall eat of it and have perfect health,
The old men shall eat of it and shall lengthen their days,
And the old women shall eat of it and shall lengthen their days.

SPEECHES NOT TIED BY CHARACTER OR EVENT TO THE NARRATIVES OF ANCIENT TIMES

[For] War Ritual

William Blackwater

I made aamina[39] *and counted the days.*
On the day appointed I took my burning brand and started toward the country of the enemy.
I came to a hill upon which there was a water hole.
I built a fire and warmed myself and wondered whether any would follow me.
One by one the people came.
In the blue evening I spread my blue council circle.
Our ceremony[40] *was of good omen:*
That the enemy forget his wife, his child, his friend.

Early in the morning I took up my burning brand and started again toward the country of the enemy.
I laid my brand beside a water hole.
When my comrades brought their game, we ate,
And our ceremony was of good omen:
That the enemy forget his wife, his child, his friend.

Early in the morning I took up my burning brand and started again toward the country of the enemy.
I laid my brand beside a water hole.
When my comrades had found me upon the gray mountain,
They brought their game and we ate,
And our ceremony was of good omen:
That the enemy forget his wife, his child, his friend.

Again, early in the morning I took up my burning brand and started again toward the country of the enemy.
I laid my brand beside a water hole.

39. Counting sticks to mark the days that should elapse before the ceremony.
40. Literally, "dreams."

The dreams of my enemy were bad:
He dreamed that he drank water he had never drunk before,
He dreamed that he ate food he had never eaten before,
That he was among people he had never been among before.

I encircled my enemy and I stepped upon a stick.
It broke beneath my feet (but the enemy did not stir).
I encircled my enemy a second time, and I saw him under a
tree within arrow range.

I sent my men ahead as scouts and they returned bringing
green stalks that had been trampled under foot,
And the bruise upon them was still fresh.[41]

Then were my warriors as wild beasts that hunt one another
and as birds of prey,
And they threw themselves against the enemy.
I looked, and behold! white rocks fell from white clouds as rain,
And from the east white whirlwinds bent until they touched the west.[42]
I looked, and behold! black rocks fell from black clouds as rain,
And from the west black whirlwinds bent until they touched the east.
I passed under the white whirlwind carrying the body of my enemy
in my arms,
And under the black whirlwind carrying the child I had captured.
I came near to my own house and the roads branched.
The captive child stared down every crossroad,[43]
But I brought him to the house of the shaman.

White drops fell from above and wet the earth,
And in it I put my seeds, and they grew,
Big stalks, broad leaves, pretty blossoms, perfect seed.
From the plants I gathered the harvest and stored it away,
And the young boys shall eat of it and have perfect health,
And the young girls shall eat of it and have perfect health,
The old men shall eat of it and shall lengthen their days,
And the old women shall eat of it and shall lengthen their days.

41. That is, the enemy had passed so recently.

42. The orator envisions bows of smoke, formed of white and black whirlwind, stretched across the sky like rainbows. Compare the "blue smoke rainbow" in the "Nasia's Twins" story, chapter 2.

43. Looking for possible escape. [Presumably "child" in this context means any captive.]

[For] War Ritual

Thomas Vanyiko

We have come together in this place, my brothers.
I broke sticks and made aamina.
I sent the message sticks among you.
You understood and I have counted the days, my relatives.

It is the day appointed and I came alone with my burning brand
to the hill upon which there is a water hole.
I build a fire and warm myself,
And I wonder whether any will meet me here.

One by one the people came.
In the blue evening I spread the blue council circle.
Our ceremony was of good omen:
That my enemy should be overcome with sleep,
That his love for his wife, his child, should be blotted out.

In the white morning I started again toward the enemy with
my burning brand.
I laid it by the river.
Our ceremony was of good omen:
That my enemy should be overcome with sleep,
That his love for his friend and his comrades should be blotted out.

In the blue evening by the sandy spring I spread the blue council circle.
Our ceremony was of good omen:
That my enemy should be overcome by sleep,
That his desire of drink and of food should go unsatisfied.

In the white morning I started again toward the enemy with my
burning brand.
I laid it by a spring of water below a tree.
I took the cup and gave it to the enemy and he dreamed dreams
of bad omen:
That he drank water he had never drunk before,
That he ate food he had never eaten before,
That he was among people he had never been among before.

I raised myself and saw my enemy under a tree within arrow range.
I overcame him without difficulty.
I returned to my brothers with power,
And my house and my land were renewed.

[For] War Ritual

William Blackwater

Around me the earth was smooth.
They raised me and set me up.
They gave me a burning brand and a roll of native tobacco.
I lit it and inhaled the smoke and blew it out.
It came from my mouth in all colors of the light.

Toward the east I cried for help to the people of that country.
And they pitied me and answered my cry.
They shook the earth as they came into my country.

Toward the south I cried for help to the people of that country.
And they pitied me and answered my cry.
They shook the earth as they came into my country.

Toward the west I cried for help to the people of that country.
And they pitied me and answered my cry.
They shook the earth as they came into my country.

Toward the north I cried for help to the people of that country.
And they pitied me and answered my cry.
They shook the earth as they came into my country.

In the east is a shining pueblo.[44]
In the center grows a shining reed.
I reached out my hand and took the reed,
And with it I bored a hole in the stone wall (of the pueblo).[45]

44. The Pima word would probably be *va'aki,* or *vaaka,* as Benedict usually wrote it. It refers mainly to the clay-walled "great-houses" made by the prehistoric Hohokam people. These exist today as ruins. Sometimes, as in this speech, the word refers to a magical place at the edge of the world, a place that still exists in good repair and that one might visit today in a dream.—*Ed.*

45. Probably sun-dried mud, not stone.—*Ed.*

Out of the hole came shining water,
And after that came shining dragonflies,
And they flew four times in a circle and returned again to the hole.

In the south is a blue pueblo.
In the center grows a blue reed.
I reached out my hand and took the reed,
And with it I bored a hole in the stone wall.
Out of the hole came blue water,
And after that came blue dragonflies,
And they flew four times in a circle and returned again to the hole.

In the west is a black pueblo.
In the center grows a black reed.
I reached out my hand and took the reed,
And with it I bored a hole in the stone wall.
Out of the hole came black water,
And after that came black dragonflies,
And they flew four times in a circle and returned again to the hole.

In the north is a yellow pueblo.
In the center grows a yellow reed.
I reached out my hand and took the reed,
And with it I bored a hole in the stone wall.
Out of the hole came yellow water,
And after that came yellow dragonflies,
And they flew four times in a circle and returned again to the hole.

On top of the yellow pueblo was Yellow Spider Shaman.
I turned to Yellow Spider for help.
He pitied me and spun his thread toward my enemy.
He bound the heart of my enemy
And the hands of my enemy
And the feet of my enemy
And threw him aside as a thing of nothing.[46]

I set out toward that place
And I swam the four waters.

46. "As a woman."

Beyond the four waters
I found the shaman and he pitied me.
He reached out his hand and plucked his reed,
And with it he scattered the food of my enemy
And scattered the water of my enemy.
Then were my warriors as wild beasts that hunt one another and as birds of prey.
They overcame the enemy.
At that victory the brush was trampled
And drops of rain fell on the earth.

I returned to my people.
I looked, and behold! the white whirlwind in the east, its top bent to the west.
I passed under with the body of my enemy in my arms.
I looked, and behold! the black whirlwind in the west, its top bent to the east.
And I passed under with the captive child.
I came near to my own house and the roads branched.
The captive child stared down every crossroad,
But I brought him to the house of the shaman.
The power of the shaman lay beside him,
But the deed of my victory stirred it up,
And the rain fell.
All this was done from the deeds of my warpath.[47]

Ritual for the First Water Allowed the Slayer in [War] Purification Rites

Probably from William Blackwater

The word of your great deed came to me, and I rejoiced at it.
Straightway I ran to the ocean and returned bringing you this water.
Four times I strengthened myself, and behold!
Red Thunder (Lightning) stood in the cup.
And before his power I fell upon the earth.

47. "This recitative is intended to show that to accomplish any great thing, all those who take part must be of one mind."

I rose and smelled the cup,
And the water was as water in which a thing had been burned.

Four times I strengthened myself, and behold!
Glittering Eagle stood in the cup.
He churned the water, and before his power I fell upon the earth.
I rose and smelled the cup,
And the water stank.

Four times I strengthened myself, and behold!
Chicken Hawk stood in the cup,
And before his power I fell upon the earth.
I rose and smelled the cup,
And the water was as fresh blood.

Four times I strengthened myself, and behold!
Coyote, our gray cousin, came from the east and stood in the cup.
He churned the water, and before his power I fell upon the earth.
I rose and smelled the cup,
And the water was as the smell of Coyote.
I rose, and in coming to you I have rested four times.
I have brought you the water.
Drink it in one draught; it has been given power by great spirits.

Notes on the Warriors' Purification

Ruth Benedict, from statements
by William Blackwater

The *first* time one kills an enemy is the only time when the tabus [rules of purification] are fully kept. "When one does not drink for four days." [That is one of the rules.]

There is no heraldry for indicating the number of war counts [kills or contacts with the enemy]. The only way to know the count is by the number of forelocks of the Apaches they [Pima warriors] have killed. These are kept in their war boxes [small, closed baskets] in their own houses.

Men who had several of these [forelock scalps], and were often spoken of as brave men, would pierce the nose and adopt the headdress of the brave, but this was never a part of the purification ceremony. The headdress was like the headdress of the Sioux but had no tailpiece.

The nose piercing was peculiar to the braves; it was not shared by *maaka* (medicine men) or by *sivanyi* (chiefs).

For the purification ceremony one chose a man as "father" who had been through it himself. Those who had been through the ceremony would come together sometimes and talk of old times, but there was no formal boasting, no group care of scalp locks.

There was no master of ceremonies; all the people came together on the sixteenth day and danced.

The scalp was raised on a tall pole, and the women relatives of the slayer gave war whoops and danced. WB has not seen a ceremony over a scalp during his lifetime, 65 years. Women do as they wish during a scalp dance (he denied any license).

Thanksgiving for Food[48]

William Blackwater

I sat upon the ground.
You gave me a burning brand and a roll of native tobacco,
And I lighted it and blew smoke from my mouth.
I took the shaman's feathers and pointed them toward the east.
From the east the winds came and crossed to the west.
After them came the white clouds and crossed to the west,
And covered the land with all the colors of the sunlight.
The big-drop rain came and dampened the earth,
But no plants grew.

I took the downy feathers of the eagle and pointed them to the west.
From the west the winds came and crossed to the east.
And after them came the black clouds and crossed to the east,
And covered the land with blackness.
The fine-seed rain[49] came and wet the earth,
And the plants grew.

48. I don't know of any specific or unique ceremony for thanksgiving. Rain, harvest, war, and *eḍa mel* ceremonies, and the speeches for them, all have elements of thanksgiving.—*Ed.*

49. *Tsuuwat djuk,* "fine-seed rain." The *tsuuwat* is a plant with very small seeds, formerly gathered for pinole. The distinction is always made between rain with large drops, which runs off the packed ground without wetting the roots of plants, and fine rain, which permeates the ground and makes for growth. [*Su:'uwaḍ,* "fine-seed," is the tansy mustard, *Descurainia pinnata;* its seeds were parched, ground, and mixed with water to form a gruel (Russell 1908:77; Saxton, Saxton, and Enos 1983; Rea 1997:223–24).]

The rabbit hunter went out with his bow and arrows.
He saw that the earth was good and that plants grew over the land.
The mountains were covered with green,
The hills were covered with yellow caterpillars.[50]
He brought them home in the evening braided in a long string.

The people came together and saw and took council.
In the early morning they started toward the hills.
Over their heads formed the black whirlwinds.[51]
Toward evening they brought home their braids of food and dried them in the wind.
The man from the fields returned home in the evening and saw these things.
The man of few words began to talk (and was happy).

Thanksgiving for Food

Kisto

Yes, you know the earth is dead.
I took shaman's feathers and pointed them to the east, and touched the wind.
From it came white clouds of all colors with lightning and thunder and rainbows.
They covered the whole land,
And green plants grew.
I took shaman's feathers and pointed them to the west, and touched the wind.
From it came black clouds with lightning and thunder and rainbows.
They covered the whole land,
And green plants grew.
The hunter went out with his bow and arrows.
He went through the brush,[52] *seeking to start the young jackrabbits.*

50. *Maakum* [a caterpillar, also called] shaman's decorations. The caterpillars were caught in large numbers, their heads snipped off, and the intestines squeezed out. They were then braided into long braids and thrown into boiling water. When the people returned home, these braids were dried in the wind and eaten. [Compare Saxton, Saxton, and Enos 1983:40 (*makkum,* "a large edible green caterpillar"); Herzog n.d.*b* (shaman's decorations, referring to the designs on the caterpillar's skin).]

51. Said to be the smoke rising from the fires on which the kettles of water were boiling for the braids of *maakum*.

52. A variety of brush called "owl's feathers."

He went to the Mountain of Many Points,
And there he saw the yellow caterpillars.
He gathered them and brought them to his home in the evening,
And threw them down before the old men.
They stirred the fire and cooked them.
With them they renewed their hearts.
The dark came and they sat close to the fire.
They moved fagots closer together.
They talked until dawn came in the east.

Women came with carrying baskets,
And young men came,
And went to the place where the yellow caterpillars were.
And (the smoke of) their fires rose like whirlwinds.
In the evening the young men returned with cooked braids of yellow caterpillars.

The man from the fields knew nothing of the good fortune.
He came home after sundown and saw them and filled his mouth.
He ate, talking meanwhile.

Recitative [Oration] of the Acquisition of Power[53]

William Blackwater

You were chosen and placed in this land.[54]
You lay down to sleep, and behold! in your dreams a shaman led you,
He led you toward the east;
He brought you to the shining house of stone.
He put his hand in, and brought out a gourd rattle and placed it in your right hand.

53. I don't know of a specific event, following the getting of a specific kind of power, where this speech would be used. People got power from going to war and, at least among Papagos, or Tohono O'odham, from killing eagles and going to the ocean for salt. Speeches were given at all these occasions, including speeches at the end directed to people who were isolated and being purified and who were likely to get "power" in the form of a vision or dream. The speech for the first water in war purification is such a one. This could be another. (Herzog [n.d.*b*] was told that it was used for curing: it was recited by the sick person's relative, usually the father, to the medicine man who had just arrived to take care of the patient. By reciting the source of the medicine man's power, the father strengthened the medicine man's self-confidence.)—*Ed.*

54. Appointed to come to this country as a human being.

He led you toward the west;
He brought you to the black river.[55]
He put his hand in, and brought out four shaman's feathers[56] *and placed them in your left hand.*

He led you then into the foothills, and there he gave you his shining heart.
He led you into the higher hills, and there he gave you his shining heart.
He led you into the mountains, and there he gave you his shining heart.
He led you into the topmost peaks, and there he gave you his shining heart.

He brought you home, and beside your path lay an animal dead.
On it you tried your powers;
You shook your gourd over it,
You shook your shaman's feathers over it,
And it came to life and ran away.

He led you continuing on your way, and beside your path lay a bird dead.
On it you tried your powers;
You shook your gourd over it,
You shook your shaman's feathers over it,
And it came to life and flew away.

Figures of Speech among the Pima[57]

Ruth Benedict

I wanted to speak this evening about the primitive development of metaphor and some of its implications in literature—how metaphors are a way of extending perceptions indefinitely.

55. "Black" here is the color associated with the west, as "shining" is with the east (in the preceding stanza).

56. The four long wing feathers tied to a stick.

57. This must be the text of a talk that Benedict gave during the time she was working on the texts. I don't know the occasion for the talk, which has not been published before.—*Ed.*

The categories of thought under which peoples perceive both the world around them and their own subjective experience are most significant as they are externalized in linguistic form. As has been abundantly shown, these categories—especially as they are developed in grammar, but also as they express themselves in vocabulary—are an intrinsic formal patterning of experience which is peculiar to any one language family and utterly inescapable by it. No perception can come, to any speaker of a particular language, except as it is already classified under its fundamental forms. The influence of this is manifested in all possible ways; the aspect chosen by one people as a grammatical classification—let us say gender or locative elements—must be repeated in every sentence until it is a weariness to the ear (as in a Bantu sentence); or the elements not chosen, no matter how much more significant, will come in for only casual and unimportant notice.

Now, it is not only grammatical categories and those of vocabulary that pattern the characteristic expression of different peoples. We have given too little attention to metaphor and have been too little concerned with its distinctive qualities and the way in which it is elaborated.

In general, people of a particular culture do not range freely over the external world in search of metaphorical images for the various kinds of experience. Just as to be intelligible they must operate phonetically with only a small proportion of the possible phonetic elements, so in the metaphors of unwritten literature there is almost always a very definite limitation, both in the facts for which images are sought and in the elements of nature where images are found.

Both of these traditionally fixed aspects of metaphor are vividly contrasted among tribes not far removed, geographically, from the Pima Indians of Arizona—for example, the Osage and the Zuni.

For the Osage we have a great body of ritual material, of which perhaps nine-tenths is an elaboration of symbols for one fact of experience—that of the twelfth chapter of Ecclesiastes, old age. Only here it is not a warning against the evil days when "the grinders cease because they are few, and those that look out of the windows be darkened." In Osage ritual all of nature is ransacked for analogues of the wrinkles, the white hair, the bowed form, the loss of teeth; and these are bestowed as blessings that the individual shall live to a ripe old age. Thus the bear gives the blessing of its toothless jaw, the elder bush of its white blossoms, the crane of its wrinkled comb.[58] Nature is realistically searched for any image that fits the traditional demands.

58. La Flesche 1928.—*Ed.*

The bear preparing its winter hiding place, the turtle floating down the river—all these seen events that figure in Osage poetry—are absent in the poetry of the Zuni. Characteristically enough, in Zuni, it is rain for which symbols are most urgently sought, but abstract notions which would be alien to Osage thought are just as prominent: the "roads of life," the emergence,[59] the "things we live by,"[60] and the directions are all symbolized. And just as the Zuni symbol usually refers to a ceremonial act—the scattering of the meal line for the road of life, the placing of the bowl of water on the altar for the lake of emergence—so it is that poetic symbolism is found in ceremonial paraphernalia and in ceremonial acts. The Zuni do not, as the Osage do, search the world of nature for their figurative images; even if this world is used, it is patterned into a series of symbols associated, for instance, with the six directions (east, south, west, north, zenith, and nadir). Chiefly they choose their metaphors from ritual things. Thus the turkey's feathers bound to the prayer stick are "the massed storm clouds of our turkey fathers,"[61] and it is the bowl of whipped-up suds on the altar that is the pile of cumulus cloud.

In the poetry of the Pima, metaphor is particularly rich. Unlike the Osage, the Pima are not limited in the experiences which they wish to express symbolically; and in the figures of speech themselves there is an open-eyed observation of nature that, by contrast, is stereotyped in Zuni metaphor.

Among these people, who are quite without the formal ceremonial and social elaboration of neighboring Pueblo groups, the cultural limitations of figurative speech give way before a habit of metaphor as a way of perceiving the entire universe. It is not only that the figures are particularly vivid and well carried out, they are very widely applied—to nature, to ceremony, to war, to creation, to the emotions. It is the working out of these metaphors that gives the distinctive character to Pima curing and war practices and to their story of creation.

Their war practices are typical. All of the images of powerlessness are used to describe a crippling of the enemy in imagination before the crippling in fact. Spider binds with his web the Apaches' hearts and hands and feet, and throws them aside disabled; Gopher gnaws their power asunder; Owl covers them with darkness so that they fall into a slumber. But there is also metaphor based on vivid picturing. According to Pima notion, the springs of the enemy are magically dried, choked with driftwood, and covered with cobwebs—

59. Of ancestors from the underworld.—*Ed.*

60. Compare "that by which we live," that is, corn (Bunzel 1932:803).—*Ed.*

61. Compare Bunzel 1932:626, 644, 694–95, 698, 710, 799, 804, 806.—*Ed.*

And their houses were filled with soot, and their footprints were covered like old, old trails.
Then there stood out the prints of their feet and their tracks were plain.
My [young men] went out and followed the clear trail of their enemy and captured him.[62]

There is also in Pima ritual a recurring metaphor that I do not know from any other American Indian tribe, though it has a kind of analogue in the biblical swords beaten into ploughshares. The idea is that a supernaturally great medicine man or woman has the power to use the most dangerous weapons of the Apache for the most domestic and peaceful purposes; and by giving the suppliant this power he (or she) makes the enemy harmless.

And I said, "I will go to the east,
I will seek out Nasia the shaman."
I groped for her through the darkness,
And I was not sure that I had found her.
I spoke to her and I said, "(Help me), you who use the bows of the
Apache for the frame of your carrying basket;
The arrows of the Apache for the shoulder pad;
The arrow shafts of the Apache for the netting hook;
The bowstring of the Apache for the string to the net;
The scalp lock of the Apache for the cording of the net;
The blood of the Apache to paint beautiful patterns upon your carrying basket."
In these words I spoke to her and she gave me her power and I went onward.

I said, "I will go to the zenith,
And I will seek out the Shaman of the Downy Nest."
I came to him and I spoke and said, "(Help me), you who use the bows of the Apache for the curved posts of your house;
The arrows of the Apache for the withes laid crosswise;
The bowstring of the Apache for the cording to make them fast;
The hair of the Apache for the thatch of your roof."
He gave me his powers and I slung them under one arm and went onward.

62. Reworded by Benedict from Lloyd 1911:141–42.—*Ed.*

I said, "I will go to the south,
To Driftwood Shaman.
And I cried to him for help and said, "(Help me), you who make the bow of the Apache the rainbow;
The arrows of the Apache the reedy desert grass;
The arrowheads of the Apache the soft down feathers (clouds);
The poison of the Apache the sacred frog spittle on standing water."
He gave me his powers and I slung them under one arm and went onward.[63]

Here is a particularly elaborate statement of the idea of magic crippling of the powers of the enemy before an act of war, and it recurs over and over in slightly different images.

As their practice of magic is carried out in varied figures of speech, so also their fundamental religious notion is a metaphor. Religious experience is symbolized by intoxication, and this is fundamental to the understanding of Pima religion. In outward act its celebration is the wine ceremony, where the fermented juice of the cactus is drunk as a sign to express this relationship. The only source of sacred power known to the Pima is the personal experience which they think of under the figure of intoxication.

"And I spoke intoxicated words"[64] is the phrase which means "power descended upon me." They carry this out in its two aspects—its sense of being uplifted and its dizziness that destroys activity. One song runs, as nearly as I can phrase it:

Our plans that are blessed by the waters of the earth till they blossom with flowers of all colors,
Our plans that are blessed by the rays of the sun till they whirl in dizziness that we may not go onward.[65]

Both are sacred blessings—one of hope, one of losing the thread.

The Pima also use metaphor to portray emotion. Sorrow and vision and intoxication are not often elaborated in primitive poetry, but in Pima they are vividly expressed:

63. Reworded by Benedict from "War Recitative [Oration]," this book.—*Ed.*

64. From the first speech of Koolhaa's son (chapter 3).—*Ed.*

65. I haven't found the source of these lines. They don't come from a speech of the orphan boy, which is the source of the phrase on the intoxicated words. Nor did a quick search through the rest of Benedict's, Russell's, and Lloyd's texts yield these lines. They read like something taken from the end of a Pima oration rather than like a Pima song. The pairing of earth and sun is uncommon in Pima song or oratory. It would be good to see the Pima phrasing for "[rays] whirl in dizziness that we may not go onward." This is what makes the lines Dionysian, and as Benedict says, their translation was not easy.—*Ed.*

Over my head sorrow was tied in fast knots,
And I lifted my hand and untied them.
In the cuttings of my hair I was entangled,
And over the dry bones I stumbled.[66]

The narrator elaborated, "He was so weak it was as if the long hair he had cut in mourning was a snare to make him stumble, and he could not lift his feet over so small an obstacle as dry bones." This is finely done, but perhaps the most striking is the setting of metaphor for the orphan's vow of revenge for the death of his father:

And I came to a water hole in the country of my enemy.
With the black paint of my face I covered the waters,
With the clipped hair of my head I covered the waters.
My own bones lay beside the water hole, and I raked them up for firewood.
I lit them, and with the bright light of my fire the whole world was painted.
The country of my enemy lay plain before me in its light.
I took a rib from my body and made of it counting sticks by which to know my days.
Of the skin of my head I made sandals,
And from my intestines a belt, and I girded up my loins.
Beside the water hole stood my own skull filled with my own blood.
I lifted it and drank.
I strengthened myself and spoke intoxicated words.[67]

The same ritual continues with a vivid expression of emotional stress that is perhaps only by courtesy a metaphor at all:

I took in my hand my torch (of the rib of his own body)
And set out over the earth.
And there came toward me my brother.
I stretched out my arms to embrace him,
And behold they closed upon my empty breast.[68]

Later on, too, comes this vivid image for ecstasy with its great events in a moment's duration:

66. Quoted from "War Recitative [Oration]," this book.—*Ed.*
67. Reworded by Benedict from the first speech of Koolhaa's son (chapter 3).—*Ed.*
68. Reworded by Benedict from the second speech of Koolhaa's son (chapter 3).—*Ed.*

Then were my warriors as wild beasts and as birds of prey.
They ran upon the enemy and killed them without effort.
I heaped around the enemy all that was theirs and gathered it into the compass of my hand (destroyed it).
I turned myself, and behind me the trees I had brushed were still in motion,
And the water I had stirred (at the water hole in drinking) was still stirred,
And the stones over which I had stumbled were still rolling against each other.[69]

There is no opportunity to read to you what is perhaps the most perfectly carried out metaphor, the image of the creation of the universe as the building of the dome-shaped little hut which was the traditional Pima house. Every step of the traditional process is given. The measuring worm breaks itself into lengths for the roof beams, the gopher gives the dirt from his holes to pack the dome, and—

Then I lit tobacco and smoked, and the smoke floated upon the dome,
White clouds upon the sky.
And from them rain fell and watered the earth,
And in the soil I planted my seed.
And it grew, big stalks, broad leaves, pretty blossoms, perfect seed.
From the plants I gathered the harvest and stored it away,
And the young boys shall eat of it and have perfect health,
And the young girls shall eat of it and have perfect health,
The old men shall eat of it and shall lengthen their days,
And the old women shall eat of it and shall lengthen their days.[70]

69. Quoted from the first speech of Koolhaa's son (chapter 3).—*Ed.*
70. Reworded by Benedict from the end of the Rain Ceremony oration, this chapter.—*Ed*

REFERENCES CITED

Note: the abbreviation RFB refers to the Ruth Fulton Benedict Papers, Vassar College Library, Poughkeepsie, New York.

Babcock, Barbara

1993 "'Not in the Absolute Singular': Rereading Ruth Benedict." In *Hidden Scholars: Women Anthropologists and the Native American Southwest,* edited by Nancy Parezo, pp. 107–28. Albuquerque: University of New Mexico Press.

Bahr, Donald

1998 "Mythologies Compared: Pima, Maricopa, and Yavapai." *Journal of the Southwest* 40(1):25–66.

n.d.*a* "Bad News: The Predicament of Mythology." Manuscript in the author's keeping.

n.d.*b* "Temptation and Glory in One Pima and Two Aztec Mythologies." Manuscript in the author's keeping.

Bahr, Donald, Juan Gregorio, David Lopez, and Albert Alvarez

1974 *Piman Shamanism and Staying Sickness.* Tucson: University of Arizona Press.

Bahr, Donald, Lloyd Paul, and Vincent Joseph

1997 *Ants and Orioles: Showing the Art of Pima Poetry.* Salt Lake City: University of Utah Press.

Bahr, Donald, Juan Smith, William Smith Allison, and Julian Hayden

1994 *The Short Swift Time of Gods on Earth: The Hohokam Chronicles.* Berkeley: University of California Press.

Benedict, Ruth

1924 Research Proposal 2. Ruth Benedict Papers, Vassar College Library, Special Collections Dept., Poughkeepsie, New York.

1931a (1981) *Tales of the Cochiti Indians*. Introduction by Alfonso Ortiz. Albuquerque: University of New Mexico Press.

1931b Folklore. *Encyclopedia of the Social Sciences,* vol. 6, ed. Edwin R. A. Seligman, pp. 288–93. New York: Macmillan.

1934 *Patterns of Culture.* Boston: Houghton Mifflin.

1935 *Zuni Mythology.* 2 vols. New York: Columbia University Press.

n.d. Pima Mythology. Typescripts, manuscripts. RFB, boxes 80 and 81 (folders 80.1–80.25 and 81.1–81.18). Vassar College Library, Special Collections Dept., Poughkeepsie, New York.

Briscoe, Virginia

1979 "Ruth Benedict, Anthropological Folklorist." *Journal of American Folklore* 92:445–76.

Brotherston, Gordon

1992 *Book of the Fourth World: Reading the Native Americas through Their Literature.* Cambridge: Cambridge University Press.

Bunzel, Ruth

1932 "Zuñi Ritual Poetry." *Forty-seventh Annual Report of the Bureau of American Ethnology, 1929–1930,* pp. 611–835. Washington, D.C.

Caffrey, Margaret

1989 *Ruth Benedict: Stranger in This Land.* Austin: University of Texas Press.

Culin, Stewart

1907 "Games of the North American Indians." *Twenty-fourth Annual Report of the Bureau of American Ethnology, 1902–1903,* pp. 3–809. Washington, D.C.

Deacon, Desley

1997 *Elsie Clews Parsons: Inventing Modern Life.* Chicago: University of Chicago Press.

Evers, Larry (editor)

1980 *The South Corner of Time: Hopi, Navajo, Papago, Yaqui Tribal Literature.* Tucson: Suntracks, University of Arizona.

Fewkes, J. W.

1912 "Casa Grande, Arizona." *Twenty-eighth Annual Report of the Bureau of American Ethnology,* pp. 25–179. Washington, D.C.

Gifford, E. W.

1933 "Northeastern and Western Yavapai Myths." *Journal of American Folklore* 46:347–415.

Hare, Peter

1985 *A Woman's Quest for Science: Portrait of Anthropologist Elsie Clews Parsons.* New York: Prometheus.

Hatto, Arthur

1999 *The Mojave Heroic Epic of Inyo-kutavere.* Helsinki: Academia Scientiarum Fennica, FF Communication no. 269.

Haury, Emil

1976 *The Hohokam, Desert Farmers and Craftsmen: Excavations at Snaketown, 1964–1965.* Tucson: University of Arizona Press.

Herzog, George

1936 "A Comparison of Pueblo and Pima Musical Styles." *Journal of American Folklore* 49:283–417.

n.d.*a* Pima Indian Myths. Typescript. Archives of Traditional Music, Indiana University, Bloomington.

n.d.*b* "Remarks to Pima Speeches." Typescript. RFB, folder 81.9.

n.d.*c* "Remarks to Pima Stories." Manuscript. RFB, folder 81.9.

Hieb, Louis

1993 "Elsie Clews Parsons in the Southwest." In *Hidden Scholars: Women Anthropologists and the Native American Southwest,* edited by Nancy Parezo, pp. 63–75. Albuquerque: University of New Mexico Press.

Katz, Israel

1980 "Herzog, George." In *New Grove Dictionary of Music and Musicians,* vol. 8, edited by Stanley Sadie, pp. 527–28. London: Macmillan.

La Flesche, Francis

1928 "The Osage Tribe: Two Versions of the Child-Naming Rite." *Forty-third Annual Report of the Bureau of American Ethnology, 1925–1926,* pp. 23–164. Washington, D.C.

Lloyd, J. William

1911 *Aw-aw-tam Indian Nights: Being the Myths and Legends of the Pimas of Arizona.* Westfield, N.J.: Lloyd Group.

Luckingham, Bradford

1989 *Phoenix: The History of a Southwestern Metropolis.* Tucson: University of Arizona Press.

Mead, Margaret (editor)

1959 *An Anthropologist at Work: Writings of Ruth Benedict.* Boston: Houghton Mifflin.

1974 *Ruth Benedict.* New York: Columbia University Press.

Modell, Judith

1983 *Ruth Benedict: Patterns of a Life.* Philadelphia: University of Pennsylvania Press.

Parsons, Elsie Clews

1928 "Notes on the Pima, 1926." *American Anthropologist* 30(3):445–64.

Rea, Amadeo

1997 *At the Desert's Green Edge: An Ethnobotany of the Gila River Pima.* Tucson: University of Arizona Press.

Russell, Frank

1908 "The Pima Indians." *Twenty-sixth Annual Report of the Bureau of American Ethnology, 1904–1905,* pp. 3–389. Washington, D.C. Re-published with an introduction by Bernard Fontana, University of Arizona Press, Tucson, 1975.

Santamaría, Francisco J.

1978 *Diccionario de mejicanismos.* 3d ed. Mexico: Porrúa.

Saxton, Dean, and Lucille Saxton

1969 *Papago and Pima to English, English to Papago and Pima Dictionary.* Tucson: University of Arizona Press.

1973 *Legends and Lore of the Papago and Pima Indians.* Tucson: University of Arizona Press.

Saxton, Dean, Lucille Saxton, and Susie Enos

1983 *Dictionary: PapagoPima–English, English–PapagoPima: O'otham–Mil-gahn, Mil-gahn–O'otham.* 2d ed. Tucson: University of Arizona Press.

Spier, Leslie.

1933 *Yuman Tribes of the Gila River.* Chicago: University of Chicago Press.

Tedlock, Dennis.

1987 "Walking the World of the Popol Vuh." In *Recovering the Word: Essays on Native American Literatures,* edited by Brian Swann and Arnold Krupat, pp. 469–96. Berkeley: University of California Press.

Underhill, Ruth

1936 *Autobiography of a Papago Woman.* Memoirs of the American Anthropological Association, no. 46. Menasha, Wisc.: American Anthropolgical Association.

1938 *Singing for Power.* Berkeley: University of California Press.

1939 *Social Organization of the Papago Indians.* Columbia University Contributions to Anthropology, no. 30. New York: Columbia University Press.

1940 *Hawk over Whirlpools.* New York: J. J. Augustin.

1946 *Papago Indian Religion.* Columbia University Contributions to Anthropology, no. 33. New York: Columbia University Press.

Underhill, Ruth, Donald M. Bahr, Baptisto Lopez, Jose Pancho, and David Lopez

1979 *Rainhouse and Ocean: Speeches for the Papago Year.* Flagstaff: Museum of Northern Arizona Press.

Zumwalt, Rosemary

1988 *American Folklore Scholarship: A Dialogue of Dissent.* Bloomington: University of Indiana Press.

1992 *Wealth and Rebellion: Elsie Clews Parsons, Anthropologist and Folklorist.* Urbana: University of Illinois Press.

INDEX

C

Q

R

ABOUT THE EDITOR

Donald Bahr, born in Iowa, educated at Harvard, and employed as an anthropology teacher at Arizona State University, has spent forty years studying the language and culture of the Pimas and Papagos, or Akimel and Tohono O'odham, of southern Arizona. He generally produces his work in coauthorship with members of those communities, often, as in this case, with the community members as speakers of a text and Bahr as commentator. The forms of the texts have been didactic "oral essays," prose myth stories, ritual oratory, and song. The topics have been curing, the history of the world, ancient shamanic journeys, and the feelings that recent people report hearing spirits sing about during dreams. Bahr is married and has two children and two grandchildren.